Children and Trauma

Children and Trauma

*A Parent's Guide to Helping
Children Heal*

Cynthia Monahon

Lexington Books
An Imprint of The Free Press
New York   London   Toronto   Sydney   Tokyo   Singapore

Lexington Books
An Imprint of The Free Press
A Division of Simon & Schuster Inc.
866 Third Avenue, New York, N. Y. 10022

First Lexington Books Paperback Edition 1995

Printed in the United States of America

printing number

1 2 3 4 5 6 7 8 9 10

Library of Congress Cataloging-in-publication Data

Monahon, Cynthia.
  Children and trauma: a parent's guide for helping children heal / Cynthia Monahon.
      p.   cm.
  Includes bibliographical references.
  ISBN 0-02-921666-4
  1. Psychic trauma in children.   I. Title.
  RJ506.P66M66   1993
  618.92'85210651—dc20   92-46318
                                                             CIP

For Ed and Caley
and in memory of
my father, Richard M. Monahon, Sr.

Can't nothing heal without pain, you know.
Toni Morrison, Beloved

Contents

Introduction

There was a time when I knew little about children's terror. My training as a psychologist had prepared me to understand only the ordinary fears of children. When I finished graduate school, I knew something about why monsters hide under children's beds and the nature of bogeymen who lurk in their closets at night, but I knew little about real terror in children's lives. Moreover, I never set out to learn about childhood trauma. But one after another, children came to my office following horrific events that had left them deeply shaken and changed. One girl of three had watched her father fatally shoot himself while loading his gun. A little boy had his foot severed in a lawnmower accident. A ten year old had spent two days in a cave, unable to move with a broken leg, waiting for rescuers to find him. While bicycling together, a group of girls had watched their good friend be hit and dragged to her death by a truck. These children were not plagued by fantasied monsters and bogeymen; their terrors were all too real. They taught me about what it feels like to be young, helpless, and terrified. Working with these and other traumatized children, I have learned something about taming the terrors that can linger mercilessly after a traumatic event.

Each traumatized child whom I have seen in therapy has been accompanied by at least one frightened and worried parent. These parents have also been my teachers. They have taught me—painfully—about their own suffering with the reality of a child's trauma. Not one of these parents ever felt prepared for the reality of living out this nightmare. Regardless of their own shock and concern, however, these parents knew that they had to go on being parents, courageously and creatively finding the ways to help their children heal. I have come to count on parents as the child's best allies in recovering from traumatic events.

Parents seldom feel powerful or confident when faced with the task of caring for a traumatized child. When single shocking events tragically introduce horror into a child's life, parents often feel immobilized by feelings of helplessness. These head-on encounters with trauma tend to undermine the very feelings of power and hope that children and their parents need for healing to occur. But healing from childhood trauma can and does occur. Recovery is not magical, and in most instances it is not speedy. It begins with parents' discovering that their children need them more desperately than ever to help restore a sense of safety and normality to their lives. Children look to their parents for so much: love, reassurance, understanding, hope, and humor. Often children need to borrow on their parents' patient belief that the hurt and fear will diminish over time. Through gentle and skilled care for their frightened children, parents are also able to recover what a child's trauma has often shattered: their own sense of power as protectors and healers for their children.

One of the first parents who taught me about parenting a traumatized child never came to my office. This mother, Weesie, has been my dear friend and colleague for many years. Despite the thousands of miles that separate us geographically, Weesie and I have maintained our friendship through a correspondence that most frequently chronicles the mundane struggles and joys of balancing work and mothering. Trauma has always been an interest in our professional lives but never in our personal ones. Then, seven years ago, a letter arrived that was different from the start:

Dear Cynthia,

This has been a long hard winter here. Shortly after I sent you the Mary Gordon article, in which she talks about her feelings that she couldn't possibly accept the death of one of her children, my Annie came within moments of dying. This is even hard to write about but perhaps I need to, now that there is a little time and distance. This happened without warning or preparation. One day Annie was a happy thirteen month old baby, crawling and babbling, and the next morning she awoke with a fever and vomiting—nothing too unusual in a baby. But she just didn't seem well to us. Two calls to the doctor produced nothing other than the customary Tylenol. That afternoon, Frank was changing her when he lifted her T-shirt and noticed some little purple spots. He called and luckily the person on call for our Dr. was a Fellow in infectious medicine and she recognized this dreaded disease—Annie had a form of meningitis called meningococcus. We raced to the hospital because the purple spots are the beginning of hemorrhaging. Within minutes, Annie was in shock.

We sat for six agonizing hours with doctors racing in and out of Annie's room but of course we weren't allowed in. No one said anything but we knew it was dreadful. Finally we got to see her in the intensive care unit with every bit of life support equipment there is. She was doing nothing but nothing to manage her own body—machines were running everything from her breathing to her feeding and peeing. It is a blur. Frank remembers some of it and I remember other bits and we talk occasionally and fill in the gaps for each other, although each of us is most comforted by not having too many gaps filled in.

The wonderful news is—Annie made it. I lived and breathed and slept and sat at her beside in mask and gown with well-scrubbed hands until I learned to decipher every blip on the screen. As the days passed, Annie got rid of one piece of equipment after another. It is funny, but as each thing went, I felt scared. They had been the only thing that told me she was alive and breathing for days. I felt that maybe they were being premature. Could she really live without the machines?

Slowly, as Annie improved, she needed us there so much. At first, I was there for me—Annie didn't know the difference but I couldn't bear to stay home. Every time the phone rang I found my heart sinking into my feet. What if the hospital is calling? So I just sat there beside her for my sake.

Then Annie rallied and at first I was devastated again. I expected her to come right out of it and be the Annie I once knew. Instead she was almost autistic-looking. She wouldn't relate at all. After one long night of crying and worrying that she had been forever damaged, I began to try to think it through as a social worker might. I knew that I was probably expecting far too much. She had been in intense pain and I had not been there to protect her from it. I decided I needed to start over from the very beginning and not expect her to give to me but to give all I could to her. So we sang. Singing was so much preferred to talking because it was safe. We found all the old mobiles and stuffed toys from the earliest months. Cynthia, it worked. Day by day, Annie began to come out of it—at first tentatively and then more and more she began to trust again. Or I should say she began to discriminate the good guys from the bad guys. Anyone with a folder in hand or stethoscope around their shoulders was greeted with a resounding howl. We were smiled at finally. We did have to go back to the beginning and work through each stage in her development again.

Today, Annie looks so well that we can almost forget this happened. She lost ground developmentally but is coming. She's back to where she left off and then some. She's happy and related but still shows some bits of psychological trauma. She flinches, for instance, if I go in to cover her in the middle of the night. I try to think through the effects of a horrible experience like this at such a young age and wonder what its impact will be. For now, she remembers less than Margie who just turned five. As you can imagine, this was a trauma of a different order for Margie. She was suddenly abandoned by all as we stood at Annie's bedside. She was bewildered and confused and scared that it could have happened to her and pleased, at the same time, to be rid of baby sister. A whole set of conflicting and complicating feelings. That is a whole letter in and of itself.

We play and play hospital at our house and Annie is surpassing all of us in her recovery. I will need much time to heal—this was the scariest thing I have ever been asked to go through. With Annie doing well at last, Frank and I find ourselves blowing up at each other over trivial things now that the crisis is past.

We'll have to wait and see about our trip to the beach. Do you know, I feel frightened sometimes of traveling with Annie. I think, my heavens, what if we had been too far away from a major medical center? It's just going to take me time to get back to the everyday run-of-the-mill problems and perspective.

Fondly,

Weesie

I don't save all of Weesie's letters, but this one I could not bring myself to throw away. Weesie so elegantly explains what occurs when trauma suddenly bursts the bubble of protection and safety surrounding a child. Every member of Weesie's family was deeply shaken by Annie's close escape from death. Fear for Annie's life was followed by new fears when this spunky toddler was transformed by illness, pain, and repeated medical assaults on her body. Annie needed to be actively wooed back to her former self. To pull her back into relatedness again, Weesie creatively and patiently found the old games and toys from early infancy that Annie could respond to. It was hard work, undertaken at a time when Weesie and Frank were exhausted by fear and sleeplessness. The trauma of Annie's illness dominated the household for many months, permeating the children's play and the parents' thoughts and dreams. Everyone had to learn to live with a new sense of fragility and danger, and it was a long time before anyone took much interest in small, routine matters.

Caring for Annie and tending to her older sister's fear and anger required energy and determination. At first, Weesie and Frank were overwhelmed with their despair that Annie would be damaged forever. Then Weesie began to realize what she had to give to Annie. Despair turned to hope—blind hope, really. Neither Frank nor Weesie had any way of knowing what degree of recovery Annie would be capable of, but their hope launched their battle for her.

Most parents do not have the social work training that helped Weesie quickly recognize and respond to Annie's psychological and physical trauma. They know little about children's reactions to terrifying events and are unprepared for the many changes that trauma can usher in for their children and themselves. Bridget's mother, for instance, was totally confused and devastated following the loss of their home to fire when her five-year-old daughter seemed like a different child—withdrawn, fearful, uninterested in playing with friends. Allie's mother and father were shocked when they watched their angelic seven year old turn into a tyrant in the months after Allie had witnessed an elderly man being run over by a car in front of their apartment. For Jeremy's parents, the task of parenting was complicated by grief. Four-year-old Jeremy had stood nearby and watched as his younger brother fell to his death from a third-story window. Jeremy became obsessed with dying and slept with an arsenal of toy guns beneath his pillow; his screams pierced the night for months when he woke from his unrelenting nightmares. These children felt helpless in the face of events that had suddenly obliterated their sense of safety in the world. Their parents also felt helpless—helpless in being unable to prevent harm to their children and helpless to heal their terror. Feelings of helplessness mark the territory of trauma.

I have spent a good deal of time with parents trying to deal with the impact of various traumas on their children and on themselves. My job is to serve as a coach for these parents and, when needed, as a therapist for their children. Parents often ask for something they can read—some guide that will help them find the path they need to follow in helping their children heal.

Although much has been written for professionals on childhood trauma, there is little directed to parents about traumatic incidents other than abuse in children's lives. When more parents began calling me than I could possibly see regarding their children's traumas, I decided to write a letter that I could mail to the many parents whom I had time only to talk to on the telephone. I thought it might be helpful for these parents at least to know what they might expect in their children's behavior and to have a few tips regarding the ways they could help their children's recovery. More than anything else, I wanted parents to understand the meaning of trauma in their children's lives. I did begin this letter to parents but found it difficult to write. There was a lot to say, and I worried about leaving something out that might be of help. In the end, I wrote not a letter to parents but this book.

The chapters in this book offer a map to the unfamiliar territory of parenting traumatized children. I hope that this map will help parents to recognize the effects of trauma on children and make the commitment to the unquestionably hard work of parenting that goes so far in restoring a child's sense of safety and balance. There is some order to the map as I have laid it out, but it need not be read in any particular order. Chapter 1 explains psychological trauma from the child's point of view—a perspective that children need their parents to understand. In chapter 2, various experiences of childhood trauma are briefly described to help parents draw a line in their own minds between stress and trauma. The signs of trauma in children's behavior are reviewed in chapter 3, to help parents recognize and understand the long- and short-term effects of trauma for their child. These indicators of trauma are summarized in a chart at the conclusion of the chapter. In chapter 4, parents may find some beginning answers to their questions about why individual children have such different reactions to traumatic events and the factors that can influence their reactions. Chapter 5 focuses on the various compelling and often surprising ways a child's trauma can affect the lives of all family members.

Many parents may find it a long wait before getting to chapter 6, which reviews concrete and practical ways children can be helped to cope and heal. Parenting a traumatized child well is not simply a matter of following do's and don'ts. Much of a child's healing depends on the understanding and acceptance parents convey to children. For this reason, the bulk of the book is aimed at helping parents understand their traumatized children. Parents who are having difficulty managing particular problems with their children's behavior, however, may want to skip right to this chapter.

Chapter 7 contains guidelines on when to worry about children's reactions to trauma. The guidelines are offered to help parents with the difficult decision about whether a child needs professional help. For parents of children who are in therapy or needing therapy, chapter 8 explains the various approaches to child treatment and the crucial role parents play in this therapy.

Throughout this book are the stories of children who have encountered both mild and truly dreadful horrors. The parents whom I could locate have all generously given permission for their children's experiences to be described in ways that protect their privacy. Reading about these children's experiences can provide a perspective on the range of traumas children encounter. Some parents will conclude that their own child's trauma has been mercifully mild. Other parents will find company in the descriptions of children whose lives have been interrupted by more severe traumas. Reading about these children's experiences is not easy. To understand childhood trauma, it is necessary to travel through it, painful and disruptive as it may be. The most important points are summarized at the end of each chapter to make skimming easier.

There is nothing magical about children's healing from the wounds of terror. Love alone is seldom enough. Love must be put to work—the hard and patient work of parenting a traumatized child[1]. There can be no minimizing the impact of trauma on the lives of children and their families. Yet there is no reason to discuss childhood trauma without hope and optimism for child victims. In the Afterword I discuss my work with children and their families a bit more personally and look at the sources of my own hope and optimism. Parents who do the hard work of caring for a traumatized child need to know that living with memories, even horrifying ones, is possible for both their child and themselves.

Many children whom I have never met have been much on my mind while writing this book. I know them only from newspaper accounts of tragic events that have surely transformed their lives. The headlines while I have been writing have been particularly alarming: children caught in the violence of the Persian Gulf, children victimized by hate crimes in New York City, children who witnessed their Los Angeles neighborhoods erupt in deadly violence, children in the state of Washington whose classrooms were shelled by bullets, and most recently, the many child victims of hurricane Andrew. I know that these children's fears will not go away just because a grown-up tells them that it is "safe again." Experiences of terror echo longer and louder in children's lives than most parents anticipate. Children's memories of trauma can be tyrannical. It is seldom possible to notice an exact day that a trauma's echo gets quieter. Healing from trauma is so gradual that small changes are difficult to detect and there is no set timetable to the workings of horror upon the minds and lives of children. The healing distance of time is always a factor in recovery. If time alone could simply and effectively heal the wounds of psychological trauma, however, there would be less need of a guide for parents faced with the challenges of parenting a traumatized child.

Is This Book About Your Child?

This book is about every child who has been suddenly overwhelmed by an extraordinarily terrifying situation that he found himself helpless to cope with. *Extraordinary, unpredictable, sudden, overwhelming, shattering, transforming:* these are the key words that define trauma.

This is not a book about children's ordinary fears, such as going to the dentist. If, however, a girl was in the dentist's chair when an out-of-control car smashed through the office wall, then this book would be quite relevant. Traumas generally involve such improbable and hard-to-believe incidents. How probable is a car driving through a dentist's wall? About as possible as the car that crashed into a little girl's bedroom at midnight several months ago in Connecticut when a drunken driver failed to negotiate a turn.

Many parents will want to know if this book addresses the needs of abused children. The answer to parents of abused children is a qualified yes. Yes, many children who have been victimized by abuse are described here when their reactions are similar to children traumatized by other one-time events. And no, this is not a book written primarily for parents of abused children, nor does the book discuss the full range of child abuse in all its complexity.

This book addresses a wide variety of single-incident traumas, ranging from dog bites to disasters. Although the experiences of trauma vary, the effects on children have distinctive similarities. There are several types of childhood trauma, however, that are so distinct that they could not be well addressed by inclusion in this text. Children who have been repeatedly abused and children who have been incestuously abused, two groups that often overlap, have an experience of trauma that is unique.

The effects of repeated abuse are cumulative and generally involve radical distortions in a child's relationship to a trusted adult perpetrator. A chronically abused child may have many of the same posttraumatic reactions and behaviors as a child who has encountered a single traumatic event, but these reactions are complicated by relational wounds and the child's complex accommodations to long-term, generally secretive abuse. The difference between single and repeated incidents of abuse is not unlike the difference between simple and compound bone fractures. Both involve serious insult from a similar type of impact, but effective healing depends on recognizing the critical differences between these injuries.[2,3]

This book best addresses the needs of children whose abuse, whether mild or severe, has involved one or very few incidents involving a perpetrator who has had little prior importance to anyone in the family, including the child. Throughout the book, I have noted where the needs and issues of children recovering from single incidents of abuse differ from the handling of other types of single-incident trauma. At times I give examples of children who have been repeatedly traumatized by abuse to illustrate various reactions to trauma but I do not intend this book to meet the full needs of parents and caretakers of chronically traumatized children. There are many good books about abuse written specifically for parents that address this subject in all its complexity. Some of them are listed in Further Readings for Parents and Children, at the end of the book.

Understanding the Experience of Trauma for a Child

Trauma occurs when a sudden, extraordinary, external event overwhelms an individual's capacity to cope and master the feelings aroused by the event.[1] By its very nature, trauma is the occurrence of the unthinkable. Surprise and horror combine in one event to shock the totally unprepared child. The real event may be of very brief duration; it then becomes an emotional event that the child may struggle to come to terms with over a long period of time. If all traumas could successfully and permanently be forgotten by children, as we wish they could be, the aftermath of childhood trauma would be of less concern than it is. But children are not generally blessed with the capacity to erase their traumas from memory.[2]

Occurring suddenly and unforeseen, trauma can interrupt the most casual moment. It was during one such a casual moment, while taking a walk with her parents that Marcie learned about trauma.

Five-year-old Marcie was fond of her family walks through the quiet residential neighborhoods of their small town. This particular day was unusually beautiful, and the three of them were glad to have some weekend time to be out together. Quite unexpectedly, a disheveled woman walked straight up to Marcie and grabbed her in a very tight hug. Marcie screamed for her parents to help her. Unbelieving and alarmed, her parents repeatedly commanded the woman to let their daughter go and tried to pull her away from Marcie. Finally, the woman released the tearful child and ran away, leaving the family shocked and trembling.

For many weeks, this little girl retold the story of her terrifying encounter with this woman. Her parents found themselves retelling the story quite frequently as well. Marcie had numerous nightmares about being grabbed by hideous monsters and was clingy and fearful whenever she left her home.

Within a month, Marcie seldom mentioned her scare. Her nightmares disappeared, and she resumed her prior adventurous and spunky approach to life, with one exception: she refused to walk on the street where she had met the strange woman. Two months after their scare, Marcie's parents felt that they and Marcie had largely recovered from this experience.

Marcie's experience is a good example of a mild trauma. Her encounter with this frightening woman was shocking and terrifying, but it was also brief and resulted in no physical harm or permanent change in her familiar and protected world. Yet, as with all other traumas for children, Marcie's scare changed her expectations of safety in the world. She had to question her own safety in a new and unwelcome way. Her parents went back and forth between feelings of rage and sorrow watching their own small child worry about safety in the very neighborhood that they had carefully chosen as a safe place to raise a family. Over a relatively short time, however, Marcie was able to master the feelings of fear and helplessness that this incident had powerfully aroused.

Many parents wish their own child's trauma had been as mild as Marcie's. It is often difficult for parents to sort out how severe their own child's trauma has been. Carrie's experience involved more severe trauma.

Out with her mother on an errand, three-year-old Carrie had no reason to be on guard for the lunging attack of a german shepherd. Unnoticed by Carrie and her mother, the dog appeared suddenly from behind a shed and attacked instantly. Neither Carrie nor her mother had time to defend themselves. As the snarling dog locked Carrie's head within its jaws, Carrie's mother screamed for help and tried to restrain the dog. This dog's attack was vicious; it caused severe pain and facial mutilation. Carrie was overwhelmed with terror.

At first, Carrie's terror was of the dog and the pain. Later what Carrie would repeatedly recall with fright were her mother's screams for help, her mother's rage at the dog's owner who finally appeared to subdue the dog, the sound of the dog's snarling as it ripped open her cheek, and the smells of the doctor's office where she sat, frozen with shock, while her face was stitched.

Carrie's memories echoed in her nightmares and play for over a year, long after her face had healed. Once a confident and resilient child, Carrie was temporarily transformed into a fearful little girl. She became afraid of all dogs and would panic walking with her mother if she saw any dog at any distance. Her fear of dogs then enlarged to include fear of all animals. Carrie's fear focused on the animals' teeth. Ultimately she became fearful of going outside at all. Carrie's resolution to avoid the outdoors—and thereby avoid attack—was not a reasoned decision; she was simply terrified of going outside. Her solution, a phobia (or extreme fear) of the outdoors, helped her control her fear of further trauma, but it did not release her from this fear. Even within the safety of her home, Carrie remained fearful: she panicked when she encountered pictures of dogs and other animals with large teeth in her books. Like many other children who have experienced a severe trauma, the wish to avoid the memories and feelings of the trauma resulted in Carrie's designing her life around the wish to forget and avoid. Her efforts to avoid were both unsuccessful and unproductive: the terror continued to visit Carrie in her dreams, and she repeatedly reenacted the dog's attack in her play. As Carrie narrowed her world to the hoped-for safety of her own home, opportunities for normal growth and recovery were increasingly unavailable to her.

Severe psychological trauma, like Carrie's dog attack, sets into motion a series of predictable reactions and psychological mechanisms in a child's efforts to cope with and master an extraordinary event. Following a trauma, children become fearful of further trauma. They temporarily lose the sense of immunity to danger that we hope will color most children's basic trusting stance toward life. Rather than embracing life with a sense of openness, a traumatized child may suddenly need to retreat defensively. Like Carrie, severely traumatized children frequently go to extremes in order to control their fear that trauma will be repeated.

The difficulty of the actual trauma is compounded by the memory of that trauma. The memory of trauma is persistent for children. Adults sometimes erase the conscious memory of a trauma, but children rarely do[3]. Children over two years of age often maintain an indelible memory image of a traumatic event, complete with recall of incidental details that can come to have great and surprising meaning to them. These memories are similar to a snapshot of the event that freezes certain visual and sensory information into a lasting image. The fact that children cannot always verbally describe these memories, due to age and circumstance, can be deceptive[4]. The memories may be plentifuly evident in young children's play and reactions to events, locations, or people associated with the trauma.[5] These images have a haunting power to reevoke the feelings and experience of trauma for children.

Long after the original trauma, specific sights, smells, sounds, tastes, and physical sensations can remain powerful reminders of the experience. Little bits of memory, a smell or an image, serve as triggers that activate a child's fuller recall of trauma. When a memory of trauma is suddenly triggered in this way, the child can become quickly overwhelmed with feelings of present danger and fear. This is a flashback-like experience. Generally children do not experience the full-blown flashbacks of adults that involve a total loss of contact with reality. Some very severely traumatized children, however, are triggered into episodes of such terrifying recall that temporarily they are unable to recognize the people around them. Regardless of how much is triggered by a reminder of a trauma, children are very upset and disrupted by these experiences of recall that may occur in the midst of some pleasant activity. For parents and caretakers, such dramatic incidents of a child's sudden fearfulness can be particularly confusing. A parent cannot always know or understand exactly what the child is responding to with such fear, and children are not always able to pinpoint what set them off.

Nicky was a three-year-old child whose path seemed to be mined with memory triggers following his severe battering by his stepmother. As Nicky and his therapist walked toward the office playroom for his first visit a year later, the halls of the clinic were filled with the whirring sound of early morning vacuuming. Before reaching the office, Nicky suddenly froze with a look of pure terror on his face and then began screaming, "No vacuums, no noise." There was no doubt from Nicky's terror and driven need to silence the vacuum

that some bit of his traumatic memory was associated with the vacuum's noise. It was not until many months later that anyone understood that the "hurting stick" that Nicky frequently mentioned
referred to a vacuum attachment that had been used to beat his
shins.

Nicky's reaction to the sound of a vacuum suggests the power of
memory for a child who has experienced psychological trauma. It
is not just the original trauma that children struggle to master.
Memory itself can become the enemy, causing children to go to
great lengths to avoid encountering anything or anyone that is associated in their minds with the original trauma. These memories
carry the renewed experience of terror and the very real feeling
that the trauma will be repeated. This fear of fear can drive a child
to avoid ever larger spheres of activity in an effort to avoid both
memories and feelings.

Like Carrie following the dog's attack, children who have experienced psychological trauma frequently appear to be stuck in their
efforts to cope. Rather than moving forward developmentally, they
seem to stand still, avoiding the normal risks and activities that
nurture growth. So much energy is expended trying to manage
feelings and memories that too little may be left to resume the normal work and play of being a child.

As every parent knows, children need to play. They need to play
for pure pleasure and to solve problems and express feelings.
There is always some work being accomplished, however subtly, in
a child's spontaneous play. Children use play to help them master
everyday life, often playing out real-life situations that have caused
them some transient distress or anger. A young child who has been
punished for decorating a wall with crayons might be observed
several hours later putting her doll in a time-out chair with stern
words of warning about writing on the wall. This play occurs
without undue anxiety for the little girl; the doll's pretend session
in time-out helps to relieve traces of her own guilt about her earlier misbehavior. Similarly, young children play "doctor" with
their dolls and animals following an anxiety-provoking visit to the
doctor's office.

Children who have been traumatized similarly turn to play for
help in mastering an overwhelming event, but their play can take

an entirely new direction and form. Following a trauma, a child's play may lack ease and joy; the "player" may look anxious, driven, and too involved. This play is a deadly serious affair, involving concrete and literal reenactment (replay) of the trauma or slightly disguised versions. The play of traumatized children often does not look or feel "playful"; it looks and feels like the hard work that it truly is.

Three-year-old Sam began therapy three days after his mother's murder. After briefly glancing at the play materials in the therapist's office, he immediately emptied the dollhouse of all its furniture, which he then reassembled on a table in the exact layout of the rooms in his family's apartment. During each of his first twelve sessions of therapy, Sam relentlessly recreated this floor plan in great detail, always including the steps to the attic where his mother had been found murdered. Sam's play was serious, driven, and exacting, seeming to give him little pleasure or relief, yet he continued it week after week without variation.

As he played, Sam whispered bits and pieces of his own experience the night of his mother's murder. He recalled the violent altercation that had occurred before he had been put to bed. He told of calling for his mother's help the next morning when he woke with a wet bed. "But she didn't answer me," explained Sam. "She couldn't talk."

It took many weeks of play before Sam let a small doll representing himself climb the play attic stairs to find the dead mother. Through this repetitive play, he was able to explain what no one at the time had understood: Sam had in fact been the first one to find his mother.

Sam was engaging inpost-traumatic play.[6]post-traumatic play is marked by repetitiveness, seriousness, and lack of relief for the child. With very young children,post-traumatic play is often obvious. Older children tend to be more secretive in their reenactments.[7] During the initial phase of therapy, Sam looked stuck as he struggled to come to terms with both his loss and trauma. In his need to master these events and memories, he seemed not to notice the many other toys that usually delight children of his age in the playroom. Sam's psychic energy was available only for play that might assist him in coping with his trauma. Later in therapy, Sam abandoned the dollhouse furniture and moved on to much more diverse play. This change was the first signal that Sam was beginning to come to grips with his trauma.

A frightening encounter, a dog attack, physical abuse, witnessing the events surrounding a mother's murder: these situations exemplify a range of childhood traumas brought on by single overwhelming events. The concept of psychological trauma ranges over a broad spectrum of very mild to severe reactions in children. Frequently the nature of the traumatic event determines the severity of the child's reaction—but not always. Some children have severe reactions to seemingly mild or moderately severe traumas, and others endure severe traumas with relatively mild reactions. It is interesting to speculate on the reasons for some children's surprising reactions—personality, temperament, previous history—but there are no absolute explanations. More important is the need to understand the unique meaning and experience of a trauma for each child. The empathy the child experiences from loved ones and caretakers is a critical beginning for healing.

Trauma, A Childhood Wound

Mild or severe, a traumatically frightening event matters deeply to a child. Even when parents wish to forget what has occurred to their child, the child remembers. In fact, the child needs to remember—over and over, detail by detail—as part of the healing process. Children remember through retelling, through play, and through their post-traumatic fears, dreams, and unusual behaviors. These memories intrude unwelcomed; the child has not the least wish to remember. All of these varied forms of remembering are indications of the trauma's force but also part of the child's internal struggle to heal and master the trauma.

A trauma is a psychological wound to a child. The wound is often invisible, internal; no X rays define the damage. Most parents feel far more comfortable tending to a child's broken leg than to psychological trauma. An X ray can tell exactly where the fracture occurred and how serious a break it is. Even with a very serious fracture, knowing precisely what the problem is helps parents cope and support a child through the long and difficult healing process. With trauma, there is less certainty and precision of prediction, which generates more anxiety for parents. It is hard to wait patiently for a traumatized child to begin looking and feeling like herself again. Nagging at parents is their agonizing worry about whether the child will ever truly recover.

All wounds take time to heal. Children need to be given this time when the wound is a trauma just as much as they would when the wound involves broken bones. The early period of healing can be extraordinarily difficult for the entire family. There are many unanswerable questions for parents to tolerate, but there is also much that they can do to comfort and support the child. For most parents, knowing that they are finding ways to help and understand their child in turn helps them cope with their own worries and fears for their child.

Points to Remember: Understanding the Experience of Trauma for a Child

A trauma is an extraordinarily frightening event that overwhelms the victim with feelings of terror and helplessness. Unable to cope and unprotected against the force of terror, the child's encounter with defenselessness can create memorable emotional pain, confusion, and behavioral disruption.

The experience of a trauma is forcefully imprinted on a child's memory in ways that everyday experiences are not. Children struggle with lingering thoughts, feelings, and visual images of a trauma long after the event is over and their safety has been assured.

Traumatic memories are hard to shake and distressing. These memories and feelings intrude in children's daily lives in alarming and disruptive ways. The memories can be set off by some random triggering reminder encountered by the child, or they can intrude willy-nilly and unwelcomed in the child's daydreams and thoughts.

Children experience dread that the trauma will recur and have difficulty believing that it will not be repeated. They often use their play to help them master their experiences. The child's play efforts to control and master events over which she felt helpless are often unsuccessful, leaving her anxious and unrelieved.

Trauma causes psychological wounds. Healing from the wounds requires time and depends heavily on the understanding, support, and protection provided by parents and important other caretakers.

Sources of Childhood Trauma

It is common for parents to refer casually to a child's difficult experience as being "traumatic," but many trying and even startling situations which children encounter fall instead into the category of normal stress—for example, going to the dentist, moving to a new town, undergoing planned routine surgery, or enduring the taunts of another child. Children can have strong responses, emotionally and behaviorally, to these stressors, but they are seldom traumatized by them. The outcome of experiencing this normative stress, in fact, is generally positive when children can develop a sense of mastery in overcoming temporary and manageable adversities.

Trauma differs from ordinary stress in childhood in several ways. First, it generally occurs suddenly, leaving a child no opportunity mentally or physically to prepare for it. Moreover, the events are unusual, unpredictable, and outside the range of a child's typical experience. A hallmark characteristic of trauma, for both child and adult victims, is the extreme feeling of helplessness aroused. Avenues for coping and making the situation better are not evident or available. The suddenness, unpredictability, and overwhelming nature of the experience combine to create an emotion of terror.

Accidental Injury and Severe Illness

When childhood accidents are severe, resulting in life-threatening or extensive injury, the potential for trauma is high. Frequently, the concerns about the child's physical welfare or survival are initially so intense that little attention is paid to the child's emotional reactions. Severely injured children themselves also tend to put their initial energy into their physical recovery and may show more delayed emotional reactions to trauma.[1]

Accidents that result in repeated or painful medical procedures, hospitalizations, or disfiguring injuries have a strong likelihood of creatingpost-traumatic stress for children. Injured children have difficulty letting their memories of a trauma settle when they are repeatedly reminded of their experience by the ongoing need for medical procedures or when their injury has transformed their physical sense of themselves.[2] Accidents that involve prolonged periods of intense terror as a result of lengthy rescue operations are typically strongly imprinted in a child's memory. Children involved in accidents that have claimed the lives of others have the additional burdens of grief and survivor guilt to bear in their recovery.

Children with chronic or severe illnesses can experience aspects of their illness or treatment as traumatic. Cancer victims who undergo invasive and radical medical treatment have been found to show various signs of post-traumatic stress.[3] Necessary medical treatments can create severe reactions of helplessness and immediate or delayed trauma responses for children.

Catastrophes and Disasters

Weather-related disasters and community catastrophes—floods, tornadoes, earthquakes, volcanoes, hurricanes, fires—have an immediate, life-changing impact on all affected family members.[4] Environmental disasters, such as Three Mile Island, have been shown to result in post-traumatic stress for adults and children.[5] Victims of weather-related disasters suffer from immediate and long-term psychological distress following the devastation of their homes and communities.

Disasters and catastrophes most often hit entire families and large segments of the community. Some experts suggest that recovery from these calamities may be eased by the shared nature of the ordeal and the positive effects of community involvement in reconstruction efforts.[6] But others disagree, pointing to the destruction of the community as a loss of a major resource for residents' coping.[7] The impact of disasters that stem from human irresponsibility or callousness may well be more devastating for victims than those exclusively caused by the random forces of nature.[8]

Every disaster has unique aspects in terms of community-wide reactions and recovery. Whether the larger community responds with resilience or despair, the impact of a disaster will predictably have a wide range of impact on individual children and adults. Certainly children's different accounts of the same disaster clearly show how unique each child's experience truly is.[9] The extent to which a child is directly exposed to life threat, visions of destruction and death, isolation, injury, and personal loss will have an impact on recovery. When whole families are victimized by disaster there are opportunities for mutual support in coping but the children are exposed to the anxiety of living in a family that may be physically dislocated as well as psychologically disrupted.[10]

Physical and Sexual Abuse

Childhood physical abuse is a source of trauma for children. Children who are victims of adult violence frequently develop various emotional and behavioral signs of trauma. A single incident of physical abuse usually creates a different outcome than repeated incidents over time for children. Children who are extensively and repeatedly physically abused are prone to the most disabling and severe symptoms of chronic post-traumatic stress. The continuum of physical abuse ranges from a single incident of physical abuse to the prolonged suffering of children tortured in the secrecy of their homes or in punitive institutional settings.[11]

Child sexual abuse is a source of trauma for countless numbers of children. When children's bodies are used to meet adult sexual needs, there is enormous potential for physical and psychological trauma. The phenomenon of sexual abuse is widespread and involves extremely diverse incidents of misuse, ranging from mild single incidents of private touching to severe incidents of rape and ritualized degradation for children. Sexual abuse may also involve repeated incidents of progressively more severe abuse which occur secretively in the context of important and powerful relationships between a child and an adult over many years. All sexual abuse involves gross misuse of adult power and violation of a child's right to depend upon adults for care and protection. Sexual abuse that is accompanied by threats, betrayal of trust, violence, physical injury, pain, or terrifying sadistic ritual involves the most extreme psychological assaults on children.[12]

Interpersonal and Community Violence

The soaring level of community and domestic violence has increasingly involved large numbers of children as direct and indirect victims.[13] Within the family, children are traumatized by witnessing violent or sexual assaults on loved ones. Children of battered women who witness countless acts of violence against their mothers may show severe signs of post-traumatic stress even when they themselves may be exempt from physical abuse.[14]

Community violence involves child victims and child witnesses in terrorizing incidents. Hate crimes against children, motivated by rascist or religious beliefs, have drawn national attention to one devastating source of violent childhood victimization[15]. Shootings in schoolyards and other community settings are dramatic, highly publicized examples of violence involving child victims. In the 1984 Los Angeles schoolyard sniper shooting, nearly all of the children on the playground at the time of the shooting showed signs ofpost-traumatic stress a month following the incident. Not just the children who were at school during the shooting were plagued by nightmares, but also children who were away from school that day and had to imagine their friends or siblings being fired on.[16]

Schoolyard slayings and single incidents of dramatic child-directed violence receive a great deal of media attention. There is less publicity, however, around the impact of high levels of violence on children living in neighborhoods where violent crime is common. These children are particularly vulnerable to experiencing incidents of genuine danger in their local communities; murder, stabbing, shooting, and rape are routine realities in the lives of inner city children.[17] Community violence is becoming a source of chronic trauma for our most vulnerable children whose exposure to violence is too frequently paired with the deprivations of growing up in poverty. What little we know as proved "facts" about children living in high-crime districts suggests that the experience is not unlike living in a war zone.[18]

Single Terrorizing Experiences

At times children have unusual experiences that are hard to categorize with other traumas of childhood. A child who is taken hostage or kidnapped, for instance, may be terrorized by threat, enclosure, and sudden separation without ever directly experiencing physical violence. Any surprising, overwhelmingly frightening event that a child feels helpless against may cross the line from fright to trauma.

The Child Witness: Observation as a Source of Trauma

To witness an act of intense personal violence is clearly traumatic. A child witness is captive in a passive role and able to attend fully to the horror of the act. These children struggle with vivid memories of the images and sounds of the scene, often focusing in their recollections on one particular worst moment.[19] Child witnesses take in the totality of the situations they observe. Their minds become flooded with impressions of both the attacker's aggression and the anguish of the victim's emotional and physical suffering, and they struggle with their inability to intervene and save the victim. Even very young children who observe acts of violence commonly experience guilt in retrospect over their failure to rescue the victim. These child witnesses often experience strong wishes to take revenge on the aggressor.[20]

Children often watch gruesome scenes of violence between people they trust and love. The more personal these acts the greater is the potential for trauma.[21] Recovery is particularly complicated when a loved one is involved. When the violence results in death of a parent, disruption of home and caretaking, or involvement in interminable criminal proceedings, the child faces the multiple stresses of dealing with loss, trauma, and family disorganization.

These children are clearly the co-victims of the traumas they observe. They carry with them indelible vivid memories and visual images of the victim's pain. While observing personal violence may be more devastating for a child's basic sense of safety, witnessing accidental harm to another also seriously threatens a child's sense of security.

Parent Loss and Trauma

Loss of a parent is a terrible blow, requiring a long and gradual period of grieving and recovery before a child's sense of well-being is restored. Children's grief can be complicated in various ways. The inability to understand the finality and reality of death, for instance, can complicate experiences of loss for very young children.[22] Trauma also complicates bereavement. A child who has watched a loved one's sudden death or been exposed to horrifying scenes of mutilation or profuse bleeding can have extraordinary difficulty coming to terms with loss. Children who face the dual challenge of mastering loss and trauma often need special help to cope with traumatic memories before they are able to truly grieve.[23]

Sources of Retraumatization

Certain traumas carry a high risk that children will be retraumatized by their experiences following the initial trauma. Traumas that carry a social stigma, such as sexual abuse, and those that expose a child to further physical or emotional pain have strong potential to re-evoke or re-create a traumatic experience.

When physical injury requires painful and lengthy medical procedures, there is little control over the necessary sources of further trauma. In many situations, however, a parent's watchful efforts can prevent or limit additional distress. Parents can help buffer an injured child from experiencing further emotional pain by their comforting presence during hospitalizations and by educating medical staff about a child's particular needs and sensitivities. Helping a child prepare for invasive or painful procedures, transforming treatments into games, distracting with activities and stories, preserving every possible connection to friends and treasured activities, and remaining calm and optimistic in the child's presence are other ways that parents shield injured children from further trauma.

Two potential sources of retraumatization are encountered when the trauma is a public event, involving the legal system and the media. Sadly, some children are exposed to further trauma within their homes when the overreactions of loved ones compounds their fright and worry. Sexually abused children are particularly vulnerable to encountering reactions in others that complicate their recovery.

When Trauma Involves the Criminal Justice System

When Bridget watched as her best friend, Jan, was pulled into a car that sped away, she remembered four of the license plate numbers. Her information led to the arrest of the couple who had taken Jan to a secluded lake, where she was raped and left tied to a tree. A year and a half later, when Bridget and Jan were both nine years old, the girls were the star witnesses in the prosecution's case to convict the couple. Bridget's nightmares returned several weeks before the trial was to begin; Jan was terrified of going to court. Despite many reassurances, Jan firmly believed that the couple would hurt her in the courtroom if she told the judge what had happened at the lake.

When a child's trauma has involved a crime, involvement in the machinery and procedures of law enforcement can be a mystifying and troubling experience. In spite of increased awareness of children's special needs in the legal community, and increased efforts to humanize the process of investigation and prosecution, involvement with the legal system is still generally an uncomfortable one at best for both the child victims and family members. At its worst, children and their families can experience further traumatization as they negotiate through the unfamiliar processes of the legal system.

Children and their parents tend to be extremely uneasy interacting with police investigators and district attorneys. For many small children, the police are simplistically equated with catching the "bad guys." To be interviewed by a police officer usually arouses some feeling in children that they themselves have done something wrong, despite many reassurances to the contrary. In many ways parents have a similar reaction. Most parents have never had reason to go beyond the front door of their local police department or the district attorney's office. Finding themselves part of a criminal investigation is an insult to their identity at a time that many cherished notions about themselves and their family life are in disarray. This involvement with the legal system can aggravate parents' feeling that a single event has wrought enormous changes in the way they see themselves, their child, and their life in the community.

Engagement with the legal system around the issue of a child's trauma plunges the family into a world of professionals and assumptions that can be confusing and stressful. Parents rightly worry about the impact of a child's having to testify in court and the uncertainty of trial outcomes even when credible testimony has been presented. They worry about the effect on the child of keeping the trauma as a forefront issue during the very long period of time required to prepare for trial. The much-delayed time lines of trials are too frequently at odds with the internal time line of children's recovery from trauma. To heal, children generally need to distance themselves emotionally from the trauma over time. But the courts are not generally responsive to a child's need to cope with and confront a trauma in the early phase of recovery and then to begin the process of encapsulating the experience and distancing from it emotionally. Prolonged preparations for legal proceedings and the actual proceedings themselves interfere with the child's natural process of healing by continually reevoking the memories and feelings of the trauma.

In some situations involving trauma to a child, there is no real choice (or no alternative) to involvement with the legal system. But sometimes parents do have a choice about pressing charges or proceeding to trial. Is there a right decision regarding involvement of a child in the legal system? Not that I know of. Parents must weigh the relative meaning of many factors in making this decision: the protection of their child from further distress, the child's and family's need for a just response to a frightening crime, the importance of swift and severe consequences in disrupting the cycle of child victimization, the protection of other potential child victims in the community, and the family's own emotional resources to endure further stress.

Many parents have found it helpful to consult with an attorney knowledgeable in the particular area of law involved as a way of obtaining information before making decisions. A child's therapist or mental health consultant can also be asked for an opinion on the child's capacity to tolerate whatever is anticipated in a particular court proceeding. Parents need to know that it is all right to put

a severely traumatized child's need for protection first in the deci-
sion-making process regarding court proceedings.

Involvement in the legal system carries with it a large degree of
stress for family members. Many parents find the feeling of helplessness and lack of control difficult to tolerate in their dealings
with the legal system. The law offers no guarantees of protection
for children or of just outcomes, and this lack of certainty can result in additional anguish for parents and children.[24] On the other
hand, the legal system offers the possibility of returning a sense of
power and justice to victimized children and their families. For
some children, the opportunity and experience of testifying can
help restore their sense of power and give some sense of closure to
an experience of trauma.[25] If this sense of empowerment could be
guaranteed for children in courts, testifying would be recommended more frequently and with less ambivalence.

The legal system has created a buffer to the stress it produces by
creating victim-witness programs whose staff members offer concrete and emotional assistance to the victims and witnesses of
crimes. In recent years, victim-witness advocates, patient and caring prosecutors, and child-sensitive judges have been key in transforming many children's and families' experience with the legal
system. And still there is much to learn about helping children and
families benefit from their experience with the legal system.

The Media

When the media are involved in a child's trauma, the experience
can be negative and memorable. Families coping with an immediate crisis need privacy, and the timing of the media's "need to
know" fits poorly with a family's need to retreat. The intrusion of
reporters and the printing of inaccurate or unwanted material can
feel injust and insensitive. When photographers and film crews in-
vade a family's privacy or pictures are published without family
permission, the experience of powerlessness is reinforced.

> When thirteen-year-old José was badly beaten on his way home
> from work in an incident that heightened tension between the
> Hispanic and white communities of a small city, his parents were
> horrified to read a profile of their son in the newspaper two days
> later. The reporter, who had interviewed some of Josés teachers and

fellow students, detailed their son's record of detentions and even his struggles with math. The quotations from other students described his "explosive temper" and his "tough guy attitude." Nowhere in the article was there any mention of José's superior pitching for his Little League team or his after-school job as a youth counselor-in-training. José's parents read this article in the intensive care unit where they waited and worried about their son's recovery from his beating by five older teenagers.

Families who need and want protection from the media can appoint a friend or relative as spokesperson to provide information to media interviewers. At times, the media can be helpful to families in providing clear information to the community or in correcting previously published incorrect information. Some families have a need to speak out in the media about a situation involving a child's trauma, although this is seldom true in the period of immediate crisis.

The media vary in their degree of sensitivity to families who have been victimized by an event considered news. The pressure to get information into print, regardless of the impact on the families involved, is not the same in rural areas as it is in urban centers where many media sources compete heavily for their stories.[26] Tabloid reporting approaches are poorly tolerated in small communities but are a reality to be contended with in urban areas. The intrusiveness and damage that can occur for families from irresponsible and sensationalized reporting techniques are obvious and lamentable.

Sexual Abuse and Retraumatization

Parents who realize that their child has been sexually abused initially react in a number of ways. Feelings of rage, disbelief, horror, disgust, and guilt are common. Because of the social stigma attached to sexual crimes, parents sometimes are reluctant to talk about their child's abuse outside the family, which can result in families' feeling isolated and unsupported. Sometimes families are truly avoided by friends or relatives who are unable to believe or cope with the fact of abuse occurring close to home. When families feel abandoned or blamed, the task of recovery is far more difficult. Whether with or without the support of friends and relatives, managing and controlling distress is the most important and the most difficult work parents have to do following a child's abuse.[27]

A child's disclosure of sexual abuse may bring the abuse to an end, but it can also expose the child to experiences that create further, and sometimes intense, distress. Children are at risk for retraumatization when their disclosures are not believed, when they are blamed for the abuse, when their disclosure results in placement away from the family, when they are subjected to multiple intrusive interviews, and when their parents' distress is so severe and dramatic that the child feels frightened and responsible for the parents' pain.[28] The sources of further trauma are also great when a child's disclosure results in real-life consequences the child never imagined or even wanted—for example, when a perpetrator is arrested or a child is involved in interminable preparations for trial during a time when the child needs to put the abuse behind him or her.

Parents of all sexually abused children need to keep the child's ongoing vulnerability to further stress in mind following a disclosure. The child's experience of others' reactions and the consequences of the disclosure appear to determine a great many of the lasting meanings a child gives to an incident of abuse.[29] Children can learn the meaning and shameful feeling of stigmatization following an episode of sexual abuse, or they can learn that this has been a bad experience that the important people in their lives are able to cope with and talk about in ways that are similar to their responses to other problems. Children can learn that there is something so powerfully distressing and unspeakable about their experience that their caretakers are devastated—or they can see that the experience has generated concern and protection for them but no loss of their loved ones' availability and responsiveness. The child can learn about her own strength and bravery in telling and coping—or she can learn that she is powerless and damaged. At every step along the way once a child discloses sexual abuse, the choices made by parents and those in the legal and social service systems make a lasting difference in how a child interprets and feels about the experience. It is a weighty responsibility for distressed parents and others carrying power over a child's life to make these choices and decisions with the child's best interests in mind.

Following an incident of sexual abuse, the child needs time and space to cope with her own feelings. A child who feels compelled to worry about and respond to a parent's anxieties and feelings has a much harder task of coping. Sharing all one's feelings openly with a child can create an enormous burden for the child, who may easily feel responsible for a parent's distress.

Limiting further distress for sexually abused children is not an easy job for parents but it is possible. Parents can help protect their sexually abused child from further stress by:

- Talking and dealing with the child calmly, using matter-of-fact language about the abuse.
- Letting the child know that she is not alone, that there are other children who have been touched in ways they're not supposed to be by grown-ups.
- Expressing pride and gratitude that the child was brave enough to tell about the abuse.
- Reassuring the child that the abuse was not her fault in any way.
- Accepting all the child's feelings about the abuse and the abuser, including the positive feelings.
- Being available to talk with the child at any time.
- Working to keep routines as normal at home after the abuse as possible.
- Protecting the child from contact with important relatives or friends whose distress, blame, or other inappropriate reactions will be disturbing to the child.
- Finding other adults to talk with freely about all the many feelings the abuse has stirred up.

Sometimes parents can only pretend to be calm and reassuring when they are first dealing with the impact of a child's abuse; they need to hold back their own strong reactions and focus on the child's needs. Parents who feel overwhelmed by a child's abuse or are unable to gain control over their feelings should seek professional help.

Points to Remember: Sources of Trauma

Trauma involves a sudden, extraordinary experience of overwhelming terror. It needs to be distinguished from more ordinary frightening experiences of childhood. These frightening experiences are upsetting to children but generally involve more common events that a child can anticipate, actively cope with, and experience comfort and support in enduring.

There are various sources of childhood trauma: sexual molestation, physical violence, witnessing incidents of community or domestic violence, accidental injuries and severe illness, catastrophes and disasters, and exposure to single, terrifying experiences.

Children who witness traumatic events are as vulnerable as the direct victims of trauma to disruptive distress and the intrusion of traumatic memory.

The death of a parent is a severe loss for a child but does not automatically involve trauma for a child. The child's actual experience of a parent's death must be understood in detail in order to know whether the child has experienced trauma in addition to loss.

When trauma and personal loss combine in a child's experience, grieving is complicated by the need first to work through memories of trauma.

Some traumas carry particular risks that a child will be further traumatized. Sources of retraumatization for children include involvement in the legal system, intrusion of the media, and the overreactions of loved ones to traumas that are difficult to accept, such as sexual molestation.

Children learn the lasting meanings of their traumas, in part, through the reactions of the people they love and depend on most.

The Signs of Psychological Trauma

Each child's encounter with trauma is unique. The particular aspects of the trauma itself interact with all that is special and characteristic about the individual child to create that child's response. There are few absolutes that parents can rely upon when it comes to predicting their child's response to a trauma. Parents must observe their child closely during the following weeks and months to discover the meaning and impact of the experience.

Generally children react to psychological trauma quite rapidly, showing some strain within a few days of the event. Some children, however, show no immediate signs of trauma and appear to be unfazed in the long run as well. Regardless of a child's first reactions, there is a tendency for traumatic memory to resurface unpredictably over time, causing distress and disruption for a child. This "time-bomb" effect needs to be considered by parents who find that their child's behavior is initially free of any signs of traumatic impact. Studies suggest that some of these symptom-free children will develop delayed responses, particularly in situations of severe trauma.

Certain groups of children predictably show delayed reactions. Children whose trauma has involved physical injury, for example, may take longer to react to the psychological aspect of their trauma.[1] The more serious the physical harm involved, the more a child will tend to invest energy and anxiety in the physical recovery. Coping with bodily trauma seems to take precedence for many injured children, leaving the emotional aspects of the trauma to be dealt with once the body has regained its strength. The three-year-old boy who had the memorable encounter with a vacuum cleaner in my office had been hospitalized for extensive injuries following physical abuse by his stepmother. He showed no signs of psychological trauma, and over the course of his ten-month hospitalization, the nursing staff assumed that he had forgotten the cause of his extensive injuries. But once he was discharged to a secure and loving relative's home, he became suddenly and overwhelmingly symptomatic. He began to have periods of terrifying recall for his abuse and described these haunting memories with harrowing and bizarre detail, leaving no doubt regarding their authenticity.

A second group of children who frequently show a delayed response are those whose trauma had a secret aspect to it. Children who have been sexually molested and threatened into secrecy may not show a full reaction until they have disclosed their secret and found assurance of safety. Children holding on to a secret trauma often withhold their emotional responses to it until the secret is at last free. In retrospect, parents may recall disturbances in a child's behavior prior to a disclosure, but the more dramatic symptoms of a child's painful coping with the memories of the trauma may not be fully evident until after the disclosure.

Whether immediate or delayed, the signs of psychological trauma include a wide range of observable reactions and behaviors. Few children will exhibit all of these signs, and some will show none of them. Most, however, will give indications of their distress through one or more behaviors and reactions.

Fears and Anxieties

Extreme fear, usually experienced as terror, is central to psychological trauma. This fear by its nature is difficult to shake. Children tend to reexperience their original state of terror in ways that disrupt their sense of self and safety long after the event. This distinctive traumatic fear can hold with a remarkably strong and long-lasting grip, causing intense dismay and concern for parent and child.

Many children fear and believe that the original trauma will occur again. Terrified once, they search for signs that will prepare them for a reccurrence of the trauma. More than anything else, they want to avoid a surprise return of the state of terror. Adults may have difficulty understanding just how compelling this fear of the trauma repeating can be for a child. Children lack the perspective to appreciate the probabilities of events occurring or not occurring, and they are little comforted by reason. In the child's mind, there remains too good a possibility that the trauma will recur.

This obsessive fear of further trauma can create a state of perpetual fearfulness that may seem tragically maladaptive from a parent's perspective. But this state of internal preparation affords the child a needed sense of readiness and power. It is as if the child is thinking, "If only I could be ready, this horror could not surprise and overwhelm me as it did before." At all costs, then, the child seeks to undo the original feelings of helplessness. Unfortunately, the child's internal state of readiness too often is one of fright and anxiety. Reasonable explanations of the low probability for recurrence of a trauma are not initially reassuring to a child gripped by posttraumatic dread.

When a bolt of lightning struck the playing field of a boys' soccer game in Illinois, one child was killed, and several of the other ten to thirteen year olds were injured. The children had quite varied reactions over the next four to eight weeks. A few showed no signs of distress, most had mild or moderate reactions of distress, and a small group experienced very severe reactions.[2] The children were plagued by various fears. As might be expected, fears related to storms were the most frequent and intense for these children. The children were also afraid of sleeping, animals, noises and disasters, the supernatural, bodily penetration, death and dying, enclosed spaces, people, embarassment, and separations from parents.

Fear takes many different forms following a trauma. Some children become pervasively fearful. Others develop specific, isolated fears. Fearfulness can be expressed in panic reactions to specific triggers or in separation anxiety with caretakers. For some children, fear is expressed through their physical responses in startle reactions and generalized nervousness. One group of children, the fear deniers, make desperate and constant proclamations of invincibility. The various faces of fear need to be understood when helping a child recover from trauma.

Pervasive Fears

Pervasively fearful children appear to have undergone a personality change following a trauma. These children are suddenly fearful of many aspects of their everyday experience. Routine activities that they may have enjoyed in the past can appear fraught with potential danger. Separations from parents, new activities, and other ventures into the unknown may be particularly difficult.

Some of these children appear to approach daily life as if it were a minefield requiring utmost caution and attention. Their wariness is similar in many ways to a soldier's negotiating a minefield. The children feel they must be on guard constantly for signs of danger. This state of perpetual caution can be perplexing and disheartening to parents. It may be helpful to recall that a child's excessive caution and fear serve the purpose of a mine detector.

Specific Fears

Specific fears following a trauma may or may not be directly related in content to the trauma itself. Like the soccer players, many children develop acute and overwhelming fears of specific objects, sounds, or surroundings associated with the original trauma. They can react with full panic to reencountering some aspect of their trauma in the months, and sometimes years, following the original fright. For the children whose soccer field was struck by lightning, every storm had the power to re-evoke their fears and memories for many months following the incident. So real was the threat of storms for one of these boys that he retreated to the safety of his basement, where he sat huddled and cringing in a corner, wearing a football helmet.[3] At times a child's fear centers on one central terror-inducing object. Little Carrie, for instance, became intensely fearful of all dogs following her dog bite. Other children become fearful of only the particular kind of dog that bit them. Sexually molested children often develop fears of people who share certain characteristics with the molester. It is not uncommon for children to react with total terror or complete withdrawal when confronted with the object of a specific traumatic fear.

> Tanya seemed unable to let go of her fear of "big boys" for many months following her molestation by a teenaged babysitter. She

talked about teenagers constantly and asked many questions about them. She wanted to know, for example, exactly at what age children become teenagers and how to tell if a teenager will make a good babysitter. When families with teenaged boys visited at Tanya's house, she became anxious for days in advance and withdrew to her room during the visit. She was only mildly suspicious of teenage girls.

Some children's fears appear unrelated in content or meaning to their actual trauma. Fears of the dark, of going to sleep, of being alone, of monsters, "bogeymen," spiders, or the supernatural are typical of children's fears following a trauma.[4] Children may focus their dread on particular fears that seem to have little to do with their specific experience. The extent of these fears and the timing of their appearance shortly following a trauma are the links that permit parents to recognize more general fears as signs of trauma.

Sudden Panic or Distress

Sudden terrifying events can imprint themselves on all of a child's senses in a powerful way. Visual impressions, sounds, smells, tastes, and skin sensations associated with the traumatic event appear to be absorbed by the memory of a child in particularly vivid form. Long after the occurrence of a trauma, a child may have an extremely strong reaction to encountering some aspect of this sensory memory for the event. A strong smell or some specific sound can set off, or trigger, the child's recall of her trauma. These sensory triggers are not always obvious to a parent, nor can a child always pinpoint or describe the source of sudden distress.

For the child, the sudden intrusion of traumatic memory set off by a sensory trigger can come close to creating a full reexperiencing of the trauma. The child may panic, believing, and acting as if, the trauma is recurring. Although children are much less likely than adults to experience full-blown flashbacks, even one flashback is extremely confusing and disorienting for the child as well as the parent. One very young and severely abused boy experienced repeated flashbacks when being diapered during the first year following his abuse. The smell of a particular diaper rash cream appeared to be a trigger in all of these incidents. During these episodes, he would suddenly start screaming and writhing, yelling, "Don't, Poppy; don't punch me. You cracked my head." For up to fifteen minutes, the child was unable to discriminate his gentle foster father from his abusive biological grandfather.

Sensory triggers can be so subtle that parents may not be able to identify them. The triggers that have power over very young, non-verbal children can be the most difficult to identify. Although there is little research available on this phenomenon, clinical experience suggests that it is this youngest group of children who are most powerfully panicked by sensory triggers.

Separation Anxiety

Fear of separation from parents or other trusted caretakers is a particularly common reaction for children of all ages following trauma, although the younger the child, the more likely that separation anxiety will be observed. Parents may note fretful clinging, following a parent around the house, resistance to babysitters, or marked reactions to separation involved in attending school or day care. A child's difficulties with separation immediately following a trauma may be mild or quite severe. The separation fears are signals that feelings of safety are temporarily available only in the presence of a parent or trusted caretaker. For some children, this means not letting a parent out of sight even at home. Children may even follow parents into the bathroom. Other children may feel secure within their homes but become clingy whenever they venture outside. Trauma can temporarily destroy a child's prior inner conviction of safety, leaving her dependent on the physical presence of trusted caretakers.

Separation anxiety can affect older as well as young children following trauma. The need for company to ensure feelings of safety is particularly intense for young women who have been raped or assaulted, but it is not uncommon following other traumas as well.

Maggie was a brilliant young girl in her sophomore year of boarding school who had been viciously attacked by her cousin's doberman. The dog had done severe damage to Maggie's ear, resulting in numerous painful reconstructive surgeries. A year following the dog's attack, Maggie was embarrassed to admit that she was unable to cross the rural school grounds by herself. Dogs ran loose at this school, and she was terrified of encountering them. She found herself choosing courses on the basis of her best friend's schedule so that she would have a companion on the way. Midyear, Maggie suddenly decided to leave this school which she had loved and return to the public high school in her home town. Overwhelmed by the feelings of danger that invaded her days and disturbed her nights, Maggie simply wished to be closer to home.

Startle Responses and Nervousness

Children of all ages, including infants, may show dramatic or subtle startle responses—a sudden involuntary shuddering or tensing of the body—to sounds. It is as if the child's body is recalling a pain, a fright, or a danger without the child's conscious awareness of the memory. The sounds triggering the startle response might be specific, such as an ambulance siren, or difficult to isolate with any specificity.

For some children following a trauma every sound or sudden movement becomes too meaningful. A child who is constantly attending to miscellaneous sounds in the environment is on guard for what those sounds might indicate regarding potential danger. This hypervigilance is common among traumatized children. The capacity to screen out random noises, which is so vital to concentration, has been temporarily disrupted. The child is left vulnerable to feeling bombarded by sounds or slight changes in the environment. Hypervigilance may combine with startle responses or unusually strong physiological reactions to events that recall some aspect of the trauma. This general state of anxiety early in the recovery period can interfere with a child's attention and pleasure. School performance can be especially affected by a child's inability to concentrate.

Fear Denial

Some children may insist all day long that they fear nothng at all— and then collapse in terror of the dark at bedtime. The extent to which these fear-denying children go to convince themselves and others of their power and immunity is a clue to the extent of their underlying fearfulness. Children who vigorously deny their fears are most likely to go to extremes in overidentifying with powerful and aggressive characters in their play. They may insist on taking the roles of the scariest characters and may want to watch the scariest movies. When confronted with gentle suggestions that all children have fears of some things, they will protest with great conviction. Fear deniers are so desperate for a sense of power that they devote their days to convincing themselves and others of their invulnerability.

Geordie was eight when he was pushed off the side of a pool by some boys who had been picking on him. He had never learned to swim and nearly drowned. For the following eight months, Geordie was a classic fear denier. He became unusually rough with the other children in his third-grade class and began to take on the role of the bully on the playground. After school he worked on dare-devil tricks with his bicycle and skateboard. Once a fairly careful child, he now seemed to have no concern about his physical safety.

Geordie developed a new interest in horror movies. He had seen one once at a friend's house and now began collecting as much information as he could gather from friends about the plots and characters of these films. Much to his parents' dismay, Geordie talked about these movies all the time, sounding like an experienced viewer. At home, he sought out the scariest videos he was permitted to watch and replayed "the good parts" (the worst and scariest) over and over. His favorite characters were always the villains. He begged to be allowed to watch "911," a gory and frightening television show about actual emergencies. "They don't scare *me*," Geordie would proclaim with great pride.

At night, Geordie was a different fellow entirely. He was extremely fearful of going to bed and frequently had terrifying nightmares. He slept for months with his light on and kept his plastic sword collection within easy reach of his bed. It took many months before Geordie could begin to acknowledge his very real fears.

Behavioral Regression

Children typically react to stress, mild or severe, with a temporary setback in age-appropriate skills and behaviors. Most parents have plentiful experience with the ebb and flow of mild regression under stress in their children's lives. During a family vacation, the stress of change and unfamiliar surroundings may result in a child's difficulties sleeping or an unwelcome explosion of temper tantrums. The first anxiety-provoking weeks of kindergarten may create sufficient tension for a five-year-old child to resume wetting the bed after two years of being dry at night. A ten-year-old who is shuttling back and forth between two newly divorced parents may be particularly whiny and demanding every Sunday night upon returning to his primary residence. Parents typically treat these regressive responses for what they are: throwbacks to old behaviors under stress.

Regression is one way children under stress cope. Given the unmanageable stress involved in trauma, it is not surprising that many children show marked regressions. They may lose some developmental skills, their inner controls over aggression, and their capacity to comfort themselves. These skills and controls have been gained with difficulty over the years, and they are particularly vulnerable to weakening under stress. Toileting accidents are common for young children following a trauma, as is a return to nighttime wetting or thumb sucking for elementary school-aged children. Young children may lose recently developed language skills or show a marked slowdown in language development. Less frequently, children may become completely mute—literally "scared speechless"—following a trauma. Aggressive acting out with other children and loss of control over anger are common. The acting out may appear directly related in content to the trauma or may simply be a generalized loss of control over angry feelings.

The loss of a child's ability to self-comfort takes many forms. A child who has previously been well able to tolerate small disappointments or frustrations may be unable to handle the frustration of a drawing that does not come out well or to wait for a parent to get off the telephone without screaming her displeasure. Mild rebuffs from friends may be reacted to as cataclysmic events.

A child's capacity to self-comfort generally goes unnoticed until it disappears. It is easy for parents to take for granted a child's ability to keep an even keel throughout the normal difficulties and frustrations of a typical day until the child falls apart from exhaustion at bedtime. When the child dissolves into a tantrum or fit of weeping over something as trivial as pajamas that do not go on right, parents watch the child's self-comforting capacity collapse dramatically. The child is just too tired and fussy to remind himself that if he tries again the pajamas will go on fine. After a trauma, some children feel this fragile all day long.

When a child's capacity for self-comforting breaks down, life can feel difficult for all members of a family. Parents often feel that the child is making constant demands for comfort, help, and reassurance. This is exactly what is occurring. Parents are called upon to respond as they used to when the child was younger. For the parents of elementary school-aged children, it may be difficult to recall the many years they spent actively helping their children cope with moment-to-moment frustrations when they were much younger. Regressed children are frequently described by their parents as excessively irritable and needy. For some children, the irritability is mild; for others, it can be raging.

Toileting Accidents

Many routinely stressful events in children's lives wreak temporary havoc with the achievement of toilet training. Most parents have some experience with a child's wetting the bed or not making it to the bathroom at least once during a disturbing or exciting time. Less commonly, children have bowel accidents under stress. Following a trauma, a temporary period of toileting accidents is quite normal for young children. Children who have experienced genital trauma can be more vulnerable to having toileting accidents.

A brief return to bedwetting following a trauma is of relatively mild concern, as is infrequent and temporary daytime wetting. Prolonged frequent daytime wetting or deliberate urination in odd places for a toilet-trained child over four years of age can be more worrisome indicators of the child's inner distress. Similarly, frequent and prolonged bowel accidents in a fully trained child can signal the intensity of a child's struggle with overwhelming feelings.

Unwanted Images and Thoughts

Following a trauma, children frequently experience unwanted visual imagery from the event that can be extremely disturbing and distracting. Bits and pieces of the traumatic scene return, as if on automatic replay, entering a child's consciousness randomly. Children describe repeatedly seeing a disturbing image of the trauma in their minds. Images that involve the sight of greatest horror are often the ones that haunt children. This relentless replay in the mind's eye can be torturous, accompanied as it often is with recall of sounds and other sensations.

Traumatic images can intrude at any time: at school, while lying in bed waiting for sleep, or at odd moments with no apparent trigger. Children do not ordinarily tell their parents what is going through their minds; they need to be asked.

The intrusion of imagery and thoughts can occur with disturbing frequency and insistence. The child can feel trapped by this relentless internal barrage that powerfully reevokes feelings of panic and helplessness. Children who become fearful of going to sleep or sleeping alone following a trauma may be afraid of a deluge of images, feelings, and thoughts that they fear will intrude when they close their eyes. Often these children are correctly fearful. The drifting of the mind just before sleep seems to invite the return of unwelcome, highly visual memories.

Loss of Pleasure in Enjoyable Activities

During the first weeks or months following a trauma, children temporarily may lose their sense of pleasure in activities that have previously been guaranteed to delight them. A child who is distracted, overwhelmed, or extremely fearful is not as free to engage with humor and energy in normal playful activities. They may engage in their favorite activities but with an unusual sense of seriousness. The capacity for pleasure returns only gradually as children begin to feel psychologically safer and more distant from the trauma.

Retelling and Replaying of Trauma

Children may appear driven to retell the story of their trauma and to reenact the experience in play. Frequently the retelling is blurted out at odd moments, as if the story was under pressure to be released. The child does not welcome interruption or redirecting of his story. This need to retell can appear insatiable, the story may need numerous retellings for the child to experience some control over it.

The retelling is generally factually accurate regarding the central events and salient details, although over time, some aspects of the child's memory may become embellished with wishful fantasy— perhaps new details to the central story that wishfully recount the child's heroism or efforts to foil the danger. Some children describe the duration of time involved in the trauma as much longer or shorter than it was in reality. These distortions appear to be related to the intensity of the experience.[5]

Children find various ways to retell their frightening memories. Drawing and other art activities provide ready vehicles for reviewing and retelling. Given a blank piece of paper or a lump of clay, insistent memories pushing for expression often emerge.

Post-Traumatic Play

All children use play to solve problems and worries of everyday life, generally finding relief and mastery in their efforts. Typically this play is accompanied by light and easy feelings; it is indeed "playful," even when populated by monsters and superheroes.

Post-traumatic reenactment in play frequently lacks both pleasure and relief. It has a seriousness and intensity uncharacteristic of typical play. Children may recreate the entire scene of the trauma with exacting detail or play out only fragments of it. Some of this play involves themes and content related to the trauma but does not exactly replicate the actual events of the trauma itself. Using props and toys, the child seems to need to review in play what happened again and again. Like the retelling, the play is often a repetitious and driven exercise in gaining control and mastery over events by which the child felt helplessly victimized. For children who assume roles of power and mastery in their reenactment play, parents may see some relief coming from this play. The traumatic play of many children, however, seems to repeat the original experience of helplessness and fails to relieve or satisfy.

Many children try to undo the most difficult aspects of a traumatic event through play. Like a scriptwriter, the child has full control over the outcomes of the story. The child can have her victim rescued at the last moment before a deadly accident, or she can become the rescuer instead of the helpless victim or observer. Children who have never found words to describe the ways they wish they had been able to overcome a trauma may express these wishes and plans of action through their play.[6] Similar to adults following a trauma, children often retrospectively search for any actions they could have taken to defeat the traumatic force. Parents can often see their children taking this belated action in their play. Bad guys are bopped to unconsciousness by bionic three year olds; a brother is pushed out of harm's way at the last moment before the deadly impact of a car's crash. Sometimes these attempts to undo the horror of an event are obvious, while others are more subtle.

> In Sam's last session of therapy, he returned for the first time in months to re-creating the scene of his attic where he found his murdered mother. With great seriousness, he set up the stairs and had a little boy doll walk up them to find his mother. In this enactment, however, three-year-old Sam had the boy doll pick up his mother and lovingly carry her down the stairs to help. "I will take care of you," the little doll whispered sweetly to his mother. Thus, Sam's wish for a better ending in which he powerfully rescued his mother from death was played out in the hush of a secret plan he had nurtured for many months.

> Nine-year-old Collin was unable to talk about his infant brother's accidental death, which he had observed. But in his first session of play therapy, he suddenly began talking about a young child whom he had seen swimming without supervision. Collin described his fantasized heroic rescue of this child from the water in great detail. Only later in therapy could he describe the helplessness he experienced as he watched his brother's fall from a fourth-story window.

Preschool children tend to be open and unself-conscious in their play reenactments, older children may seek more secretive circumstances for reenactment. Very young children are more likely to engage in solitary reenactive play than older children, who have greater opportunity and need to engage other children in dramatic play.

When children play out the events and themes of a trauma with other children, their playmates may become distressed. Parents need to maintain an awareness of their child's play and its possible dangerousness or scariness for all involved following a trauma. This is particularly true of severe traumas involving acts of wanton aggression and violations of adult power. A child can terrify himself and his friends reenacting scenes or threats of violence in play.

> Lindsay was a strong and seemingly fearless child of five before her encounter with a night intruder at her home. Woken in the middle of the night, Lindsay had been quickly gagged and roughly tied up by a man wearing a ski mask before she could make any noise to awaken her parents. Her father woke up just as the intruder, his bag full of silver and other valuables, was leaving. Lindsay's father found her, wide-eyed with terror, bound to her bed.
>
> In the weeks that followed, there were two developments that worried Lindsay's parents no end. First, Lindsay was unable to sleep in her own room. Her panic began to mount at dinnertime each evening and culminated in her tearful insistence that she be allowed to sleep with her parents.
>
> Second, at school, Lindsay underwent a disturbing transformation as she developed a new reputation as the class ogre. She made threats to sneak into her friends' homes at night and kill them in their sleep. She created harrowing verbal descriptions of what she could do to several of the smaller children. Her small friends required little convincing of her seriousness or of her power to carry out these threats. Here was a group of children who were already fascinated with the malevolent power and aggression of superheroes. The terrorizing of this traumatized little girl in their midst was too real and believable.
>
> To combat their own fear, a band of "villains" joined with Lindsay in her mission to frighten the "scaredy-cats" in the class. Parents began reporting that their children were having nightmares. A crisis in the classroom ensued. The teachers themselves began to feel helpless and anxious with the unusual events unfolding before them.

While only one child in this class had actually experienced the trauma, fifteen classmates and their teachers all felt the impact of Lindsay's terror and sense of helplessness. This contagion effect is not an uncommon consequence of a child's post-traumatic play and reenactment in schools and neighborhoods but it often goes unrecognized.

Post-traumatic play is a hallmark of psychological trauma. There are some children, however, who cope with their experience without any trace of the trauma being observed in their play.

Withdrawal and Constriction

When the world feels newly dangerous and unpredictable following a trauma, many children look for ways to play it safe. They may hold back and avoid involvements that feel risky. The need for caution can dampen children's spirit and spontaneity. Even play can seem dangerous to children who feel a strong need to avoid any activity that could trigger reminders of a trauma. Play requires children to get close to a variety of feelings as they engage in the pretend. Some children need to wall themselves off from experiencing feelings; play can be a threat to their self-enclosure. This turtle-like approach to self-protection can create worrisome personality changes in a child.

> For several years after watching his sister's drowning during a hurricane, five-year-old Duncan had periods of nightmares and daytime recall that were so disturbing to him that his behavior transformed during each of these periods. Often the bouts of recall began when it was rainy or windy. Over time, his mother noticed that Duncan would stop his usual wild and fun play for the duration of each of these episodes of recall, which generally lasted four or five days. During these sieges of memory, Duncan would avoid any toys that might be used for dramatic play. Safer for Duncan at these times were passive activities like watching videos, which helped him avoid feelings altogether. He spent a good deal of his time shadowing his mother around the house. His return to free play at the end of these bouts became a signal for his mother that he was once again on track.

Sleep-Related Difficulties

Sleeping patterns are always vulnerable to the impact of stress and change. In the wake of trauma, sleep patterns are frequently disturbed. Children may be fearful of going to bed or sleeping alone. They may have difficulty falling asleep or staying asleep. They may awaken very early in the morning—or sleep unusually long hours. Nightmares and disrupted sleep are particularly common.

Immediately following the trauma, nightmares can be frequent and intense. Elements of the actual trauma may appear in the content of the nightmares, or the dreams may be about seemingly unrelated fears. A sexually molested child of seven, for instance, dreamed repeatedly of a terrifying "tickle machine." Other children's nightmares are populated with spiders, monsters, or "bad men."

Less common than nightmares are night terrors and sleepwalking resulting from trauma. Night terrors occur during a normal period of partial wakening when the child makes a transition from one stage of sleep to the next. During a night terror, a child may look and act terrified or extremely agitated. He may let out blood-curdling screams and act in a panicked, uncontrolled fashion, or may thrash around, attempting to get away from unseen danger, with no evident response to his parents' presence or voices. The screaming, thrashing, and crying can continue with no response to comforting for up to an hour. Although the child's eyes are wide open, the child is in fact not fully awake or responding. Night terrors end as mysteriously as they begin. The child begins to relax, yawns, and will now respond normally to parents' help and encouragement to go back to sleep. These episodes are enormously disturbing for parents whose "help" is restricted to keeping a child physically safe during the wild thrashing.[7]

Night terrors are not the same as nightmares. First, children have no memory of a night terror's occurring. At no point can they explain the object of their fear or confusion or describe dream content. For parents, there is a very strange feeling to night terrors which does not accompany a nightmare. In contrast, children having nightmares can be roused rather quickly, usually can describe something about the nightmare, and are comforted by their parents' attention and reassurance.

Sleepwalking involves a less intense partial awakening from sleep than that of a night terror. During an episode of sleepwalking, a child may get up, seek out her parents, or wander around the house with a blank stare. The child has little awareness of her surroundings but may be able to converse briefly. She rarely appears fearful and will respond to a parent's efforts to return her to bed. It was on a sleepwalk one evening that one young client urinated in the bathroom wastebasket and then returned calmly to sleep in his own bed. Incidents of urination in odd spots are fairly common for boys during sleepwalking.

Sleep disturbances during periods of partial awakening from deep sleep occur fairly commonly during children's first six years and are not necessarily indicators of trauma. There does appear to be a relationship, however, between stress and episodes of night terrors and sleepwalking. For parents, the management of sleep terrors in particular can be quite stressful. The child returns to sleep with no memory of fright, but the parents are left fully awake and usually quite frightened by the intensity of the child's wordless inner storm.

Personality Changes

The massive assault on a child's inner resources that trauma involves may result in new directions for a child's personality and development. These changes can be temporary or long-lasting, depending on many factors that interact in complex ways to influence a child's development. Children's attitudes and thoughts about themselves, their lives, and the people around them can change. Even for very young children, trauma can cause a reevaluation of basic assumptions and expectations.

A child's increased self-preoccupation following a trauma is often noticeable and bothersome to parents. Children who are recovering from trauma have little reserves of energy for gracefully solving disputes or sharing with siblings. Their capacity to tolerate minor rejections is limited. Parents frequently complain that their children seem excessively "selfish" and "uncaring" in their interactions with others. The self-centeredness of a traumatized child, however, is one of the common temporary personality changes associated with their limited frustration tolerance and inner preoccupation.

Trauma can corrode a child's sense of trust in the goodness and safety of the world. Some children show temporary alterations in their level of trust but gradually return to their prior openness over time. For others, distrust is restricted to specific situations associated with their trauma. For some children, the corrosion of trust can result in unchildlike wariness, suspiciousness, or pessimism that appears as a transformation in the child's character. For these latter children, the constant state of dread and distrust, if left unattended, can become a way of being in the world.

Studies of children kidnapped at gunpoint and buried in a bus for sixteen hours of a twenty-seven-hour ordeal in Chowchilla,

California, revealed that many of these child victims developed specific changes in their personalities over the years following their trauma.[8] They often lacked the sense of great possibility and optimism about the future that generally characterizes children's expectations. They also lacked a sense of immunity to disaster and tragedy that most children usually have in healthy quantity. Following a human-induced trauma, a child's lack of trust and faith in people, or in specific groups of people, can result in changes in the personality of a previously open and trusting child.

Are the personality changes during the first stages of recovery permanent? There is no general answer to this question. The intensity of a child's initial reactions to trauma and the degree of dramatic changes in personality do generally lessen considerably over time. Although research has yet to show which children may be more vulnerable to strong and lasting personality changes, it appears likely that these changes are primarily associated with only the most severe traumas, including traumas that involve repeated incidents of exposure. (Other factors that influence the child's lasting recovery are discussed in chapter 4.)

Complaints of Aches and Pains

Children may channel their worries and fears into concerns expressed about their bodies. Small cuts or scrapes may be invested with great meaning and energy; for example, a child may react with disproportionate hysteria to a small bump or injury. Some children complain of vague aches, pains, or illnesses for which no medical cause can be found. These overreactions and complaints may occur for a surprisingly long period following a trauma, or they may be limited to the initial period of recovery.

A child who develops excessive unrealistic concerns about her body is finding a particular way to say, "I'm hurting." Since children are not generally comfortable or skilled in talking about psychological pain, bodily concerns provide them with an outlet for their distress.

Ian was three and a half when he watched his dog be hit and killed by a passing truck. His parents were quite concerned that their son seemed to be having no reaction to the dog's death, although they had been devoted friends. Instead of seeing the grief they expected, they heard long, realistic lectures from their precocious little scientist about the "ways of nature." Ian seemed to go along with their efforts to involve him in the burial as if to appease their need to "do the right thing" during this difficult time. As the family marched solemnly across their field to the prepared gravesite, carrying their lifeless pet, Ian tripped and fell over a stick. The fall appeared to be a minor one, but his cries were piercing. The cries turned to sobs as Ian collapsed in his mother's arms and finally expressed his full sense of loss for his beloved dog.

Ian's overreaction to a slight injury is a good example of the way a child turns to anxiety over his body to find relief for the real source of his distress. For many children, however, the connection between psychological pain and complaints of physical aches and pains is not so obvious or dramatic as Ian's.

Misinterpretation of the Cause and Meaning of a Trauma

When an unthinkable terror occurs, the child's natural reaction is to find some way to explain and understand it. This is not at all unlike an adult's searching efforts to come to terms with the meaning of trauma. Children generally do poorly at using reason and common sense when they attempt to find meaning in life events. Instead, they tend to depend on magical thinking and readily believe that events result from something they have done, thought, or wished. The younger the child is, the more comfortable she will be accepting irrational and impossible explanations for events. A self-centered interpretation of events characterizes the thinking of all young children. It is only around the age of seven that children gradually develop the ability to consider the role of forces outside themselves as primary influences on reality. Even eleven and twelve year olds, however, can lose their grip on reality-based cause-and-effect thinking in the face of trauma. Adult survivors of disasters and other traumas also settle for improbable explanations and interpretations when attempting to find some meaning in these life-changing events.

Magical thinking and self-centered interpretation frequently combine to create some highly unlikely private explanations and meanings. Commonly these explanations involve the child's idea of just punishment for misdeeds. The child's attempts to make sense of a trauma too often end in self-blame.

Does a brother get killed on a ferris wheel because of an older sister's fury at him several hours earlier? For eight-year-old Sara, this was a perfectly plausible and terrifying explanation of her brother's tragic death. Can the momentary angry thought, "I wish Grandpa was dead," result in Grandpa's fatal stroke several weeks later? Four-year-old Eric was quite convinced that his thoughts and wishes had this deadly power following the sudden death of his grandfather. For five-year-old Eddie, his molestation by a trusted babysitter was explained as punishment for his own badness. In his mind, the babysitter purposely selected him for victimization because, in his words, "I was a very bad boy."

While these common misinterpretations frequently involve the child's own self-punitive feelings, they can also involve distortions of a child's positive self-concepts. For example, another five year old who was molested by a babysitter reasoned that she had been selected because she was the "prettiest" of all the girls for whom this young man babysat.

Parents are often not aware of their children's mistaken convictions regarding the cause of their traumas. Children frequently hold their thoughts and explanations private and suffer from them silently. Some secret, self-blaming interpretations are held with enormous unspeakable shame. Often it is a child's peculiar behavior or emotion that directs parents to the underlying fantasies and beliefs causing distress.

Children's misinterpretations often appear to be cruelly self-blaming when viewed from the light of reason, but they offer the child an odd sense of comfort. Any explanation is better than the alternative belief that horrifying things can occur willy-nilly. Even very unpleasant and shameful explanations of a traumatic event offer some measure of control for children who struggle with the helplessness and senselessness of a frightening event.

Accident-Proneness and Recklessness

Some children seem driven to tempt fate following an event that perhaps demonstrated the most disastrous workings of fate. Driven daredevil behavior and accident proneness are evident in some children's behavior following a trauma. The children whose recklessness with their own bodies is most notable are those whose trauma involved physical harm to themselves or to someone else. These children may not be at all aware of their physical risk taking or of their inner preoccupation with physical harm. Parents and teachers, however, may notice an unusual number of bruises or may be quite alarmed at the stunts a child suddenly attempts. When the recklessness seems driven, it is appropriate to be truly concerned and take precautions for a child's physical safety.

Anniversary Reactions

The fate of memories of trauma is curious. Although the memories of horror fade in intensity over time, they can be cued by the reminders of calendar year markers—birthdays, holidays, changes of season, or seasonal activities. These occasions spark memories that can take on a renewed power that is often disorienting and frightening. Underlying a child's anniversary reaction is the fearful and magical sense that one year or five years later, the trauma might recur.

Children who appear to have recovered fully may respond to an anniversary reminder with signs of stress, sometimes similar in nature to their original reactions. Regression and preoccupation with the trauma can be surprising and disquieting for the child and for the parent, each of whom wants to believe that the trauma is now behind them, forgotten or buried. It is helpful to recall that, regardless of a child's freedom from symptoms, trauma generally remains latently present in memory. There are times when these memories may need to reemerge and be reexamined.

If a child has been free of anxiety and symptoms, a sudden change in behavior a year after the original trauma can come as a surprise. Most parents are taken off guard by the return of symptoms or renewed intense retelling of the story. It is often difficult for the child and parent to identify anniversary reactions. Although they are disturbing and disruptive, they are generally short-lived and have little long-term impact for a child who has been coping relatively well.

Subtle or unmistakable anniversary reactions may occur for many years, frequently without the child's being conscious of their origins. One young man of twelve was surprised to identify in therapy that he had had unusual difficulties in school every year during November since the age of four when he had witnessed his baby brother's accidental drowning. The school record confirmed that this boy had become unraveled each November since kindergarten. For roughly a month each year, his academic work and behavior had disintegrated. The anniversary calendar cue for this boy was his own birthday, which had preceded the baby's death by a week.

> Five-year-old Jimmy knew when a year had passed following his molestation by a babysitter. He recalled that the lilacs had been in bloom. When the lilacs bloomed again the next spring, Jimmy began talking about how "cute" his dad's penis was. To his parents' dismay, he began telling anyone who would listen the story of his molestation after months of not mentioning it at home.
>
> Across town, another five-year-old, Ben, reacted to spring with renewed thoughts of his run-in with a babysitter the previous year when he had been locked and left in a closet for several hours. Ben suddenly requested the stuffed pig he had received just after this disturbing incident. This pig, which he had used to cope with the trauma, had spent the prior eight months neglected at the back of his closet. But it was again needed to help Ben cope with the return of memories occasioned by the first anniversary of his trauma.

Behavioral Signs of Sexually Abused Children

Sexually abused children may show any of the signs already described as general reactions to trauma—or none of them. In various studies of sexually abused children, there is consistently a group, ranging from 21 percent to 60 percent, who show no behavioral disturbance that might be seen as an indication of abuse.[9] The absence of behavioral signs of abuse never rules out the possibility that abuse has occurred or that it has had an emotional impact.

Age-inappropriate sexualized behavior is one of the few reliable and distinguishing characteristics that differentiate sexually abused children.[10] These children have more specific sexual concerns and behaviors than children in general or children traumatized in nonsexual ways. Very young children may enact adult sexual scenarios and behaviors in their play with other children or with their dolls and stuffed animals. They may be excessively curious about or overly preoccupied with sexuality. Some children are driven to expose their genitals to others or engage in a sudden, unusually high level of masturbation. Aggressive attempts to undress, sexually touch, or attempt intercourse with others are not uncommon. When a tendency toward secretive post-traumatic play combines with intense sexual preoccupation, the child is vulnerable to repeating the abuse with other children in ways that can create chaos and further victimization throughout a neighborhood. A child who feels internally driven to do to others what was done to her requires extensive parental supervision and therapeutic help.

More subtle impacts of sexual abuse have to do with the child's sense of herself and her body. Sexual abuse can introduce children prematurely to sexual sensations that they are developmentally unprepared to contend with. This awareness of sexual sensation can be confusing and overstimulating. Children may react to an incident of sexual abuse with extreme worry about harm or damage to their genitals. One little girl of six confided after her pediatric genital examination that she thought the doctor would find her "all broken in there." Children may develop negative associations to their bodies that can feel newly disgusting or "bad" as a result of the abuse. Feeling sexually aroused and feeling that one's body is "yucky" or damaged are not easy feelings for children to put into words. Sometimes they express these feelings through sexualized behaviors, which signal their concerns and need for help.

Parents need to be cautious in making assumptions about the meaning of sexualized behaviors. Children between the ages of fifteen months and six years go through various periods of heightened interest in sexuality: they are fascinated with their own bodies and those of others; they masturbate; they want to touch mommy's breasts; they may undress and run giddily around the house naked; and they are intensely interested in the naked bodies of others. With young children, the task of sorting out normal sexual interest and behavior from indicators of abuse is complicated for both parents and professionals.

Reading the Signs of Trauma

The signs of trauma comprise the ways in which most children express inner pain, confusion, or distress. Most of these signs are not unique to traumatized children but are common responses of children undergoing any serious stress. The fact that children exhibit similar behavioral signs in response to many different situational or developmental stresses complicates a parent's task of understanding the source of distress. When these signs appear suddenly, very close in time to a traumatic event, and there is no other significant stressor present in the child's or family's life, it is fair to assume that some aspect of the trauma is causing the behavioral disruption. When the symptoms appear many months or years following a serious trauma or when trauma is combined with ongoing significant stresors in the child or family's everyday life, parents may need the help of a professional in sorting out the source of the distress.

Even when parents are quite confident that the behavioral signs they see in their child are tied to a trauma, understanding the exact nature of the child's distress can be difficult. Many children have been brought to professionals following encounters with mild trauma due to the parents' concern about their behavior and long-term welfare. At times, children are found to be coping relatively well with mildly traumatic situations but are reacting instead to the heightened level of worry and fear in their parents. Other mildly traumatized children are found to be much more significantly distressed by ongoing custody or marital conflicts that may have preceded a trauma by many years than they are by the single event of a recent trauma. Sorting out the meaning of a child's symptoms that carry no flags identifying their origins can be tricky indeed.

Nonetheless, the signs of trauma and stress are flags to pay attention to. Often the behaviors of traumatized children are the only indicators parents have of a child's distress. Like a fever that sounds the body's alarm of illness, many of the behavioral indicators of stress in children have a dual function: they signal a problem and indicate that the child is trying to cope with the problem. The child's success in coping with and mastering the trauma frequently depends on a parent's capacity to attend to and accept the signals of distress. Once the behaviors and feelings are understood, the task for parents of supporting the child's recovery becomes clearer and easier.

Points to Remember: The Signs of Psychological Trauma

Children have a limited number of ways to express inner distress. Most children under the age of eleven are unlikely to talk freely or at any length about uncomfortable or painful feelings. When children are distressed, the feelings are most likely to be seen as changes in their behavior.

The changes that parents see in children's behavior following a trauma often occur immediately. Some stress responses emerge gradually over time or arise long after the actual trauma in either anniversary or delayed reactions.

The behavioral signs of trauma serve as flags for parents of the child's inner struggle to come to terms with a shocking experience.

The signs of trauma vary according to the child's age. The following tables are developmental charts that summarize the signs of trauma as they typically appear for children of different ages.

TABLE NO. 1
Developmental Guidelines: Children's Reactions to Trauma
(Infancy to Two and a Half Years)

General Trauma Reactions	Sexual Abuse—Specific Reactions*	Memory for Trauma	Parental Support
Disruption of sleeping and toilet-ing	Unusual concern/attention to own or other's private parts	Memory of trauma may be evident in behavior or play	Maintain child's routines around sleeping and eating
Startle response to loud/unusual noises	Demonstration of adult sexual behavior or knowl-edge through behavior	Snatches of incomplete memory or visual im-ages may remain in memory and be given verbal description by toddlers	Avoid unnecessary separations from im-portant caretakers
"Freezing" (sudden immobility of body)	Sudden, intense masturba-tion		Provide additional soothing activities
Fussiness, uncharacteristic crying, and neediness	Inappropriate private touching of others		Maintain calm atmosphere in child's pres-ence
Loss of acquired speech and motor skills	Genital pain, bruising, in-flamation, bleeding, dis-charge, or diagnosis of sexually transmitted disease		Avoid exposing child to reminders of trauma
Separation fears and clinging to caretakers			Expect child's temporary regression; don't panic
Withdrawal; lack of usual respon-siveness			Help verbal child to give simple names to big feelings; talk about event in simple terms during brief chats
Avoidance of or alarm response to specific trauma-related re-minders involving sights and physical sensations			Give simple play props related to the ac-tual trauma to a child who is trying to play out the frightening situation (a doc-tor's kit, a toy ambulance, toy dog, etc.)

* These behaviors and symptoms are not in themselves conclusive evidence of sexual abuse but are frequently noted in sexually abused children of this age.

TABLE NO. 2

Developmental Guidelines: *Children's Reactions to Trauma*
(Two and a Half Years to Six Years)

General Trauma Reactions	Sexual Abuse—Specific Reactions*	Memory for Trauma	Parental Support
Repeated retelling of traumatic event	Sexualized play with toys or other children	Memory of at least some visual images from traumatic event is likely for youngest children; many demonstrate recall in words and play	Listen to and tolerate child's retelling of event
Behavioral, mood, and personality changes	Unusual concern about or attention to own or others' private parts		Respect child's fears; give child time to cope with fears
Obvious anxiety and fearfulness	Uncharacteristic, at times intense, masturbation	At the older end of this age range, children are more likely to have lasting, accurate verbal and pictorial memory for central events of trauma	Protect child from reexposure to frightening situations and reminders of trauma, including scary T.V. programs, movies, stories, and physical or locational reminders of trauma
Withdrawal and quieting			
Specific, trauma-related fears; general fearfulness	Inappropriate and/or aggressive touching of others or sexualized relating		
Post-traumatic play often obvious	Sudden, specific fear or mistrust of males, females, or particular places		Accept and help the child to name strong feelings during brief conversations (the child cannot talk about these feelings or the experience for long)
Involvement of playmates in trauma-related play at school and day care			
Regression to behavior of younger child			Expect and understand child's regression while maintaining basic household rules
Loss of recently acquired skills (language, toileting, eating, self-care)			Expect some difficult or uncharacteristic behavior.
Separation anxiety with primary caretakers			

(continued)

Developmental Guidelines: Children's Reactions to Trauma
(Two and a Half Years to Six Years)

General Trauma Reactions	Sexual Abuse— Specific Reactions*	Memory for Trauma	Parental Support
Loss of interest in activities	Physical indicators: genital pain, bruising, bleeding, inflamation, discharge, diagnosis of sexually transmitted disease		Set firm limits on hurtful or scary play and behavior
Sleep disturbances: nightmares, night terrors, sleepwalking, fearfulness of going to sleep and being alone at night			Avoid nonessential separations from important caretakers with fearful children
Confusion and inadequate understanding of traumatic events most evident in play rather than discussion			Maintain household and family routines that comfort child
Unclear understanding of death and the causes of "bad" events			Avoid introducing new and challenging experiences for child
Magical explanations to fill in gaps in understanding			Provide additional nighttime comforts when possible: night lights, stuffed animals, physical comforting after nightmares
Complaints about bodily aches, pains, or illness with no medical explanation			Explain to child that nightmares come from the fears a child has inside, that they aren't real, and that they will occur less and less over time
Visual images and unpleasant memories of trauma that intrude in child's mind but will seldom be discussed spontaneously			Provide opportunities and props for trauma-related play

TABLE NO. 2 (continued)
(Two and a Half Years to Six Years)

General Trauma Reactions	Sexual Abuse— Specific Reactions*	Memory for Trauma	Parental Support
Loss of energy and concentration at school			Use detective skills to discover triggers for sudden fearfulness or regression
Fear of trauma's recurring			Monitor child's coping in school and day care by communicating with teaching staff and expressing concerns
Increased need for control			Listen for a child's misunderstandings of a traumatic event, particularly those that involve self-blame and magical thinking
Vulnerable to anniversary reactions set off by seasonal reminders, holidays, and other events			Gently help child develop a realistic understanding of event
			Remain aware of your own reactions to the child's trauma
			Provide reassurance to child that feelings will diminish over time
			Provide opportunities for child to experience control and make choices in daily activities
			Be mindful of the possibility of anniversary reactions

* These behaviors and symptoms are not in themselves conclusive evidence of sexual abuse but are frequently noted in sexually abused children of this age.

Developmental Guidelines: Children's Reactions to Trauma
(Six Years to Eleven Years)

General Trauma Reactions	Sexual Abuse—Specific Reactions*	Memory for Trauma	Parental Support
Repeated retelling of traumatic event	Engages in explicit sexual behaviors with other children or attempts to engage older children or adults sexually	Child is likely to have detailed, long-term memory for traumatic event	Listen to and tolerate child's retelling of event
Obvious anxiety and fearfulness			Respect child's fears; give child time to cope with fears
Specific post-traumatic fears	Verbally describes experiences of sexual misuse	Factually accurate memory may be embellished by elements of fear or wish; perception of duration may be distorted	Increase monitoring and awareness of child's play, which may involve secretive reenactments of trauma with peers and siblings; set limits on scary or hurtful play
Post-traumatic reenactments of traumatic event that may occur secretly and involve siblings or playmates	Excessive concern or preoccupation with private parts and adult sexual behavior		
Fear of trauma's recurring	Sexualized relating to adults		Permit child to try out new ideas to cope with fearfulness at bedtime: extra reading time, radio on, listening to a tape in the middle of the night to undo the residue of fear from a nightmare
Intrusion of unwanted visual images and traumatic memory that disrupt concentration and create anxiety, often without parents' awareness	Hinting about sexual experience		
	Sudden specific fear or mistrust of males, females, or specific places		
Loss of ability to concentrate and attend at school, with lowering of performance	Verbal or behavioral indications of age-inappropriate knowledge of adult sexual behavior		Reassure the older child that feelings of fear or behaviors that feel out of control or babyish (e.g., night wetting) are normal after a frightening experience and that the child will feel more like himself or herself with time
"Spacey" or distractible behavior			

TABLE NO. 3 (continued)
(Six Years to Eleven Years)

General Trauma Reactions	Sexual Abuse—Specific Reactions*	Memory for Trauma	Parental Support
Behavior, mood, or personality changes			Encourage child to talk about confusing feelings, worries, daydreams, mental review of traumatic images, and disruptions of concentration by accepting the feelings, listening carefully, and reminding child that these are normal but hard reactions following a very scary event
Regression to behavior of younger child			
Toileting accidents			Maintain communication with school staff and monitor child's coping with demands at school or in community activities
Withdrawal and quieting or excesses of aggression and limit testing			
Loss of interest in previously pleasurable activities			Expect some time-limited decrease in child's school performance and help the child to accept this as a temporary result of the trauma
Sleep disturbances: nightmares, sleepwalking, night terrors (rare for this age), difficulties falling or staying asleep			
Complaints about bodily aches, pains, or illness with no medical explanation			Protect child from reexposure to frightening situations and reminders of trauma, including scary television programs, movies, stories, and physical or locational reminders of trauma
Concern about personal responsibility for trauma			

(continued)

TABLE NO. 3 (continued)
Developmental Guidelines: Children's Reactions to Trauma
(Six Years to Eleven Years)

General Trauma Reactions	Sexual Abuse— Specific Reactions*	Memory for Trauma	Parental Support
Acute awareness of parental reactions; wish to protect parents from their own distress			Expect and understand child's regression while maintaining basic household rules
Frightened by intensity of own feelings			Expect some difficult or uncharacteristic behavior
Vulnerability to anniversary reactions set off by seasonal reminders, holidays, or other events			Listen for a child's misunderstandings of a traumatic event, particularly those that involve self-blame and magical thinking
			Gently help child develop a realistic understanding of event
			Remain aware of your own reactions to the child's trauma
			Provide reassurance to child that feelings will diminish over time
			Provide opportunities for child to experience control and make choices in daily activities
			Be mindful of the possibility of anniversary reactions

* These behaviors and symptoms are not in themselves conclusive evidence of sexual abuse but are frequently noted in sexually abused children of this age.

Developmental Guidelines: Children's Reactions to Trauma
(Eleven to Eighteen Years)

General Trauma Reactions	Sexual Abuse—Specific Reactions*	Memory for Trauma	Parental Support
Trauma-driven acting-out behavior: sexual acting out or reckless, risk-taking behavior	Sexually exploitive or aggressive interactions with younger children	Acute awareness of and distress with intrusive imagery and memories of trauma	Encourage younger and older adolescents to talk about traumatic event with family members
Efforts to distance from feelings of shame, guilt, and humiliation	Sexually promiscuous behavior or total avoidance of sexual involvement	Vulnerability to flashback episodes of recall	Provide opportunities for young person to spend time with friends who are supportive and meaningful
Flight into driven activity and involvement with others or retreat from others in order to manage inner turmoil	Running away from home	May experience acute distress encountering any reminder of trauma	Reassure young person that strong feelings—whether of guilt, shame, embarrassment, or wish for revenge—are normal following a trauma
Accident proneness			
Wish for revenge and action-oriented responses to trauma			Help young person find activities that offer opportunities to experience mastery, control, and self-esteem
Increased self-focusing and withdrawal			
Sleep and eating disturbances; nightmares			Encourage pleasurable physical activities such as sports and dancing

(continued)

TABLE NO. 4 (continued)
Developmental Guidelines: *Children's Reactions to Trauma*
(Eleven to Eighteen Years)

General Trauma Reactions	Sexual Abuse— Specific Reactions*	Memory for Trauma	Parental Support
Acute awareness of and distress with intrusive imagery and memories of trauma			Address acting-out behavior involving aggression or self- destructive aspects quickly and firmly with limit setting and professional help
Vulnerability to depression, withdrawal, and pessimistic worldview			Monitor young person's coping at home, school, and in peer group
Personality changes and changes in quality of important relationships evident			Take signs of depression, accident proneness, recklessness, and persistent personality change seriously by seeking help
Flight into adulthood seen as way of escaping impact and memory of trauma (early marriage, pregnancy, dropping out of school, abandoning peer group for older set of friends)			Help young person develop a sense of perspective on the impact of the traumatic event and a sense of the importance of time in recovering
Fear of growing up and need to stay within family orbit			Encourage delaying big decisions

*These behaviors and symptoms are not in themselves conclusive evidence of sexual abuse but are frequently noted in sexually abused children of this age.

4

Factors Influencing Children's Reactions to Trauma

Children's reactions to trauma can be puzzling. Why does one child quickly pick up the pieces and go on with her life, looking relatively unscathed, while another becomes bogged down in difficulties that seem to color her entire world? There are too few solutions to this puzzle, although some tentative answers are emerging from current research. There remains the very simple fact, however, that children are impressively different from one another in their reactions to all major life events.

It may be helpful to think of children's responses to entering kindergarten, a high-stress event for even the most nonchalant child. In any group of beginning kindergartners, there are those who adjust by becoming quiet and withdrawn and others whose level of overactivity threatens to disrupt the entire class. Some of these children begin wetting their beds or sucking their thumbs during their first few months of school. A number of them, however, are happy and secure within the classroom. Just as children have very different reactions to routinely stressful events like starting kindergarten, their reactions to trauma are similarly diverse. Nevertheless, there are some protective factors—certain characteristics of the child and family—that appear to insulate or buffer children from the most disabling effects of exposure to severe stress and some risk factors, that contribute to a child's vulnerability.[1] While the emerging research on children's resilience is not based exclusively on traumatized children, the findings are helpful in thinking about the forces that influence children's varied responses to trauma.

Characteristics of the Child

Protective Factors

Children who bounce back readily from difficult situations are often those who have shown easy-going responses to minor stressors from early on in life. These children appear to be endowed biologically with an ease of adaptability when presented with a range of challenges and stressors. Some children simply have temperamental assets. Another protective factor is intelligence. Children not only use their ability to reason and comprehend in coping with stress and trauma, but they also generally have more satisfying experiences in school, which can contribute to their self-esteem.

A child's sense of self may well affect any long-term response to severe stress. Children who are basically self-confident and see themselves as having an impact on the course of their own lives tend to master difficult situations with more ease than children who lack confidence and self-esteem.

Children are also protected to some extent by the support they experience outside the family. Those who are well connected to their friends and to helpful adults in their communities may find it easier to master highly stressful experiences.

A child's age can affect vulnerability. Young children may be more vulnerable to situations that in any way threaten their care-taking relationships but less vulnerable to situations they are as yet unable to understand fully. With age, children develop more problem-solving abilities and are generally more able to tolerate separations and loss. Older children, however, develop the ability to grasp the larger implications and meanings of a sudden, overwhelming event and may have much stronger reactions to situations in which distress comes in part from their understanding of the events.[2] A two year old who weathers a hurricane by his mother's side is likely to emerge from the experience with less distress than his seven-year-old sister who can better appreciate the random destructive force of the storm.

In some situations toddlers and preschoolers do have briefer, and less severe, reactions to trauma than older children. There is a strong temptation to assume that all small children are buffered by age, innocence, or limited memory against the impact of traumatic experience. Clinical experience and studies that have looked closely at individual children under the age of five suggest that the common assumption that younger children are better protected against trauma is often more of a wish than a reality.[3] Young children may not have words to describe their memories of trauma, but these memories are often disturbingly evident in their behavior and play.

Gender can be related to how children react to stress of any magnitude. Boys tend to react with more aggression and acting-out behaviors; their reactions are quite evident. Girls tend to respond more inwardly; the sadness and anxiety they frequently experience are less disruptive and less easily observed by parents and others. In general, studies find girls to be more resilient developmentally than boys during early and middle childhood years but more vulnerable during adolescence.[4]

Risk Factors

A child's resilience depends on what prior demands have already been put on him to cope with extraordinary situations. Protective factors can wear thin with too much use. Prior experiences of trauma or severe stress and the child's emotional health just prior to the occurrence of a trauma can have a bearing on the capacity to cope. Children who have been dealt many difficult blows of fate can become worn out by these repetitive demands for coping. If there have been numerous important losses or other prior traumas in a child's life, the child's capacity to absorb further stress may be limited. Similarly, children who have been putting all their resources into mastering a rocky period in their individual development just prior to the occurrence of a trauma may be less prepared to cope than a child who had been thriving during a relatively easy developmental period. A child who encounters a trauma in the midst of mourning for a recently lost grandparent, for example, is likely to have lower reserves for coping.

Family Characteristics

Protective Factors

Parental care has a primary influence on children's resilience.[5] Close and loving relationships with parents and other family members buffer children from catastrophic stress. The family who can supportively respond to a child through the endless small and large acts of caring and love contributes measurably to a child's healing. Families whose members are warm and supportive toward one another in general provide a positive environment for recovery. Parents who are able to accept a child's posttraumatic distress and changed behavior without overreacting or needing to see immediate recovery tend to communicate their support clearly to children.[6] Even in families whose relationships are conflictual, children who have at least one close loving relationship with a parent often do better handling various stressors than those who lack this one special connection.[7] Loving relationships are buffers that strengthen us all against life's adversities. For children, the family's role as a buffering and healing force cannot be overemphasized.

Alongside loving care, families provide much more to children coping with trauma or major stressors. Family members, particularly parents, serve as important role models for coping and overcoming negative life events.[8] By demonstrating their own useful and reasonable ways to deal with difficulties, parents teach these approaches to children. Children pay close attention to their parents' behavior and readily pick up on a parent's attitudes, emotions, and expectations. The confused child who is trying to figure out how to make sense of a traumatic event looks for cues in his parents' responses to the event. When the child can see that parents view the situation as manageable and have some strategies for dealing with it, the child feels more empowered to do the same.

A family's support network is important.[9] Families that can readily find support from extended family, their church, or their community are more likely to have resilient children. It does not matter particularly where the support comes from; what appears to matter is that the support is there, that it is solid and enduring, and that families are able to accept and use it. A family's struggle to respond to a trauma is a lonely experience, similar to the loneliness of grief following the death of a beloved family member. The supportive responses of friends and family touch that loneliness in a way that begins to heal the sense of severed connection. Connection with others is clearly a universal source of help and hope.

Risk Factors

The importance of a family in a child's recovery can work to increase or decrease a child's resilience under stress. Children are often more vulnerable to the effects of negative life events when their families are troubled by serious problems such as parental conflict, prolonged emotional turmoil, or a member's substance abuse. It is less obvious, however, that a family's isolation from supports within the community is associated with children having a harder time recovering from major stress.[10] To some extent, the value placed on the independence of the nuclear family in American society may blind us to the importance of the family support system in counteracting negative life events. The support received by various family members, and particularly by parents, translates into support for the child's recovery.

Types of Trauma and Effect

The specific nature of the trauma itself has some influence on the extent and severity of children's reactions. Many single traumatic events, for instance, have different and less severe long-term impact than trauma that a child is repeatedly exposed to over time. The idea that all one-time incidents of trauma in childhood are less devastating than repeated incidents is false, however, given that some single events that children are tragically exposed to are so horrific.

Certain aspects of the trauma itself can influence the severity of children's reactions. Speculatively, some of the features of childhood trauma that may contribute to the severity of children's reactions include the following:

1. *The duration of the traumatic event.* Single traumatic events of long duration may create greater distress for children than relatively brief events.

2. *The presence of interpersonal violence or threat of harm.* When traumas involve intentional malicious acts of human beings rather than natural forces or accidents of fate, children may be more negatively affected.[11]
3. *The degree to which the child experiences a situation as immediately life threatening.* Children who perceive themselves to be closer to life-threatening danger may react more strongly than children who see themselves to be at some distance from danger or those who lack awareness of the actual danger.[12]
4. *The exposure to traumas involving loved ones as the victims or perpetrators of terrifying harm.* Trauma that threatens a caretaking relationship multiplies a child's psychological injuries and can leave a child without a safe harbor for recovery.[13]
5. *The involvement of temporary or long-term physical injury to the child.* Disfigurement, hospitalization, and frightening medical procedures can repeatedly rekindle a child's anxiety and traumatic memories, creating a profound sense of loss and damage.[14]
6. *The child's perception of the outcome of the trauma.* The child who perceives that the original trauma resulted in a series of negative events and life changes may experience greater long-term distress than the child who sees the trauma as a single unusual event followed by little change in his or her basic emotional or concrete life circumstances.
7. *The extent of disruption the child experiences in basic caretaking and the family's functioning as a result of the trauma.* When the child's primary healing environment, the family, is massively disrupted emotionally or physically, recovery can be complicated by loss and chaos.[15]

There is nothing simple about predicting the impact of trauma. Because this impact draws from the complex interaction of so many factors regarding the child, the family, and the trauma itself, various factors can combine uniquely for each child. For instance, it would make sense to expect that a child who is momentarily terrified by a man who briefly jumps naked out of the woods before running away will have less to come to terms with than the child who is abducted, bound, and taken hostage overnight. Although both children are returned to their parent's care physically unharmed, we might assume that these two children will respond differently and that the abducted child will have more difficulty recovering. Until we know more about these two children, however, and become familiar with the entire picture of the circumstances, the children's perceptions of their experiences, and their family's reactions, it would impossible to know how each will fare in recovery.

I always think of Sam when I am trying to understand how the many complex facets of a child's life and an incident of trauma combine to produce particular responses. Sam's overt reactions to his mother's murder did not make a lot of sense. As described in chapter 1, over the course of twelve hours, three-year-old Sam witnessed a violent argument involving his divorced mother and a boyfriend and then woke up the next morning to disquieting silence in his home. After some searching, he found his mother's body. Following the murder, Sam went to live with his father, a very calm and devoted man. Sam said nothing about having seen his mother's battering or finding his mother's body. All the grown-ups assumed that Sam had slept through the events that had led to his mother's death. Not surprisingly, Sam was uncharacteristically withdrawn and clingy for several days and subsequently had several nightmares over a three-month- period.

Sam's external reactions to trauma and loss were extremely mild; his behavior gave his father little cause to worry. Sam's strong internal reactions to these events became evident in his play, however. He chose the enclosure of the play therapy office to reenact and work through his experience. Perhaps Sam wished to protect the important grown-ups in his life from more distress. Maybe he sensed that these grown-ups hoped that he had been asleep the entire night of the murder and so had been spared any knowledge of the events that took months to reconstruct. Whatever his motives, Sam contained his outward reactions to trauma and loss. To this situation of horror he brought his own natural resilience. Sam had a history of bouncing back from difficulties and was blessed with an easy-going temperament. He had always been a "go-getter" who threw himself into learning each new skill and loved being "a big boy." Contributing to this resilience was Sam's history of receiving sensitive and thoughtful parenting.

Sam did his work of healing and grieving quietly and intensely in therapy over the course of one year. On the surface, he appeared to be fully recovered within three months, according to all the adults who knew him well. But at this point in therapy, Sam's play was still riddled with traumatic memories. Despite the considerable trouble that travel to therapy involved, Sam's father agreed to let him continue therapy even when it might have appeared that Sam had no further need of it. When he ended therapy, Sam was truly ready to end. Since then, he has had no difficulties in his development. Now nine, Sam is a leader, an athlete, and a popular classmate in his fourth grade. He is able to visit the memories of his mother's death with sadness but without reevoking the terror.

Sam's story reveals a lot about children and trauma. Sam brought his natural resilience to the double-barreled task of coping with his trauma and his grief. Although externally he seemed to be coping fairly well shortly after his mother's death, he was inwardly struggling with the memories of the night of his mother's murder and with his nearly invisible grief. It is easy to forget that children who are doing well on the outside may be suffering inwardly. Sam's inner pain was recognized and accepted. It is also common to believe that some life tragedies are too severe ever to be overcome. Sam has survived and thrived.

In every study that reports a trend in children's reactions to trauma, there are plenty of individual children whose reactions differ from the trend. Following a tornado or flood affecting the lives of many children in a community, children seldom react identically. There are usually children who have very brief, mild reactions and those with more severe, long-lasting reactions. Because parents have to take care of children, and not trends, it is important to remember that ultimately what matters is each child's unique reaction to a frightening event. It is unfair to expect individual children to fit the predictions that research studies suggest. Some children will have big reactions to relatively small events. Other children will have seemingly minimal reactions to big and terrifying events. These reactions may occur more inwardly, or they may be disruptively evident in behavior. It is interesting to ask why a child responds in a certain way, but it is not always a help-ful question to dwell on. More useful to ask are "how" questions: "How is my child reacting to this event?" "How can we help her feel safer right now?" The answers to "why" questions about a particular child's reactions to trauma will not always make sense. Fortunately, children do not always have to make sense to be well taken care of.

Points to Remember: Factors Influencing Children's Reactions to Trauma

Children's reactions to trauma can be puzzling. Some children have strong reactions to mild traumas, and others have seem-ingly mild reactions to severe traumas.

Many factors contribute to the specific reactions of a given child:

- The child's temperament and style of coping.
- The child's intelligence, self-confidence, and sense of mas-tery in the world.
- The child's age at the time of a traumatic event.
- The child's gender.
- The child's sense of connection to peers and helpful adults.
- The child's prior development and experience with stress.
- The family's ability to respond with support and protec-tion.
- The availability of helpful problem-solving role models within the family.
- The family's access to meaningful familial or community supports.

The nature of the trauma generally has a direct impact on the severity of a child's reactions. Single traumatic events of short duration that do not involve interpersonal violence or threat often have less serious and briefer impact than events of human design that result in physical harm, lasting disfigure-ment, major disruptions in a child's family and life circum-stances, or other persistent reminders of the trauma.

Trauma in the Family

Reactions of Parents and Siblings

The pain of a child's trauma echoes forcefully in the lives of parents, brothers and sisters, and other loved ones. Yet the impact on families is often disregarded, and even misunderstood, by families themselves and by friends and others who attempt to help. It is difficult to understand the intensity and the duration of the pain and worry that parents experience. Parents often report that friends and others whom they would normally turn to for support have disappointingly few ways to understand the family's distress. They may feel repeatedly misunderstood by others who advise them to "get on with their lives" or who insist, "Your child will forget about it." Other parents report that friends and family members are initially supportive and helpful but that this support disappears too soon, leaving the family feeling abandoned. Some families with a traumatized child experience true abandonment by friends and relatives; others discover that support is offered but with notable embarrassment and awkwardness. Something about the trauma itself can interfere with people's capacity to respond in helpful ways.

Most parents find themselves reeling with fear and worry following a traumatic event in a child's life. The shock embodies a powerful blow that can result in a wide range of reactions and emotions: disbelief, feelings of helplessness and horror, a wish to make sense of what may be a totally senseless event. These are the painful and lonely feelings of victimization, and they tend to be contagious. When professionals speak about "vicarious trauma" and "supporter distress," they are describing the ways in which parents and other loved ones poignantly experience feelings similar to the child's own.[1] Parents, brothers and sisters, grandparents, teachers, and day care providers are often the hidden victims of a child's trauma.

Understanding the effects of a child's trauma on all family members can help parents recognize and cope more comfortably with these effects. Recognizing the typical reactions of family members and the predictable difficulties of the recovery process can nurture parents' patience with themselves and their children.

At First...

A parent's initial worry immediately following a trauma concerns the child's well-being. If a child has been physically hurt as well as psychologically traumatized, parents focus their concern first on the child's physical recovery. Nursing an ill or injured child is a well-rehearsed role for parents. Nursing a terrified child, however, can be both unfamiliar and frightening. Few of the signs or symptoms of terror are well known to parents. It is difficult to be certain about the meaning or relative seriousness of a child's responses and behaviors. Fear may seem to be everywhere: the child's own fears and the parents' fears for the child.

Parents may experience this fearfulness as a kind of free-floating anxiety or as a pressured, single-minded concern with the child's recovery. Any unusual changes in the child's behavior or demeanor immediately following a trauma tend to intensify parental concerns. Parents may find themselves constantly distracted by worry or suddenly catapulted into states of panic and alarm. Often underlying parents' anxiety is the looming question, "What will this trauma mean for my child?" and the fear that the child's life will be tragically marred by one hapless event.

Worry about a child's long-term welfare is inevitable and understandable, but when this worry becomes overwhelming, it can interfere with the day-to-day coping that makes all the difference in a child's recovery. During periods of intense anxiety about a child, parents need to take a "one day at a time" approach and deliberately focus their thoughts on the child's specific immediate needs. When parents can focus on helping a child step by step through the various stages of recovery, they can gain confidence along the way in their ability to make a difference. Losing sight of the importance of the present and becoming consumed by global worries about the future can lead to discouragement and loss of the energy needed to tackle each day's challenges.

Worries of and About Siblings

It is not uncommon for parents to find that they need to worry about more than one child. Everyone in the family is affected when one member is struggling to overcome a frightening life event, and siblings are no exception. Parents may notice signs of stress in their other children's behavior, with the intensity of their reactions often related to the seriousness of the trauma and the relative disruption it causes in the family. The most severe reactions are seen in siblings who have witnessed a brother or sister's trauma. Given the intensity of anxiety focused on a traumatized child, it is easy to overlook the reactions of other children in the family.

Marjorie's nine-year-old daughter, April, was weepy and clingy for weeks after she had fallen through the ice on a neighborhood pond while trying to rescue her dog, who had fallen in first. Marjorie had stood helpless with other skaters, watching as a neighbor gingerly crawled across the ice reaching out a hockey stick for April to grab onto. The dog and April struggled frantically in the icy water for five minutes before April was pulled out. Marjorie whisked April immediately to the hospital, where she was treated for hypothermia. Eventually her dog was able to hoist himself out as well, and a neighbor brought word of the dog's safety to April in the emergency room.

In the weeks following the skating incident, Marjorie found herself feeling close to tears at odd moments and had begun having disturbing dreams, all of them about her children being hurt. Her three-year-old son, Tommy, had had nightmares about falling into holes every night for weeks.

When April had fallen through the ice, Tommy had been there and had seen his sister struggling in the water. A neighbor had grabbed him up and taken him away to a warming hut, and Tommy had gone home with this neighbor when Marjorie rushed April to the hospital. Later that day, Marjorie was relieved to find Tommy playing happily with her friend's son and assumed that the entire incident had had little impact on him until she realized what his nightmares were about. Then, she remembered that several days after April's rescue, she had found April's skates in the toilet. Tommy, in his reluctance to be toilet trained, had been interested in throwing many different objects in the toilet lately, and she had not given much thought at the time to the odd sight of skates in the toilet. In retrospect, she realized that Tommy had been deeply shaken by what he had seen on the ice and was trying to protect the big sister he idolized by saying, "No more skating for April."

Brothers and sisters have many different reactions to a sibling's trauma. Many feel abandoned or ignored when so much attention is going to someone else. Others become alarmed by changes in their sibling's behavior. Some children become alarmed by their parents' anxiety or depression; others feel responsible for or guilty about not preventing the harm. To one degree or another, the event of a trauma to one child in the family disrupts the sense of safety and immunity from harm for all the children, as it did for Tommy. There is the shock of awareness that it could have happened to them.

When asked how things had changed in her family since her brother's near-fatal fall from a cliff, a seven year old thought for a moment and answered, "Well, my parents don't play with us anymore." The truth was that her parents *did* still play with the children, but not as much and with less enjoyment. Like many other siblings, this little girl was beginning to throw tantrums and was defiant at school and at home three months after her brother's accident. She could find few words to describe her feelings of neglect and jealousy.

Parents are often surprised to find that their other children show signs of distress quite similar to those of the traumatized child. They may have recurrent nightmares about the trauma, or they may engage in posttraumatic play by themselves or in reenactments under the direction of the traumatized child. Through playing out the trauma, siblings can get frighteningly close to feeling the traumatized child's terror. Clear and consistent limits need to be set on trauma-related play that is too anxiety provoking for siblings.

There is a "cost of caring" for all family members following trauma.[2] Again and again we see how high this cost can be. When children described what it was like for them during a sniper attack on their Los Angeles schoolyard, what many remembered was intense worry about the safety of their brothers and sisters.³ During the hours-long wait to see each other again, the children imagined where their siblings were in the school and pictured their being shot. In the midst of the danger and chaos, children wanted to search for their brothers and sisters. One boy escaped from the playground where the danger was greatest to a protected spot in the building, but then he put himself in danger again when he left to search for his sister. Once the children were safely reunited, fears for a sibling continued to color the children's memories of the event.

Relationships between brothers and sisters are often riddled with mixed feelings. Feelings of hate, envy, competitiveness, idealization, and adoration combine with love in a volatile emotional mix. It is not unusual for children to wish some dreadful fate for a brother or sister. And when a sibling is actually harmed, the load of guilt for the ill-wisher can be heavy indeed. Children who suspect that their own powerful anger has been a magical force in creating a sibling's trauma need repeated reassurance that all children have angry wishes but that these wishes cannot in fact hurt anyone.

When a brother or sister has been hurt or terribly frightened, all the children need to be able to talk freely about the situation and their feelings at home. Children may have many questions they need to ask, and they will follow their parents' lead in talking about feelings and reactions. When parents can share their own feelings and inquire about children's feelings, the experience of brothers and sisters can be an easier one.

Parents' Experiences Following a Child's Traumatization

The occurrence of trauma to a child is a frightening and tragic event. Even learning about an unknown child's trauma through a newspaper article can be a stirring and disturbing experience. It is not unusual for strangers to contribute thousands of dollars and send letters of genuine concern when news of a child's severe trauma appears in the news media. When eighteen-month-old Jessica McClure was trapped twenty-two feet below ground in her backyard well for fifty-eight hours in 1987, this little girl from Midland, Texas, was in the hearts and minds of an entire nation. Major television networks interrupted their regular evening programming to cover her successful rescue, and a seven-ton truck was needed to deliver the mail that poured in to her from across the country. As one *Time* reporter covering her story suggested, Jessica McClure represented the central terror of every parent's nightmare: "small children, unguarded for a few moments, tumble into tragedy."⁴ In Jessica's case, her mother Reba, had momentarily run into the house to answer the telephone.

Deeply felt horror at shocking incidents of childhood trauma is rooted in the universal experience of childhood itself. To have been a child is to have known fear—to have known the feeling of being small and helpless against some real or imagined terror. Most adults have some memory of fear as a child, and a child's trauma may revive these fears and fantasies from childhood of dreadful things that could befall anyone. The old nightmares and night fears of "something bad" may be subtly re-evoked by a child's real trauma. Perhaps everyone carries these old fears and fantasies into their roles as parents, seeing their job as preventing those fears from becoming real for their own children. Those who escaped their worst fears as children, who never really met the "bogeyman" under the bed, wish the same for their children. Those who were unlucky and did not escape, whose childhoods were visited by real terror, wish to spare their own children from this memorable experience. There is nothing neutral about childhood trauma. When microphones lowered into the well relayed the sound of Jessica McClure's plaintive cries for her "Mommy," these cries stirred a universal response of empathy and distress. Part of the context in every family and for every parent when a child is traumatized is the very personal, haunting meaning of childhood terror.

When parents are suddenly confronted with their own child's trauma, they are forced to react to the unthinkable as shock waves are sent through cherished parental hopes and beliefs. As parents react and accommodate to this blast of startling reality, they generally experience some disruption in their everyday functioning. As with children, there are few ways to predict parents' specific emotional reactions. There is no right or wrong to the array of feelings that emerge. Reactions are reactions. What one does with the feelings and how they are communicated to a child, however, does have a direct impact on a child's recovery. These reactions are an integral part of responding to severe stress. Once they are recognized, they can be worked with as part of the coping and healing process that parents must go through. Certainly each parent's experience of a child's trauma is unique but a number of reactions are common and predictable.

Difficulties Coping

Many parents describe significant changes in their day-to-day ability to cope with large and small difficulties during the weeks and months following a child's trauma. They often feel disorganized, distracted, and preoccupied in ways that hinder their life at home and at work. Activities they have enjoyed can lose their pleasure and meaning.

Some parents feel lost in a sea of feelings. Others feel numb and sense themselves operating on a kind of automatic pilot. Parents frequently have difficulty putting words to their pain, and this inability to communite can increase a sense of isolation and frustration. Weepiness, bouts of hysteria, and a sense of constant fretfulness are common. Parents may find that their sleeping and eating patterns are significantly disrupted, with consequent changes in alertness or weight.

Parents are often disturbed by unwelcome changes in themselves. Many describe feeling touchy and oversensitive, reacting with undo anger and frustration with friends and family over small matters. One father noted that his rage over his daughter's injuries from a hit-and-run accident was so great that he was constantly finding targets at which to direct his anger—a line at the bank, a traffic jam, an employee's mistake. His explosiveness is fairly typical of the at-times-irrational responses parents describe in the wake of a child's trauma. This father's loss of control was in part a result of sleep deprivation. He had enormous difficulty getting to sleep for months following his daughter's accident and was unaware of the impact of this cumulative exhaustion on his coping.

These difficulties with coping can become severe enough to transform one's sense of self and the world. Troubled parents may turn to alcohol or drug use for self-medicating relief, with disastrous consequences. Preoccupation with a child's well-being following a trauma and loss of work can result in significant difficulties in job performance, which creates further anxiety for bread-winning parents. The strain of persistent stress can reduce the body's immunity to disease, resulting in vulnerability to illnesses. When worry, exhaustion, or despair reaches the point of interfering with parents' day-to-day handling of their various roles, professional help is in order. Parents may be so preoccupied with concern about a child that they do not recognize their own need for help and support. Their selflessness can backfire, however. When parents are operating on "empty," it is truly difficult to find the energy and inner resources to respond to a child's unusual neediness.

Parents need to take their own distress seriously and secure help and support. As one single–mother suggested, "Be sure parents hear that taking care of themselves is half the battle of parenting a traumatized child." This mother felt she could not have made it through the year of nursing her son without the weekly hour she had with a community counselor. After her nine-year-old son, Josh, survived being hit and run over by a truck on his bicycle, his mother often felt totally depleted by his extraordinary need for physical care and her own worry about his recovery. With no partner to share her burden, Josh's mother one day found herself weeping while she searched for a counselor in the telephone book. It took another two weeks before she could bring herself to call for an appointment. Two years later, with Josh healed and ready to play soccer again, she reflected, "Getting help for myself was the best decision I could have made. I was doing a great job taking care of Josh and a terrible job taking care of myself. When the doctors let me know he would be in bed for another seven months, I knew I wouldn't be able to keep it up without someone being there just for me. With my therapist I didn't have to be superwoman or supermom. I could just be as miserable and scared as I really felt sometimes. I don't know how it worked, but I'd go home from my appointments feeling stronger, even when I'd spent the hour just crying. I guess I leaned on my counselor, and that made me more able to let Josh lean on me."

Reviewing and Retelling

Not unlike their children, parents may need repeatedly to review in their minds and conversation the events of a child's trauma. Going over and over what happened is one way to cope and come to terms with a sudden shocking reality. The importance of having other adults to listen and understand is often a key factor in parents' healing over time. Visual images of the child's trauma or disturbing thoughts regarding the event may intrude unpleasantly and suddenly for parents, disrupting their concentration or enjoyment. For Josh's mother, the image of the truck's wheels going over her son's legs kept returning to her. These intruding images and thoughts often focus on the details of the trauma that are the most difficult to accept and integrate. Because they are the most unthinkable images, they seem to return insistently until they can in fact become thinkable.

Sense of Isolation

Feelings of isolation are common for parents following a child's trauma. Some parents feel unable to find words for their pain, regardless of how many times they may re-tell the events; others find themselves completely unable to speak about the trauma or their own experience. Feeling cut off and alone is common for parents who are acutely aware that others' lives have gone on with blissful normality while their own sense of normality has vanished. This sense of isolation is not at all unlike the feelings associated with bereavement following the death of a loved one. Life can feel so altered in such painful ways that it is easy to feel removed from the community and resentful of others.

Many parents find that feelings of isolation diminish gradually as they regain their own sense of familial normality. Those who seek support and connection with others following a child's trauma frequently credit a great deal of their healing to the availability of this support. Parents often long to talk with others whose children have endured similar traumas. Meeting and talking with these other parents can indeed provide dramatic relief and support. When available, parent support groups are enormously helpful in reducing feelings of isolation.

Disruption of Beliefs

In order to go about the business of daily life with some equanimity, all parents find ways to fend off fears that their families will encounter experiences of tragedy, pain, or terror. Parents often believe that bad things will not happen to good children. They believe that their own conscientious parenting will protect their own children from senseless accidents or incidents of victimization. However illusory they may be, these beliefs regarding the immunity of one's own children are vital and comforting. A child's trauma shatters all notions of immunity. Parents are confronted dramatically with the limits of their own power and with the limits of goodness and fairness in life. Such disillusionment involves a genuine loss that must be confronted and mourned.

Parents are seldom prepared for the ways in which their child's trauma can change their beliefs and outlook. It is a nasty shock to discover that bad things can happen to good children of good parents. There are troubling questions that need to be asked, and the answers do not come quickly. Why my child? How could this have happened to us? How did we deserve this? For parents of a child who has been victimized maliciously, there is the question of trust: How could someone do this to my child? For many parents, there is painful new doubt about the goodness of their own parenting, however unreasonable that doubt may be.

Mourning the loss of cherished beliefs takes time. Parents feel vulnerable and disillusioned during this period of mourning, which has no set timetable. For a while, the world can feel random and meaningless. Over time, however, parents find they are able to make meaning out of the most horrible experiences. They refashion their inner world to make room for the possibility of catastrophe and horror.[5]

Parents are not unlike their own children in needing to put a shattered sense of the world back together in new ways. For some parents, rebuilding trust and developing new ways to understand a world in which one's child can be hurt or terrorized is a long, painful, and often very private process, which may occur without being spoken of, even between spouses. Looking back, some parents are able to find words to describe the gradual process of rebuilding their sense of the world and themselves. They often speak about the ultimate meanings they were able to find in an event that initially seemed to have no redeeming value.

One mother's life changed the day her daughter fell fifty feet in a rock-climbing accident, but many of the changes she now treasured. At some point in the three years since the accident, she realized that she no longer worried about small matters as she once had: "I just seem to be clearer about the priorities, and I value each day a little more than I ever did before Rachel was hurt. I watched her determination to walk again. She has fought so hard. We never had a situation in this family that tested our strength or courage. I think we found out we're a pretty tough crew and, in many ways, a very lucky family to have so much to give each other. I do get more worried than I used to when I don't know exactly where my younger son is or when my husband is late getting home from work, but I feel a new sense of confidence that I can handle whatever's coming my way."

Guilt, Shame, and Helplessness

Many childhood incidents of trauma evoke feelings of guilt, shame, or helplessness. As parents struggle to come to terms with the question, "How could this have happened to my child?" the answers that arise often involve various forms of self-blame. Mothers and fathers may need to review the possible ways that they were even obliquely responsible for a child's traumatic experience. This painful searching is much like the child's own guilt-ridden quest for meaning. Parents frequently focus on the ways in which they could have prevented incidents in ways that defy logic.

There is little logic to the workings of guilt. A parent who had been somewhat undecided about sending her son to school one morning because he had mild sniffles obsessed over that decision for months following his being hit by a drunk driver on the walk to school. The reasonable conclusion that she could not have known or prevented this event was initially of no comfort to her. Parents who are searching for the ways they could have prevented a child's trauma often use the phrase "if only": If only I had gone to check on him as I meant to," "If only I had followed my first instinct and said we needed to wait for the ice to thicken," "If only I had not been so lazy and gone ahead with chaperoning the school dance." When parents are reviewing all the "if onlys" that seem to hold the key to prevention, reassurances of "it wasn't your fault" have little value or meaning.

This battle with guilt can be a necessary part of parents' own healing and coping with a child's trauma, and it can be time-consuming and extremely painful. Not unlike the child, parents may find themselves settling for any explanation for an unlikely and horrifying event. Any explanation, even at the cost of suffering the misery of guilt, may help a parent cope with the sense of helplessness and senselessness aroused by the experience. If a parent can find some way in which the trauma was her own fault, it becomes possible to believe that further trauma can be avoided. Guilt offers a kind of power, however illusory, over helplessness. This sense of helplessness is the real devil that must be struggled with when trauma has disturbed the complacency of everyday life.

Guilt and shame are often referred to as if they were identical, but they are not. Guilt visits us with less weight over specific acts we regret and that we can often find ways to correct or atone for. It is possible to forgive ourselves for guilt.[6] Shame refers to something about our whole self, something fundamentally wrong or bad about us that cannot be undone or forgiven. Typically, shame has little to do with specific events or transgressions in the present; it has something to do with being exposed for who we really are and not for any one thing that we have done. Adult experiences of shame harken back to childhood, to memories of intensely personal exposure. Like guilt, shame does not follow the rules of logic or respond easily to appeals to reason.

For parents of recently traumatized children, feelings of shame may have to do with failing to meet their own personal ideals. Most parents carry an internal guiding picture of themselves as the parents they want to be, and this idealized image is the measure against which they judge their basic adequacy.[7] Parents derive comfort and meaning when they can see that their parenting matches their internal picture of the parents they want to be. Frequently, however, parents carry another darker image of themselves as the parents they do not want to be or fear they could become. This image of the "bad" parent, modeled at times from memories of one's own parents, can have a haunting force. When a child is traumatized, the idealized image of one's self-as-parent is violated abruptly. In its place may be only the remnants of the "bad" parent image and feelings of shameful exposure. A parent may feel vulnerable not for the exposure of one misdeed but of one's whole self.

> At age thirty-nine with ten years of parenting behind her, Sally had pretty much overcome her fear that she could never be a decent parent. Her experience raising Jason and Annie had quieted her dread that she would be as abusive and neglectful as her own mother had been toward her. Her self-confidence as a parent came to an abrupt end the day Jason, her three year old, was hospitalized after drinking cleaning fluid from a cabinet she thought he could never reach. Long after he had fully recovered, Sally was unable to shake her distress over this incident. Although she tried to tell herself that accidents can happen, she was plagued by doubt about herself. She could see that Jason too was suffering from this incident, but she felt unable to help him with his own confusion and fears. For the first time in years, Sally's dreams were filled with images of her own mother hurting and insulting children. Jason's accident had reawakened the feared image of her own mother, whom she now felt no distance from. She felt exposed by this incident for who she felt she really was: a mother no better than her own. She stopped her involvement in the parent-teacher organization and pulled away from contact with her children's friends' parents.

There was nothing specific that Sally had done that resulted in her torturous feelings. Over the year of psychotherapy that Sally worked on these feelings, it was an old and powerful shame that she fought with: the shame she had felt as a child when her mother had berated her, the shame she had felt for her mother when she compared her to the mothers of her own childhood friends, and the shame of feeling that she had failed to be the kind of mother she wanted to be for her children.

Some situations of trauma arouse feelings of shame in the child that in turn stir feelings of shame in a parent. Children with disfiguring injuries often struggle with shame over their changed physical appearance. Children who feel that something unspeakably bad has happened to them are also vulnerable to feelings of shame. Parents are finely tuned to their children's feelings of shame and can suffer these feelings of shame along with them.

When the Guilt is Real

Some childhood traumas do result from the direct acts of negligence, poor judgment, or abuse by parents. A parent whose driving while intoxicated causes a severe car accident involving a child must confront responsibility for this preventable occurrence. A parent whose cocaine abuse leads to an unprecedented assault on a child must come to terms with this memory of harming a family member. A parent who has reached the breaking point due to job stress, unemployment, or unattended depression may unleash rage on a child with terrifying consequences. Incestuous abuse of a child is well recognized to be a most complex and wrenching example of preventable parental harm to a child that leaves a trail of torn loyalties and damage to the child and family.[8]

When a parent is truly at fault for a child's terror or harm, the emotional consequences can be devastating for the entire family. Parents who struggle with very real guilt and unspeakable shame over their own preventable actions require professional help for themselves and their families.

Exaggerating and Minimizing the Meaning of Trauma

Just as children find their own ways of coping, parents also develop ways of coping and defending themselves from the barrage of intense feelings that typically follows a child's trauma. Some of the efforts to cope are quite rational and conscious. A father who recognizes the stress he is under, for instance, might decide to increase his weekly exercise program because he knows that exercise has helped him manage difficult periods in the past. Other coping responses occur without any awareness of the connection between a coping behavior and the experience of stress. A different father, for instance, who finds himself unexpectedly interested in a time-consuming home renovation project that previously had held little interest for him might not recognize the connection between his child's recent trauma and his own need to occupy his time and his mind. Sometimes we make conscious choices about how we cope—and sometimes we just cope.

The ways parents find to cope can be helpful to themselves and to their children, or they can backfire by increasing the stress in the family. A father who decides to increase his exercise program might add an extra run during the week and feel less anxious and more available to support his child and family during a difficult time. Or he might end up working out at the gym five nights a week as a way of removing himself from the tension and worry at home. This latter solution would surely increase the level of tension at home. Similarly, a father who launches a renovation project at home might find a way to involve his child in the work, with the result that both father and child have a gratifying opportunity to be together and put their minds on other matters. Or the renovation project could become a consuming and isolating activity that results in the child and other family members feeling abandoned and ignored.

People generally have characteristic ways of coping. Some tend to go into action under stress, feeling best when they are actively attacking the problems. Others retreat, taking time to think or remove themselves from the problems. Coping styles include what people tend to do under stress but also how they tend to think about stressful problems.[9] How a parent thinks about a child's trauma and life problems in general appears to have a strong influence on how children recover from trauma. There is a strong tendency for parents to think about the child's trauma in ways that either minimize or exaggerate its impact and meaning. When taken to an extreme, either minimizing or exaggerating the impact of the trauma can work against the healing process.

Diana's experience of coping with her daughter's involvement in a car accident well illustrates the ways in which thoughts and coping style weave together to influence a child's healing and recovery.

Five-year-old Jill was riding home from dancing lessons with her neighbors when their car was hit by a truck. The neighbor's four-year-old child was killed instantly. Jill escaped major injuries but endured the ordeal of the collision and the horror of the emergency scene for two hours before her mother could be located. Diana found her daughter mute and frozen with fear at the police station. That evening, Jill had little to say about the accident or her friend's death. Her mother kept Jill home from school the next day and observed that she played very quietly and asked only a few questions about the accident and about dying. Diana herself was thoroughly shaken by this accident, which could have killed her child. She was also absorbed in grief for her neighbors, whom she found many ways to help and support daily in the months that followed.

Diana was no stranger to adversity and struggle. When she was a child her brother had been killed in a farm machinery accident. As a single mother, she had struggled alone to make ends meet with limited income. Diana's family of New England farmers had instilled in her an attitude of dogged perseverance in the face of adversity. In many ways, Diana expected life to throw up obstacles and tragedies, and she believed in meeting misfortune with strength and determination. At some level, she viewed misfortune as a test of individual fortitude.

As time went on, Diana continued to worry about what the accident meant to Jill but could find no signs of its impact. Jill's seeming lack of reaction to her experience was surprising and somewhat confusing to her mother. Over the next two months, Jill appeared to be doing fine at school and at home. The teachers reported no significant changes in her behavior or attitudes. When Jill's mother was offered the opportunity to work some evening overtime two months after the accident, she grabbed this chance to earn the money for a trip to the beach that Jill had long requested.

Jill's nightmares began during the evenings that she was with a new babysitter while her mother worked overtime. At first she had one nightmare each night; the babysitter decided to report the nightmares to Diana after Jill had had three in one evening. Soon after, the teacher sent a note home describing Jill's daydreaming in school. The note arrived the day Jill's mother had found a small box carefully lined with tissue holding a doll with red marker smeared over its face and hands. Artificial flowers were strewn over the doll, whose box was surely Jill's depiction of a coffin. The box had been hidden in the deepest recesses of Jill's closet.

Diana was mildly concerned about the nightmares and the dead doll. She spoke with Jill briefly about her dreams, got her a new nightlight, and instructed Jill to pay attention at school. But basically Jill's reactions seemed normal to Diana who recalled her own childhood nightmares following her brother's death.

It was not until nine months after the accident that Diana became alarmed when the teacher called her at work to tell her of several disturbing incidents at recess. Jill had been instructing her friends to play dead while she buried them in piles of coats. Several children had become frightened of being smothered during these "burials." At this point, Diana realized that the memory of the accident was distressing Jill in more ways than she realized. She recalled that the police had initially given her the name of a social worker who worked with children and took Jill for an initial appointment the next week.

After the accident, Diana relied on the coping skills she had developed over her lifetime and her own belief that one can and must overcome difficult times in life. Her perseverance helped her to move forward, attend to a mourning neighbor's needs, and resume her active and goal-oriented life as a single parent who wished to give as much as possible to her child. Her life became occupied between working overtime and helping the neighbors. This busyness may also have helped her cope with the anxiety and fear she herself was feeling about the accident. Jill may have experienced her mother's busyness as withdrawal and distance at a time that she was particularly needing attention and time.

Jill's lack of evident reaction to the accident initially was reassuring and confirming to her mother. When Jill first began to show delayed reactions to the trauma, her mother needed to minimize their importance. How entirely understandable is the power of a parent's wish for wellness in a child whose life was recently spared in a tragic accident. Like most other parents, Diana's coping was adaptive in many ways and limited in others. Jill found it helpful to see the model of her mother resuming life after the accident, and there was something comforting about the sense of normality she sensed at home. But there was also a way in which she felt lonely and frightened with her memories and unsure whether her mother wanted to hear about them.

Diana was not a "bad" parent. She was an exceptionally responsible and overburdened parent who was doing the best she could for Jill and for herself. Diana did come to see that her own coping following the trauma involved a literal blind spot—an aspect of her child's painful experience about which she dearly wished to be blind. She found that she could more easily cope with the exhaustion of overtime than she could with the pain of hearing her child's fears and memories. She avoided that pain as long as she was able to, following her beliefs in the importance of moving on and overcoming adversity. When Diana did get in touch with Jill's fears and confusion, she began to recall her own childhood nighttime fears about her brother's death and all the alarming thoughts she had had at age seven about the reasons he had died. Once she was able to recover and confront the long-buried memories of her own feelings following her brother's death, Diana was able to slow down and attend to Jill's feelings and needs in ways that strengthened Jill's coping.

During the first months following a child's trauma, parents cope. Denying, minimizing, and avoiding are all forms of coping that work well in small quantities but generally work poorly when used to excess. It would have been helpful if Diana had been able to recognize the signs of distress in Jill's play and nightmares as ones that needed her attention. Had Diana not been so intent on moving on, she might have sensed that being home with Jill at night would have been more helpful than a trip to the beach. The force of Diana's need to cope in certain ways created blind spots that complicated Jill's recovery and kept her from seeing Jill's needs clearly.

Parents can also be blinded by overreacting and exaggerating the meaning and impact of a child's trauma, as Tom and Mary did when John Henry was lost in the woods near their home for eight hours.

John Henry was a tough and spunky four-year-old. He was a bright, independent child who devoted himself to being just like his eight-year-old brother. He was both a terror and a joy to parent. Since birth he had had little need for sleep and was on the go from dawn until bedtime. John Henry had already given his parents several scares by getting into cabinets of cleaning fluids and starting the car.

On a Monday in April that Mary will never forget, she went out to get John Henry from the sandbox, where he usually played while she made dinner. There was no John Henry in the sandbox and no answer when she called to him. At first, Mary was angry that he was playing a hiding game on her. Her anger quickly turned to panic when the silence continued as she screamed for him to come out.

Mary checked with the neighbors and then called the police. It was her other son, Stuart, who discovered that Blacky, their retriever, was also missing. Tom came home at dusk from a business trip to find their rural home transformed into the headquarters for a search operation involving hundreds of neighbors, strangers, and the police. After a long night of wider and wider search through the woods, John Henry was found curled up asleep, cuddled into the side of Blacky. He was cold and groggy but unharmed. John Henry explained that he was out looking for good sticks to throw for Blacky and then lost his way home. He told his parents that Blacky protected him from the tigers in the Connecticut woods.

Over the next several weeks, John Henry stayed close to his mother's side, following her upstairs and down. At night, he wanted to sleep with Tom and Mary, who were only too happy to have him close to them. But after several weeks of clinginess, John Henry seemed to bounce back. He wanted to accept friends' invitations to play and begged to be allowed to walk to his best friend's house, where he had been allowed to go by himself for over a year. Tom and Mary would have none of it; John Henry was put under house arrest.

John Henry's night in the woods had unraveled his parents. For months, Mary's sleep was disrupted by nightmares and insomnia. Tom often woke to find Mary curled up in John Henry's bed. She knew it was silly and perhaps harmful in some way, but she had to know he was within reaching distance. During the day, she started feeling jumpy and nervous. Mary's migraines returned for the first time since she was a teenager. Tom was also deeply shaken by the incident. He found himself unable to concentrate on a trial he had to prepare for at work and started going home for lunch, something he had never done in their fifteen years of marriage. Tom decided that this independent child of theirs needed more discipline. His manner with John Henry seemed suddenly gruff to Mary, who could not find enough ways to indulge the child. An odd scenario ensued in which Tom seemed to say no to everything John Henry wanted and Mary said yes to everything. The only area of agreement between the parents had to do with John Henry's not being out of their sight.

Five months after John Henry's night in the woods, he was still not allowed any of his previous freedom, including visits to friends' houses. By this time, Mary was seeing a physician about her migraines and her anxiety. She was furious at Tom for being so hard on John Henry. Tom had stopped coming home for lunch and started working late most nights of the week, perhaps to avoid the fights he and Marying had been having. John Henry had stopped asking for his privileges back but had begun soiling in his pants and seemed more defiant than usual. It was Stuart who told his parents that everything had been a "real drag" at home ever since John Henry had gotten lost.

The experience of almost losing a child had a dramatic effect on John Henry's family and it was not abating over time. Neither Mary nor Tom could find a way to put the experience behind them, perhaps because both of them tended to overreact in general to emotional events. Tom dealt with his worry by seeking excessive control over John Henry, who became confused by his dad's sudden harshness. Mary coped with her ongoing fears of loss by being overly indulgent and protective with her son. The signs that John Henry himself was ready to resume his life as normal (with perhaps a tighter leash) were missed. John Henry ultimately came up with a signal that was too smelly to overlook; his soiling seemed to echo brother Stuart's sentiments that things were really a drag at home.

It is not unusual for parents to feel pulled toward overindulging and overprotecting a child following a trauma, nor is it uncommon for a child's trauma to be more troubling to the parents than to the child in the long run, as occurred in John Henry's family. The consequences of overreacting, however, can be problematic when the child's feelings and needs are lost in the family atmosphere of distress and worry. John Henry needed to get back to the business of being a four year old, which he did not see as scary at all. In very gradual steps, Tom and Mary needed to let John Henry have a bit more freedom, and to do this they needed to loosen the grip of their own fear. When John Henry's soiling began, Tom and Mary did change the way they were responding to him and to each other. A talk with their pastor helped them see how out of whack things had gotten at home. They started talking about the ways their lives had become dominated by one evening's huge scare and made a conscious decision to work their way back to normal family life. Very gradually over the next six months, it became possible for Mary to watch John Henry head down their sidewalk to a friend's house without feeling panic.

The question is always how a parent's particular style of coping matches the child's needs for understanding, support, and reassurance. Parents do not need to torment themselves by demanding perfection in their responses to their child. There is no perfect in parenting—just approximations of good enough. Parents who are coping well with a child's trauma in ways that promote that child's healing will have times when they cannot attend to the child or tolerate her expression of pain. There will be times that overindulging or overprotecting a child feels like the only course to pursue. Parenting always involves making an infinite number of difficult judgment calls and decisions that in retrospect one might regret. Occasional bad days and scattered difficult moments in parenting come under the heading of forgiveness. Children are amazingly forgiving of their parents, and parents need to be thoughtfully forgiving of themselves. Problems arise when a parent's style of coping is consistently at odds with a child's needs, as Tom and Mary's turned out to be, and the process of healing for everyone in a family can be delayed and complicated.

Making Matters Worse: Family and Marital Tensions

There is no good time for trauma to occur in a family, but there are perhaps better or worse times. A family may be visited by trauma during a period of familial strength and resilience or during a period when coping with stress is already difficult. Responding to a child's trauma can be particularly troublesome when it occurs during times of economic uncertainty, parental unemployment or illness, bereavement, or other life stress. Even recent welcome changes in a family—the arrival of a new baby, a recent move, a parent's job promotion—can create stress. The degree of stress in the family just prior to a traumatic event has a strong influence on the family's capacity to cope.

Most partners experience difficult seasons in their relationships. Marital stress and conflict can be aggravated or newly created by a child's trauma in ways that parents find particularly painful and perplexing. At times, marital conflict precedes a child's trauma and colors parents' experience of it. At other times, parents report that the stress of the child's trauma itself either exposes or creates fault lines and tensions in the relationship. Either way, parents frequently describe an intense need for each other's support and involvement following a child's trauma and some degree of difficulty meeting this need.

One common source of marital tension arises when each partner has a very different way of coping with a child's trauma. When one spouse reacts with very strong emotions and the other reacts with minimal emotion, both spouses can end up feeling isolated and misunderstood. Patricia Crowley, the mother of a child molested at day care, describes a common experience for many spouses in her book, *Not My Child:*

> Right from the start, Jim and I weren't good at comforting each other through any of this. We both were consumed by it, of course, but he didn't want to discuss it, while it was all I wanted to talk about. I snapped at him for not caring, he became disgusted with me for the uncontrollable fits of weeping I allowed myself each night when the kids fell asleep. It set the tone for the coldness that would pervade our marriage in the next couple of years, and as I found out later—it was a common behavioral pattern among other Wee Care parents.[10]

Gender differences in coping with emotion and relational issues may come to the fore in the opposite reactions of spouses.[11] Fathers and mothers may find themselves focusing their concern on very different aspects of the trauma or coping in distinct ways. A couple can easily become polarized when spouse's responses and ways of coping are at odds with each other. Some parents describe one spouse carrying all the sadness, while the other carries all the anger. Other parents describe one spouse needing to move along quickly away from the distressing feelings set off by a child's trauma, while the other remains overwhelmed and tuned in to all the feelings.

Many men have been socialized to cope silently and inwardly with strong emotions, while women are more comfortable expressing these emotions. Mothers can feel emotionally abandoned by husbands who are uncomfortable with displays of emotion. Fathers can feel barraged by their wives' more open expression of pain. Fathers may process the emotional impact of a child's trauma more slowly over time, showing less immediate emotion during the crisis period but being vulnerable to delayed responses of distress and depression.[12] Polarization between partners in the ways they express and cope with strong feelings does not always follow the traditional stereotypes, however. Whenever partners are polarized in the ways they express feelings and cope following a child's trauma, there is the potential for conflict and estrangement in the relationship.

It can be difficult for spouses to respect and accept their partner's different ways of responding and coping. Parents find themselves blaming their spouse for being overemotional or for avoiding all emotion. Usually both are doing the best they can given their different styles of coping. Partners need to talk about their coping styles and acknowledge the differences between them. Some partners find that while they are irritated by the other's approach to managing stress, they are also somewhat grateful for a partner's different style. When one partner is overwhelmed by feelings, it can be relieving to depend on the other partner's opposite tendencies to stay on top of the daily business of life during a period of stress. Conversely, a spouse who finds emotion difficult to express may find vicarious relief in a partner's more open expression of feelings. Whatever the differences or similarities between partners, there is a need for partners to find ways to feel that they are traveling together through a period of pain and upheaval and yet to recognize that temporary feelings of isolation, distance, and misunderstanding are extremely common in parents' relationships following a child's trauma.

Misperceptions of the Traumatized Child

Accurate perception and understanding of any situation is always more difficult when emotions run strong. Parents are vulnerable to misreading and misinterpreting children's behavior and reactions when they are in the midst of coming to terms with a child's trauma. It is a true ongoing struggle for parents to sort out the impact of a trauma on a child's behavior, reactions, or attitudes, and their heightened anxiety about the child can lead to misconstruing the meanings of a child's behavior or misperceiving the child's needs. At times, parents read too much meaning into a child's behavior, looking for impact from the trauma where none exists. Since children move on from a trauma to experience the typical childhood difficulties with everyday events, there are always opportunities for parents to agonize over the meaning of a child's fears or unusual behavior.

Parents who need to reassure themselves by minimizing the impact of the trauma will also find many opportunities in looking at the child's behavior to see that a child has been unharmed and unaffected. Even very distressed children seldom look miserable or act in unusual ways all the time. Parents who are determined to find proof of a child's well-being will generally be able to find it. "She's already forgotten about it" or "He never talks about it" are typical comments parents make when the trauma needs to be put quickly out of mind as a way of coping.

The danger of excessive minimizing or exaggerating is exactly the same: the child's real experience may get lost or misperceived. Following a trauma, children are desperate for parents simply to accept and understand their true feelings. If a child could express her feelings about what she needs from a parent, she might say, "Just stay with me, and stick this out with me. Don't go into the ozone getting so scared about me, or I'll get more scared. And don't go pretending that what happened to me was no big deal, or I'll feel like you can't handle these scary feelings I'm having. If you can't handle this, how am I supposed to?" Children can feel burdened by parents' misperceptions of them.

Most people have a tendency to either minimize or exaggerate emotional events as a way of coping. The tendency in either direction may be quite subtle or dramatic. Following a child's trauma, it can be helpful for parents to examine how their own typical tendency to either minimize or exaggerate may be influencing their perceptions of a child's functioning. As if working with a compass that is known to be off by several degrees, parents can try to adjust and correct the direction of their responses. At times, the perceptions of more distant adults who know the child well can lend objectivity to an anxious parent's view of the child's adjustment.

When Other Family Members Are Also Victims of Trauma

A child's trauma is not always the child's alone. A natural or human-induced disaster, a serious accident, a fire, or any number of other extremely frightening events can involve multiple family members as co-victims or witnesses. In the wake of large-scale disasters, families typically experience many immediate and long-term stress-related difficulties and unexpected changes.[13] Individual family members may experience nervousness, loss of concentration, difficulties sleeping, and stress-related headaches or other physical complaints. All members of the family must struggle with their fears and memories, their feelings of anger and helplessness, and an overwhelming sense of loss.[14] Following disasters and large-scale catastrophes, social disorganization and disarray as well as the loss of personal and community economic resources can work against the emotional rebuilding that must occur within families. Bitterness and intense frustration can compound survivors' difficulty in recovery if relief and aid are delayed or inadequate. Community-wide recovery is intricately interwoven with the adequacy and timing of overall relief responses.

When parents are responding to the shock of a trauma along with their children, often in the midst of physical dislocation, it can be extremely difficult to restore a sense of calm and normality within the family. Children are particularly reactive to the high level of distress and the loss of balance within their families and communities. While there is some evidence that childrens' posttraumatic reactions to natural disasters and catastrophes are often less severe than their reactions to abuse, the impact on individual children can be extreme.[15] Children suffering from posttraumatic stress following disasters and catastrophes fare best when parents can resume their roles of authority and protection relatively rapidly. Children find relief in anything that has not changed following life-transforming events and often it is the stability of the relationships and interactions with parents that first restore their feelings of well-being. Parents who expect, encourage, and accept the expression of grief and distress ease the process of healing for their children and for themselves. The capacity to accept and seek out help is a strength in families coping with overwhelming loss and change. Relying on extended family and other outside supports and taking advantage of disaster-relief resources can be important in the long-term recovery process within the family. Realistically recognizing when a family member's extreme distress requires professional help is part of successful coping that allows families to move forward with the recovery process.

When the anchors of home and routine daily life have been destroyed by disaster or calamity, the process of recovery for all family members is slow and gradual, occurring more often over years than months. In this process, families can discover unknown strengths and re-evaluate what is truly valuable in their lives as they tackle the massive problems of re-building.

Parents realistically must expect that recovery for all family members will be slow following a disaster, and that each member of the family will have unique struggles in coming to terms with experiences of loss and trauma. Because the meaning of a disaster may be very diffferent for the child victim than for the adults, it is important to listen carefully and understand exactly what the specific fears, memories, and struggles are for each child.

Special Concerns for Parents of Sexually Abused Children

Incidents of sexual abuse tend to raise a host of unusual concerns that complicate the task of parenting. The graphic introduction of adult sexuality into a child's life is itself experienced as a major violation by most parents. When the perpetrator is a known caretaker, feelings of betrayal and violation are frequently mixed with feelings of guilt and inadequacy as a parent searches retrospectively for signs that would have allowed the abuse to be prevented.

Given the sexual nature of the trauma, parents must confront their own hornet's nest of feelings regarding sexuality. Some parents are dismayed to feel that their child is contaminated or different following molestation. They find themselves dwelling on questions about the effects of abuse on a child's sexual orientation and development. A disturbing worry for some parents is whether their child will be compelled to repeat the abuse by later victimizing another child. A vicious cycle can ensue in which the parents are reluctant to share the story of their child's trauma for fear of the stigmatization that might occur. The abuse can become a family secret, leading to isolation from the friends and relatives who might otherwise have been able to provide support during a difficult time. The very secretiveness surrounding the abuse can intensify feelings of shame for family members who find the trauma to be unspeakable. How does one heal from an event that cannot be spoken of when part of the natural healing process from trauma involves retelling and repeated confrontation with the trauma? Secret traumas can delay and complicate healing for the child and the family.

Family reactions to sexual abuse have a lot to do with children's long-term recovery. The children are particularly vulnerable to suffering additional after-effects of trauma due to the nature of adult reactions. When parents overreact, they can inadvertently create or intensify a child's anxiety about the abuse. The raw and often explosive rage some parents feel after discovering their child's sexual victimization can be terrifying to the child. More subtle, but equally disturbing to the child, is a parent's perception of the child as unalterably damaged. Children are similarly confused and distressed by parents' concerns about the long-term impact of the abuse.

Parents whose own childhood history echoes the experience of child sexual abuse have unique difficulty coping with disclosure of their own child's abuse. Adult survivors must swim back and forth between their own world of revived painful memory and their child's current painful reality. For most adult survivors of sexual abuse, sexual victimization is the one experience they have been determined to prevent in their children's lives. The sense of failure that accompanies the realization that abuse has been repeated with their own child is yet a further burden for adult survivors.

Many single incidents of mild sexual abuse have much in common with other one-time incidents of childhood trauma. For children, the experience may involve feelings of confusion, helplessness, and often intense, immediate distress. For some young children, there is frequently something dark and "icky" about an abusive sexual experience. Others, who have been mildly molested without force, pain, or penetration, may feel only confused and a little "weird." There is always the possibility that an incident of abuse has involved physical pleasure for a child, as well as whatever other feelings the child has about the situation. Sexual organs are made to have good feelings, and some children experience various degrees of pleasurable arousal. A child who has experienced pleasure can become confused and ashamed if these feelings are not acknowledged.

Individual children's reactions to sexual abuse vary enormously, and are affected by the specific nature of the experience, the meaning of the perpetrator in their lives, their age, their temperment, and their prior experiences in life.[16] How each child reacts and recovers has a lot to do with the particular meaning she or he gives

to the abuse. The meanings children give to long-term and very severe abuse are often more complex and damaging to their self-esteem than the meanings children attribute to brief or mild
episodes. Frequently the meaning is different for the child than it is
for the protective adult or parent, who agonizes over the abuse.
Some of the meaning the child gives to the abuse is derived from
careful observation of parental reactions. If children detect a sense
of catastrophe in a parents' reactions to their abuse, they will generally incorporate the parent's distress in their own perceptions
and reactions.[17]

Children's exquisite sensitivity to their parents' feelings places a
burden of care on parents to respond thoughtfully and calmly.
Focusing on the child's actual experience can help parents respond
empathically and reasonably. Parents need to know what this particular incident of abuse was like and what special meanings the
child has given to it. What did this experience really mean to the
child? Was there a terrifying use of physical force? Did the child
experience physical pain? Did the child feel tricked? Was the child
threatened into compliance? Is the child now terrified that the
threat will be carried through? Did the abuse occur in the context
of a game? Did the abuser in fact seem playful and friendly to the
child? Does the child believe the abuse was her own fault? What
did the child make of this experience? What are the lingering worries, feelings, and confusions for the child? An inventory of the
child's own experience often turns out to be quite different, and
sometimes less shattering, than the parents' adult imaginings and
reactions. Once focused on the child's actual concerns and fears,
parents often find it easier to do their job of parenting and helping
the child to heal. Keeping adult reactions separate from an em-
pathic understanding of the child's experience of the abuse is difficult but helpful emotional work for parents. Like all traumatized
children, the sexually abused child needs to feel that her parents
are right there with her, understanding and accompanying her
through a difficult period.

Sexual abuse that has involved extremes of violence and terrorizing, betrayal of carefully placed trust in a caretaker, and pain or
injury for a child are among the most devastating incidents for
children and their parents to cope with. Ritualistic abuse that involves the child in bizarre sexual practices of satanic cult worship

complicates recovery for parents and children.[18] Experiences of severe abuse inevitably create so much traumatic disruption for children and their parents that professional intervention is always recommended.

There is obvious potential for a mismatch between a child's needs and the parents' reactions following disclosure of sexual abuse. Repeatedly studies find that children's sensitivity to their parents' reactions to sexual abuse affects their recovery.[19] Parents' natural reactions of distress to the abuse can create a further bind for the child. There is no easy exit from this bind, but parents need to be aware of their own impact on children. One specialist in child sexual abuse concludes that "it should not be assumed that a victimized child is destined for difficulty. It may be that by providing a calm and supportive reaction to victimization, the risks of long-term effects on the child can be completely dissipated."[20] The supportive reactions parents can give include believing and protecting the child, focusing on the child's needs and experience, accepting the full range of a child's feelings, and holding on to the image of a child's strength as a survivor.[21] Remembering that the intensity of feelings and worries will lessen with time is helpful in getting through the most difficult periods of recovery with sexually abused children.

> Ginny's preschooler had been abused by a well-trusted babysitter a year ago. Looking back, she felt that her family's life was only beginning to feel normal again one year later. Ginny described months of intense worry about her son and her agony that his sweet little life had been visited by an experience of hurt and fear. Long after her son seemed to be recovering well from this one incident of abuse, Ginny found herself constantly searching for signs of the abuse in his behavior. When he had a difficult day at school or a rough time getting to sleep at night, she could never feel certain whether she was seeing normal developmental difficulties or reactions to his molestation.

Like many other parents, Ginny mourned her losses. Her prior sense of trust and optimism had been transformed by the experience of her child's molestation. She hated living with distrust but could not shake this new awareness of evil and danger that had crept into her sense of the world. Ginny saw her own and her family's life as divided in time by trauma: the life they had known right up to the moment they discovered the molestation and the very different life they had after it. Ginny had also lost a sense of herself. She was distressed by the enduring guilt that had nagged at her as she repeatedly reviewed what she could have done to prevent the abuse. A protective parent by nature, Ginny struggled to come to terms with the raw reality that her protection had been insufficient to safeguard her little boy. Her faith in the goodness of her own mothering was deeply shaken. Twelve months later, Ginny saw herself as still healing, still getting some needed distance from an event that had shattered her most basic assumptions about life and about parenting. The pain of this one event ran through Ginny's fresh tears as she reviewed the year they had all struggled with.

A year felt like a long time to Ginny, as it would to most other parents, but time was working for her and her family in a healing way. Ginny could see that the constancy of her support had made a difference to her son. She was proud of the many creative ways she had found to help him express his big feelings about the abuse. While she still felt the grip of this experience on herself and her family, the grip was loosening and she was beginning to feel that she was ready to let it go.

Recovering Strength and Resources

There are no formulas that universally apply to all families who face the task of recovering from a child's experience of trauma. There are, however, some thought-provoking lessons that have been learned from families who have successfully coped with the invasion of trauma in their lives. Effective coping requires that parents confront the actuality of the trauma. Like any other tragic or catastrophic event in life, healing begins with acceptance. Wounds must first be acknowledged before healing can occur. Parents who model this acceptance help their victimized and non-victimized children learn to accept and confront painful realities. Horror that can be talked about and faced together is less horrible.

Parents who accurately judge their own and their children's resources to cope with and recover from trauma seem more able to cope effectively. Parents need to decide whether their existing resources as a family are sufficient to provide the support and strength needed for recovery. Realistically identifying when help is needed is critical to effective coping. Families who can accept offers of help, who find meaningful ways for others to be supportively involved, or who actively seek out assistance in the community are strengthened in their healing.

Years after their child's trauma, parents inevitably talk about time. Often they refer to the effects of time as if speaking of a friend. They acknowledge that time itself softens and heals the wounds of even the most severe trauma. These parents are not saying, "You'll get over it," a phrase that most resent hearing from well-meaning friends and family members. "You'll get over it" seems to imply that parents and families should be able to continue on as if nothing had happened.[22]

When a family is first coping with a child's trauma it can be hard to believe that the pain will change or lessen. Time does ease and change the pain, for parents and for children; it does not erase it.

The elusive entity of time heals at a pace unique for each individual. It is easy to underestimate how long it will be before some sense of normality returns. When a child has experienced a severe trauma, a year of intensely painful recovery would be an unusually short period of time. For severely traumatized children whose recovery involves extended, complex, medical, and/or legal involvement, the period of gradual healing may entail many years. But many years is not forever.

Points to Remember: Trauma in the Family

A child's trauma has enormous potential for creating family distress and disruption. Problems with coping are normal for all family members following a child's trauma. When parents know about the typical reactions of family members, it is easier to recognize problems and cope with them.

Feelings of abandonment, jealousy, intense distress, fearfulness, and guilt are not uncommon reactions for siblings of a traumatized child. Some siblings themselves show signs of posttraumatic stress in their behavior.

Depending on the severity and nature of a child's trauma, parents can experience a wide range of reactions. Anxiety, fearfulness, loss of sleep, depression, and distractability are commonly experienced by parents. When parents' reactions are severe, they can wreak havoc at home and at work.

Parents experience many reactions similar to their child's: feeling preoccupied with the trauma, needing to review and retell the event, experiencing intrusive thoughts and images of the trauma, feeling helpless and guilty, and searching for explanations.

Many parents feel devastated by their inability to prevent a child's trauma. Harm to a child can challenge parents' sense of themselves as protectors and lead parents to question their own goodness as parents.

Trauma can shatter cherished beliefs in fundamental goodness and justice. Feeling raw and vulnerable to random destructive events disrupts basic feelings of safety in the world, for parents as well as children. The occurrence of trauma can set off a painful reevaluation of many basic beliefs.

Coping for parents sometimes involves minimizing or exaggerating the importance or severity of a child's trauma. Extremes of either minimization or exaggeration can leave children feeling lonely and misunderstood.

In two-parent households, it is common for each parent to react to a child's trauma quite differently. The potential for parents to experience conflict and distance is high.

Incidents of sexual abuse are particularly disorganizing and distressing for parents to cope with. Parents need to watch their own reactions to prevent their own distress from overwhelming and frightening a child.

Recovery from a child's trauma is a family matter. Parents need to take the lead and model positive coping for their children. Encouraging open discussion of the trauma and family members' feelings, focusing on children's immediate needs in a one-day-at-a-time approach, respecting a spouse's different ways of coping, finding and using supports outside the family, and maintaining an image of the child as a survivor are helpful steps toward family recovery.

Time is a friend to families healing from a child's trauma. Memories of a terrifying event are not erased by time, but they do get easier to cope with and fade in intensity. There is no one answer for parents wanting to know how long their child's and their family's healing will take, but there is the re-assurance that time will work with the parents in their daily care for children to create a healing distance from the trauma.

The Healing Process

How Parents Can Help Their Child

When a psychological trauma intrudes upon the emotional safety of a child's life, the child feels that an invisible bubble of protection surrounding him has been violated. The child temporarily loses his prior sense of security from harm. Following trauma, it is not just fantasies and bad dreams that can be scary; real life must now also be feared. Fearful children experiencing the impact of a psychological trauma look first and foremost to protective parents and trusted adults for reassurance and support. They search for signs of comforting normality and routine in their daily life to undo their sense that life has changed in sinister and frightening ways.

Above all, most children look for signs that nothing has changed in their important relationships with parents and other trusted adults. And here is the painful paradox of parenting a traumatized child: in most situations involving childhood trauma, something *has* changed in the child's most important relationships. To some degree, most parents of traumatized children are emotionally traumatized themselves. Thus, just when the child is struggling most to comprehend and master a trauma, so are the parents struggling with their own sense of horror and pain. At the very point that the child is looking to the parent for reassurance, despairing parents may feel that they have little to give.

Finding a fit between the child's needs and the parents' own struggle can be difficult in the aftermath of trauma. Children look for emotional protection, but parents are often feeling little confidence in their ability to protect. One father saw his daughter's loss of her arm in a lawnmower accident as a line drawn in time through his family's life. As he put it, before the trauma were "the years of immunity, when we never imagined anything like this could happen to our daughter." After his daughter's accident, he mourned the loss of this sense of immunity. This was a good and loving father who found his greatest pleasure in parenting his four children. His discovery that he could not protect his child from loss and pain was a wound to his sense of himself as parent and protector. It took some time before he realized the importance of his role in his daughter's recovery.

The hard truth of this paradox is that parents cannot always prevent harm to a child, but they can always help a child cope and master that harm. Parents make an enormous difference in the speed and nature of a child's recovery from a psychological trauma. They find numerous ways to reseal the bubble of emotional safety around the child. Parents find their own healing and reassurance in their many efforts to help their child cope. When they can feel helpful and important to their child's recovery, parents can do much to dispel the feelings of horror and impotence that they have suffered along with their child.

Positive Ways to Help Children

Immediately following a child's encounter with trauma and sometimes for many months, children need lots of comforting and reassurance. This need for comfort is obvious and comes naturally to most parents. Infants and very young children are particularly in need of soothing experiences that relax and relieve the tension in their bodies: nursing, rocking, cuddling, singing and music, telling stories, peek-a-boo games, and quiet reading together.

For older children, parents need to match their comforting to their child's needs and likes. Most parents know what is particularly soothing to their child. Back rubs, for instance, which might usually only be given at bedtime, can be given during the day. Children need to calm their bodies, which are often overwrought with tension.

Special comforting at bedtime is frequently an issue for traumatized children. Beefing up the bedtime rituals with more soothing can help: an extra story, a massage or back rub, a nightlight, thinking together of some good dreams to have, or a tape recorder with favorite music or stories. Some parents have found that creating a tape of the child's favorite read-aloud story in their own voice can help a child drift off to sleep. Parents may need to lie down with a terrified child to help him get to sleep at night for the first weeks or even months. Many children are so frightened at bedtime that they plead, sometimes hysterically, to sleep in the safety of the parent's bed. This will be a hard habit to break for many children, but a child's immediate feelings of safety and comfort have to come first under these unusual conditions. Alternatively, parents can make a little bed on the floor of their bedroom for a child and let him know from the outset that he will be able to sleep there for a while and then be given help to return to his own bed.

Comfort and reassurance are also the treatment of choice for children with nightmares. Young children need physical comforting after their nightmares. Parents can remind children who understand verbal reassurances that they will be alright and that mommy or daddy will take care of them. As children get to the age of three or four, when they truly understand that dreams are not real, parents can remind them that "it was just a dream" and help them reorient to where they are in the safety of their home.[1] At night, parents should stick with simply comforting a child until she can get back to sleep. During the day with older children, parents can teach children about how bad dreams are created in the mind out of children's own fears and feelings. There are many reassuring books for children of different ages about bad dreams (see the Suggested Readings at the back of this book). Children who have frequent nightmares need to know that these are common for children who have had big scares and that they will come less often over time. Professional help is available for a child whose nightmares continue with intensity and frequency beyond the first six to eight weeks after a trauma.

Parents sometimes are concerned that their child will be "spoiled" by extra attention and comforting given following a trauma. When the extra attention involves soothing and comfort, there is no basis for worrying about a child's being spoiled. The terror needs to be directly combatted, and soothing is critical in relieving this terror.[2]

In addition to comforting, children often need basic information about what happened to them. Information should always be presented simply and in small bits, with questions answered directly and matter-of-factly in language the child can understand. Lying to a child to protect her from disturbing information generally backfires in the long run. Children can be protected, however, by giving them the information they seem to want and need at a given time as indicated by their direct questions and their concerns. Children are often not ready to cope with some of their most disturbing questions right after a trauma. Following the child's lead and signals regarding the need for specific information is often the most helpful policy.

Expect Regression

Because the force of a psychological trauma disrupts a child's psychological gains, it is normal for a traumatized child to look and act like a younger child for a period of time. Fears seen at an earlier age may reappear. A child may need a level of comforting and reassurance that strikes a parent as quite "babyish" for the child's age. Old problematic behaviors—biting, bedwetting, wishing to drink from a bottle, hitting—may return with a vengeance. These steps backward are normal and predictable for children following a trauma but can be quite disturbing to parents, who want signs that everything is all right. But clearly everything is not all right for a child who has experienced a significant trauma. Parents need to lower their expectations and remind themselves that most regression following trauma is temporary.

When children regress, parents need to match their responses to the needs of a younger child. For example, during toilet training, accidents are considered normal and children are reassured that they will gain control in time. When a child first enters school or day care, fears of separating from a parent are common, and parents usually respond with extra time and patience through the transition period, looking for supports to help a child master this challenge. Just as parents are naturally gentler and more forgiving of the difficulties of younger children, parents need to respond to regression with the same gentleness and understanding when a child has been traumatized. They need to convey a message of, "I know you're having difficulty with this now, but we can all handle this problem together until you're feeling stronger and older again." This message offers support, lets the child know that she will once again feel stronger and safer, and reminds her of her parents' belief in her basic competence.

An example involving my own child illustrates children's regression following a trauma—in this case a very minor one. When my four-year-old son had sand scratch the cornea of his eye during play at school, he had to endure a long day of acute pain, frightening procedures in the emergency room, and the scary feelings of being locked into darkness behind an eye patch. The events and pain exhausted and frightened him. That night he made the unusual request that I rock him in the rocking chair before bed, a ritual that he had abandoned two years earlier. As we began to rock, he jumped down and assembled the old and comforting stuffed animal pals that had long been relegated to the back of his closet. Stressed and frightened, he had pulled out a memory of long-ago comfort on this night when his usual need to be a "big boy" temporarily lost all its importance for him.

Respect a Child's Fears

There are few children who show no signs of increased fearfulness following a trauma. When a child develops specific fears, there is no short-term magical solution for robbing these fears of their power. Children are not generally helped by efforts to argue them out of their fears with appeals to reason or bravery. What *is* helpful to most children is an approach that says, "I know you're feeling quite frightened of_____right now," followed by an offer of help and support: "Let's think of what we can do to make this less frightening for you." A child will find it helpful to be reminded that the fear will get smaller over time and to feel that the parents can take these fears in stride. Very young children enjoy seeing pictures drawn of a big blob of scary feelings that get smaller and smaller, until only a small speck is left. Older children can be reminded of fears and challenges that they overcame in the past. When parents remind the child of other difficult situations he has mastered or endured, they offer a strong and positive image of himself to hold on to.

Most important, children need assurance early after the trauma that they will not be required to face their fears alone and will not be expected to be "brave" or "tough" during the next few months. Parents can easily become worried that a temporarily fearful child will transform into a permanently fearful child unless pushed quickly and forcefully out of this stance. The opposite tends to be true: children who feel that they cannot express their fears might be able to bury them or transform them into behavior that does not look like but still is fear. In the long run, children are helped toward true courage by acceptance and respect of their fear and gentle, practical assistance in overcoming it.

There *is* a danger, however, in giving a child's fears too much support. Following a trauma, some parents go to extremes of over-protectiveness and miss the signs that their child is ready to move on. Children need to hear that parents will help them gradually cope with their fears over time, not that they will need permanent protection. When a child balks at engaging in some activity or responds with terror, it is helpful to remind him that this is a temporary reaction: "Going to the zoo today feels too hard and scary. We will save that trip for later this year when you are feeling stronger." How different this message is for the child than, "Oh, I guess we can't go to the zoo. All those big animals are too scary for you. We'll just stay home." When a child feels unable to cope because of fears, he needs messages of hope and reassurance from parents. As with most other issues in parenting, finding the middle course between overprotectiveness and excessive expectations is the most difficult but helpful route.

Some expressions of fear should not be ignored or indulged if the child is to progress. Prolonged school refusal for school-age children and specific extreme fears or phobias that prevent the child from engaging in a large segment of normal life are best handled by parents and a professional working together. A child so riddled with fear for a protracted period of time that he or she is taking little pleasure in daily life may need psychotherapy to work through and beyond the fears.

Provide Active Help for Flashbacks and Panic

Children experiencing flashbacks and panic reactions need a combination of immediate reassurance and education. When a child suddenly reacts as if a past trauma is reoccurring, she needs to be guided gently back to awareness of the present. Many children find physical contact helpful in reorienting them: rocking, being wrapped in a blanket, holding something dear and soft (a special stuffed animal, a pillow, or a blanket).[3]

During a flashback or panic reaction, parents can talk to the child about the here and now, reminding their child that the danger is over and that she is not alone. An unresponding child can be encouraged to use all her senses to orient to the present. Parents can ask a child to identify sounds, smells, and objects in the immediate vicinity. Some children are willing to taste something. By focusing her senses on what is immediate and real, the child is less able to register the sensations and feelings of her returning memories. Instructing the child to breathe deeply (count to three "in," count to three "out") can help the child relax and refocus.[4] Squeezing something very tightly or stamping her foot can help a child reengage with the present. The child should be encouraged to express her feelings about the trauma as much as she is able to.

Both during and after, parents can explain that what is happening is the scary event replaying itself in the child's mind, just like a video. Children need to be reminded that they are truly safe now but that the movie in their minds of what happened makes them feel unsafe, just as some scary movies on television do. Children can be encouraged to learn breathing techniques for relaxation and have them ready to use against panic. One trauma specialist explains to children that "fear can steal your breath away." She teaches breathing exercises to children to empower them to take their breath back from the "robber fear."[5]

Flashbacks, once over, can leave children exhausted and depleted. Many fall asleep. Others need a quiet time to feel safe.

Provide Opportunities for Talking About Feelings

Children have just a few ways at their disposal to cope with the disturbing feelings aroused by traumatic memories: they can play these feelings out, they can act them out through various behaviors, they can struggle with them in their dreams, and they can talk about them. Talking directly about feelings is not easy for children of any age; it is most difficult for preschoolers. It is helpful, however, for children to talk freely about their feelings whenever they are able to. For parents and caretakers, this means listening care-fully for the times when a child does directly express feelings. All that children need from their parents is a simple acknowledgment of those feelings.

If acknowledging a child's feelings were easy, I'm sure it would be done more frequently. It is, in fact, quite difficult to accept what children say about their feelings. There are so many feelings we wish children would not have. For instance, if little Marcie were to tell her mother that she hated that lady who squeezed her, would her mother feel she had said enough by simply replying, "I know, Marcie. You really hated her when she did that to you"? Most parents would want to add some instructive words about "hat-ing." But sometimes when we add our own thoughts and reactions to what children tell us about their feelings, we unintentionally give them the message that we do not accept and respect those feelings. The ever-present temptation to lecture a child is one that we would all do well to resist.

Children who have been traumatized have strong feelings, many of them unpleasant and frightening to hear. If a child can say these feelings in the ways his or her age allows, it will help prevent those feelings from being expressed in more disturbing behaviors. When two-year-old George says of the man who molested him, "He's garbage. I flush him down the potty," he is explaining his angry feelings in a very mature way. George does not need to be re-minded about being nice at this moment. He needs the listening parent to say something along the line of, "Yes, George, that guy was garbage. He scared you," and, most important, "He's all gone now and won't hurt you again."

Words are among the best armaments children have in the strug-gle with their feelings following a trauma. A child can tell of some dreadful revenge fantasy in words without an ounce of real dam-age being done to anyone. When children cannot find words for their strong feelings or when their words are criticized and dis-couraged, they are more vulnerable to acting out these strong feel-ings, at the risk of real hurt to themselves or others. A child's own words for these feelings need to be listened to and accepted.

A child's feelings can overwhelm parents, who may find it im-possible to extend the acceptance and respect the child needs. Parents who have been joint victims of a trauma with their child may well find themselves in this position. Similarly, parents who experienced a similar trauma in their own childhood may find themselves too flooded with their own memories to feel able to respond neutrally to their child's feelings. When hearing and accepting a child's feelings is too difficult, it can be relieving to get some professional help for the unmet needs of both child and parent.

Expect and Tolerate Repetitious Retelling of a Traumatic Event

Children, like adults, need to retell tales of horror, and over many retellings, there is progressive relief. Many children will want to tell their parents the story of their trauma over and over. The repetition can be extremely hard for some parents to tolerate. When parents want to forget and children want to retell, a child may retreat with the impression that the story is too much for the parents.

Retelling is part of the healing. We all tame the most difficult times in our lives by creating stories out of the horror or sorrow. Children also need to tell their stories and they need a loving audience to listen, again and again, sometimes in agonizing detail. Parents eventually tend to report their surprise when they realize that their child has stopped the retelling.

Provide Opportunities and Props for Play

Like retelling, playing out of the trauma is predictable and necessary for many children. This play may be quite frequent and intense in the period immediately following a trauma. Most children do not want or need adults to join them in this play. For some children, particularly older ones, traumatic play may require privacy.[6]

Occasionally, a child's trauma involves unique circumstances that a child has difficulty replicating in play. For instance, a five-year-old girl who observed an air show accident that killed her cousin was having difficulty coming to terms with the horror of this event. No toy planes existed in this girl's toy collection. In this situation, her mother found it helped her to have a toy plane with removable pilots who could repeatedly crash over a period of months. Similarly, doctor kits, ambulances, and fire engines are generally put right to use by young children whose experience of trauma they recognize as an emergency.

Parents and professionals find ingenious ways to help children's healing through play. One gifted child care director showed up in the hospital room of her three-year-old student the morning after an emergency intubation with a special doll for this frightened little girl. The doll was reintubated hourly over the course of this child's hospitalization. Having the opportunity to do to the doll in play what had been done to her greatly relieved this child and contributed considerably to her mastery of this scary experience.[7]

Sometimes a child struggling with trauma will make an uncharacteristic request for a special toy.

> A week after being locked and left for hours in a closet by his babysitter, seven-year-old Ben insistently asked for a toy pig. His mother wasn't sure what meaning this pig had for him but responded to the intensity of his request by taking him to the store. There he picked out a stuffed pig, which he took home. His mother was a bit surprised to find that her son proceeded to hate his pig. In fact he devoted himself to despising this "stupid pink pig." It became clear that he needed something outside of himself to contain all the bad feelings and anger following his trauma, and he found a brilliant object for these feelings in an ugly pig.

Limit and Monitor the Play of Victimized Children

The play of a child whose trauma has involved victimization can present special difficulties. When victimized children reenact trauma, they may alternately take on the roles of victim and victimizer. Children who role-play extreme versions of being the hurting one or the hurt one can end up scaring themselves and/or their playmates. Victimized children therefore need their play to be watched quite vigilantly and ended if it gets out of hand.

For some child victims, the only short-term solution they can find to their feelings of helplessness and anger is to "pretend" the role of the powerful perpetrator. This role allows escape from the worst feelings associated with victimization, but if the play involves scaring and hurting siblings or friends, it needs to be stopped firmly with a reminder that "there is no hurting" and "this play is too scary." Similarly, a child who refuses all roles but that of victim needs to be limited in this play. One girl, for example, who insisted daily on being the one dragged to jail by her preschool playmates needed help in finding more active powerful roles. Because play reenactments most frequently occur with other children, at school, day care, or in neighborhoods, supervising adults need to be asked to monitor and limit the play. A child may feel driven to reenact a victimization, but it is not helpful to the child to succeed in doing so with other children. Hurtful and scary reenactive play neither feels good nor is good for children.

One of the most puzzling and challenging behaviors for parents involves the sexual play and reenactments common to sexually molested children. These children engage in many different forms of sexual play for many different reasons. Some are overtly seductive and sexualized in their interactions with adult caretakers and others. Others are driven in their sexual play with dolls and stuffed animals. Children may masturbate with no regard for privacy, or they may masturbate so intensely that they hurt themselves. Abused children may initiate sexual games and play with other children with great silliness or with intense seriousness. Most difficult for parents is a child who is driven to reenact her abuse with younger, vulnerable children in victimizing interactions.

Parents must never ignore a child's sexualized behavior. When play and interactions become sexualized following one or more episodes of sexual molestation, it is an indicator of the child's distress and lack of resolution of the experience. Preoccupation with sexuality can signal the child's concerns that need attention. Some children have learned to associate attention and affection with their own sexual behaviors and feelings. Others have ongoing concerns about their molestation that are surfacing in their play, just as other nonsexual feelings surface in play. Some children have become prematurely eroticized through chronic experiences of abuse and are trying to cope with their genuine feelings of sexual stimulation.

Many parents have great diffculty responding to the sexualized behaviors of children, even the mild ones. Parents know what to say when a child is picking his nose, but many parents find they are left speechless by finding a child touching the genitals of another child. One trauma specialist suggests that parents respond to sexualized behavior as if the child were indeed picking his nose. She recommends that inappropriate sexual play and interactions "be addressed simply, directly, and without emotional charge."[8] Parents tend to back away with anxiety, and sometimes disgust, from sexualized children, ignoring the disturbing behavior or feeling powerless over it. When they turn away, they may also turn away from the child himself, further harming his self-esteem.

What can parents say and do with sexualized and eroticized children? Children need to be told, calmly but firmly, that the sexualized behavior is not acceptable.[9] Parents can remind and show children what good hugs, kisses, or cuddling are like, and they need to talk with children about their sexual feelings and the rules about private touching. Children with lots of sexual feelings need to have them acknowledged and accepted first and then be given help coping with these feelings. Children can be given rules about masturbation—for example, that it is for private times, not for public display. Children who masturbate compulsively may need a behavioral plan worked out with a therapist to help them find appropriate times and places for this behavior. When children are involving friends or siblings in sexual activities, the play needs to be stopped and the child more closely supervised. In her therapeutic work with sexually acting-out children, Beverly James recommends explaining to children that just because they know how to perform grown-up sexual acts does not mean they may.[10] In therapy sessions, she asks children how old they will have to be to drive a car and whether they would drive a car now (at four, six, or ten years of age) if they knew how. She then compares the age rules about driving cars with the age rules about private touching. Even if children know how to do grown-up touching, they still have to wait, just as they wait for other things they want, like their driver's license. "You just have to wait" sounds more accepting and nonshaming to a sexually abused child than some of the lectures that run through parents' minds when confronting an incident of sexualized behavior.

It is hard not to shame and blame a child whose sexualized behavior worries and upsets a parent. Using concrete examples when teaching children the rules of private touch can help take the awkwardness and anxiety out of these conversations for parents and children. Children find it enormously relieving when parents can react in a matter-of-fact manner and discuss sexuality in simple ways. It is frightening and shaming for children when grown-ups react with extreme anxiety or alarm over their sexual play and behavior. Parental anxiety tends to fuel more of this behavior and maintain the overcharged nature of sexuality for the abused child. The goal is to neutralize this charge around sexuality for the child, and this is best accomplished by calm reactions.

Sexualized behavior is not generally eliminated overnight. It can take time for children to cope with their many feelings about molestation and to learn different ways of meeting their needs and answering the many questions they have about their bodies and private touching. Neutral, educational, and caring responses can go a long way in controlling children's sexualized behavior.

Expect Some Difficult Behavior

From the child's point of view, the essence of trauma is loss of control. Following trauma, many children's own controls fail them. They may cry more over little things, make angry demands, show more aggression, and test limits and rules. The difficult path for parents in responding to this behavior involves conveying understanding and caring while maintaining the rules and limits of the home. Parents should not abolish rules out of sympathy for a child who has been traumatized. Rules and limits are comforting to children; they are part of the routine they rely on to know that not everything has changed in their lives. On the other hand, it is not helpful to be totally inflexible or engage in massive power struggles with a child who already has enough struggles. Parents who can manage to respond gently but firmly have the easiest time with the testing and misbehavior.

Setting consistent limits and coping with problems of discipline tend to be the most difficult areas of parenting, under even normal circumstances. When a child's behavioral difficulties present the need for more than the usual amount of parental management, the strain for parent and child can be great. Parents who never saw themselves as candidates for community courses on parenting strategies or as likely readers of self-help books on discipline may feel the need of such additional support following a child's trauma. They are right. The parenting skills that served well before the trauma may now be insufficient because the child is truly more difficult to parent.

When children's misbehavior following a trauma results in prolonged strain between parent and child, it is wise to get some outside help. There is a danger that a child who feels guilty and bad about himself as a result of a trauma may become locked into a pattern of provoking the very punishment he fears he deserves.

Communicate with School and Child Care Staff

In most situations parents will find it helpful to let teachers and child care workers know about their child's trauma. Most teachers make genuine efforts to be helpful and understanding with a child they know has been through a horrible experience. Parents need to let teachers know of any behaviors they are specifically worried about. Teachers can also be enlisted to give helpful reports to therapists or doctors.

Sometimes parents hesitate to discuss particular situations of childhood trauma outside the family. Although sharing important information about a child with teachers is generally helpful, there are occasions, particularly in small communities, that a parent's reluctance is realistic. Nevertheless, it is still possible for parents to express regular concern about their children and inquire frequently about their progress. Parents cannot assume that no news is good news regarding their children's behavior at school. Schools and teachers vary widely in their willingness to contact a parent regarding a child's behavior. Teachers are more likely to contact a parent whom they are sure is interested in hearing from them.

Maintain Routines and Avoid the New and Challenging

Following a trauma, which is by definition extraordinary, a child finds particular comfort in the ordinary. Even special events meant to distract and please may flop in the early period following a trauma. Routine is particularly helpful to children who are openly fearful, clingy, and distressed by separations following a trauma. For these children, reading with a parent may be the special event they need rather than a trip to the new exhibit at the children's museum.

Some children have difficulty adjusting to change or new activities; others may welcome the release and distraction. Again, a child with predominantly fearful reactions to trauma should probably not be encouraged to take on new challenges unless he expresses great interest in doing so.

Family life sometimes needs to adapt temporarily to the neediness and rigidity of a terrified child. Many children, for instance, do not feel safe being left at home with a babysitter at night, regardless of what their trauma involved. If a child expresses great post-traumatic fear about being left with a babysitter, babysitters should be avoided until the child is feeling safer. When it is time to try a sitter again, a child can be involved in the planning by being given choices, or arrangements can be made to have a special well-loved adult as the sitter. Many children who have been traumatized truly do not believe they will be safe from danger in ordinary circumstances. The return to normal family life often needs to occur in small steps that gradually allow a child to rebuild confidence.

When a child's distress is most evident, it is helpful to avoid big changes or disruptions in family life. This might mean rethinking the timing of a family-oriented or business trip or postponing a move to a new house. Children who have been through a trauma cling to sameness and routine as a source of basic comfort. Even seemingly good changes can feel disruptive and unwelcome to a frightened child and can slow their recovery.

Monitor and Limit Children's Reexposure to Frightening Situations and Activities

Parents need to serve as the barrier between the child and her exposure to anything that would cause further fright or disruption. Parents need to think about potential specific triggers that a child might find frightening or overwhelming. It requires a kind of constant empathy with a child's unusual state to remain mindful of potential triggers. A child who has been attacked by a dog cannot easily cope with a visit to a neighbor's home where a dog regularly greets all comers with licks or snarls at the door. Nor does this child need or want to know about a child across town who also has been bitten by a dog. Unfortunately, triggers are not always obvious or concrete.

For most children, specific activities, places, sights, smells, or noises can evoke the memory of a trauma. These triggers need to be kept in mind by parents long after the original trauma. In the first months, when these triggers for memory can be avoided, they should be. When they cannot be avoided, it is important to help a child anticipate and prepare internally for an encounter that is likely to bring back unwelcome memories. There will always be situations in which some trigger takes a child and a parent by surprise. Rain, sudden large noises, or just the presence of clouds in the sky can panic child victims of storm disasters who believe the storm is still out there, waiting like some angry monster, to attack again. Taken off guard by such reminders, children may react with obvious panic or with more subtle withdrawal, quieting, or freezing. Some children respond to traumatic triggers with sudden aggressive outbursts. It is helpful when a parent can calmly help a child identify a trigger and then reassure the child of his or her safety at that moment (e.g., "That did sound like the big dog that bit you, but that is a different dog you're hearing who is far away and tied up").

Although children need careful limits to be set on their exposure to frightening experiences early in recovery, many children seem to seek as much "scary stuff" as they can find. Some children attempt to master fear through reexposing themselves to it. This search for power and mastery through reexposure to fear is similar in nature to repetitive post-traumatic play. Left to their own devices, children do not always choose opportunities for mastery wisely. They need help to figure out which activities will promote feelings of mastery and which situations will reexpose them to overwhelming terror.

The child's at-times insistent need to take on situations that evoke fear can create difficult challenges for parents. One father who has struggled hard to find activities and toys that would help his son feel strong but also safe after their house burned to the ground, felt that he was continually being trapped by this four year old's driven requests for the implements of power, many of which turned out to be overwhelming for the child. In the father's words, "I just wanted him to be able to feel some of that power that he seemed to be asking for." For this child, however, the arsenal of weapons he had begged for was too frightening for him to handle early in his recovery. There are no hard and fast guidelines regarding what children need to avoid. A different four-year-old, for instance, found target shooting with his various toy guns to be exactly the safe outlet he needed for his feelings of rage and powerlessness. Children vary enormously in their capacity to manage the feelings evoked by their exposure to scary situations and play, and parents need to attend to the impact of activities and play on the child.

Seemingly routine activities can expose children to heightened levels of fright. Frequently childrens' television programming, videos, and adult television shows (including the news and commercials) contain elements of violence and scary themes that are inappropriate for traumatized children, particularly young ones. Children will not always censor these programs themselves, despite the level of fear aroused in them. They may instead become nearly addicted to certain fear-arousing programs or videos. Nine-year-old Catherine, who suffered severe injuries in a car accident, pleaded with her parents to let her watch "911," a television program that graphically covers emergencies of all kinds. Catherine's interest in this program seemed desperate to her parents, but they soon discovered that she was unable to manage the fear she felt watching it. Her agitation at bedtime and her nightmares following the program were clear signals that Catherine was being overwhelmed and that the program needed to be put off-limits. It is doubtful that Catherine would have come to the same conclusion about the impact of this program, given the strength of her interest in it. It is up to parents to set firm limits on what a child can tolerate and to give babysitters and relatives clear instructions regarding what a child can and cannot watch on television.

Use Detective Skills When a Child Suddenly Regresses or Becomes Fearful

Parents of very young trauma victims or quite severely traumatized children frequently report wracking their brains to discover the cause of sudden regressions or fearful reactions in their children. Toddlers and preschoolers have few ways to let parents know exactly what might have frightened them or taken them off guard. Severely traumatized children tend to have multiple triggers for their fears, making it difficult for parents to identify them. Parents can always ask children about the source of their fright, but children cannot always answer. It can be helpful to think back through a child's recent experience to identify something that might have set off a reaction related to the original trauma. At times specific school activities can inadvertently stir children's fears.

> Four-year-old Patty became frozen with fear on a class trip to the local hospital. She complained of a "bad smell" in the hospital and cried that she wanted to leave. Disturbing memories of her own hospitalization at age two and a half were powerfully reevoked in a way that Patty could not explain by this field trip. Later that day she began limping, favoring the same leg that had been badly fractured when she was trapped beneath the falling debris of her home during a tornado.

Provide Physical Outlets

The memory of trauma is often lodged in children's bodies and physical experience. Following various types of trauma, many children end up feeling ashamed about their bodies. Others hold enormous tension in their bodies. Children need to be offered good and fun physical activities as part of their healing process. Good choices of activities depend on the child; sports and activities that a child is either very good at or has a lot of fun doing are recommended. Many girls and boys love gymnastics, in their backyards and at a gym. Baseball is a good activity for children who need to whack something. It's hard for a child who is doing something active and fun to feel like a victimized wimp. Traumatized children need physical experiences of their bodies that are incompatible with the negative feelings they may now be having about and in their bodies.

Physical outlets are also important for children who have difficulty controlling their anger.

> Teachers described Brian, at ten, as the angriest boy in his class. Everyone in the school knew Brian had a lot to be angry about, but that did not make handling his outbursts any easier. Seven months previously, Brian had watched his terminally ill father shoot himself. His battle with the images of his father's suicide and his feelings of rage and guilt created storms of temper that could be triggered by the smallest frustrations.
>
> Brian was a strong and well coordinated boy. With his father's encouragement, he had always been involved with the town Little

League and soccer teams. After his father's death, however, he told his mother he wasn't interested in playing any sports. For months, he seemed interested only in watching television and playing Nintendo.

Brian started therapy with a male therapist nine months after his father's death. Over time, Brian began to look forward to his sessions with Dr. Fred. Brian began spending part of every therapy session playing basketball and catch and clearly wanted to show off his talents for Dr. Fred, whom he was able to impress genuinely.

Several months after starting therapy, Brian's mother reported that he had begun practicing batting at home again and now accepted invitations to play instead of staying home to watch television. At school, Brian was encouraged to earn extra outside time playing ball with one of the teacher's aides as a reward for controlling his temper. His outbursts all but disappeared over the next six months. When spring rolled around, Brian was ready to try out for the baseball team. Two years after his father's death, when Brian was ready to end therapy, he made a special request: he wanted Dr. Fred to watch him play at one of his games as a special celebration for completing therapy.

Like Brian, many other children find that sports offer a way to express their angry feelings safely while giving them something to feel good about themselves and their bodies. Children do not necessarily need organized sports or activities. Part of what was important to Brian was Dr. Fred's attention and admiration. Parents can also make a special point of reminding children about how strong and capable their bodies are. Children generally give parents lots of "watch me!" opportunities to comment on their skills and strengths. Following a trauma, these admiring comments have special meaning to children.

Keep Anniversary Reactions in Mind

Calendar-related events can trigger memories of trauma for children. Holidays, birthdays, special annual events, and seasonal changes have tremendous power to reevoke the memories of trauma for children, as well as for adults. A year after a trauma, everyone in the family may just be beginning to enjoy a returned sense of normality when the child's memories and feelings surrounding the trauma may intrude again without warning.

The triggers for anniversary reactions can be very slight and insignificant or quite transparent. For one four-year-old, the sight of acorns falling to the ground was so strongly associated with her first autumn visit to the therapist the previous year that her face momentarily resumed a look of frozen terror. For another child, the annual arrival of snow threw him off balance each year for several years. He had been resuscitated while lying in the snow following a nearly fatal accident. Later it became evident that this three year old had a vivid partial memory of his resuscitation. He recalled people screaming, "He's dead. He's dead," and explained, "They sucked on my mouth. It was cold. I was in the snow."

Unless parents expect these anniversary reactions, they can easily be misunderstood. For both parent and child, anniversary reactions tend to sneak up unidentified, causing confusion and distress. A child's initial behavioral reactions to a trauma may return in force during the anniversary period. Parents as well may find themselves reexperiencing distress or unusual reactions around the anniversary of the trauma. Even parents who are prepared for and aware of the possibility of anniversary reactions tend to be surprised and taken off guard.

Listen for a Child's Distortions and Misunderstandings of a Traumatic Event

Children frequently misunderstand and misinterpret the events preceding and surrounding a trauma. Children's tendency to find the cause of a trauma in their own misdeeds can lead to complicating guilt and perplexing behavior. They do not always state clearly their distorted understanding of why their trauma occurred.

Clues to a child's misinterpretations of a trauma can sometimes be found in their behavior. A little girl who was molested when she took a short-cut to school against her mother's instructions became excessively "good" following her trauma. She logically concluded that the appearance of the "bad man" in her path was a punishment for her own failure to follow instructions. Her belief that her misbehavior had brought about the visitation of this punishment was profound. While most parents would not be overly alarmed by a child's sudden conversion to "good behavior," this particular little girl needed reassurance that her molestation was not her fault and did not result from any badness within her. Without that reassurance, her misinterpretation of the trauma would leave her directing her anger inward rather than more appropriately directing that anger at the man who was truly responsible.

Like the little girl who vowed to "be good," children often come up with curious and improbable ways to keep themselves safe following a trauma. The therapist Beverly James describes these magical thoughts in the child's words: "I'll be safe if I'm watchful, if I'm tough, if I'm smart, if I'm good, if I pray, if I keep clean, if I make a sacrifice, if I don't need anybody, if I hide, if I run away, etc."[11] Children want to believe that their own magical actions will serve them as amulets of protection.

At times children's misinterpretations of the causes of a trauma are connected to their private feelings or behavior, of which parents have no knowledge. As the child reaches back in memory to the time preceding the trauma, he or she may recall some feeling or event that seems to explain the experience. A young boy who was terribly angry with his dad prior to a car accident that left his father paralyzed later maintained an absolute conviction that his angry feelings had resulted in his father's injuries.

It is common for young children to believe in their own great and dangerous power. Up to the age of six or seven, they must struggle with the possibility that their own aggressive or hostile wishes have the power to do real harm to the people they love and need most. Older children should be more immune developmentally to the power of magical thinking, but the impact of trauma often is forceful enough to undo their capacity for logical thinking. Teenagers and adults also settle on magical explanations for terrifying events, including the retrospective discovery of omens that have preceded the events.[12]

Be Mindful of Your Own Reaction to a Child's Trauma

In the intensity of anxiety over a child, parents sometimes disregard their own reactions to a child's trauma. Mobilizing all their energies to cope with and help the child, their own strong feelings and reactions can build up insidiously, along with exhaustion. For both the child's sake and the parent's own welfare, these strong feelings about a child's trauma need to be acknowledged and attended to. Otherwise, the stored up guilt, rage, sadness, and anxiety can create havoc in parents' personal lives and complicate the work of parenting a traumatized child.

Traumatized children need calm parents. "Calm," however, is the last word most parents use to describe their feelings when first facing a child's trauma. Nevertheless, the child has a serious dilemma when parents are emotionally overwhelmed or unavailable. Parents' own suffering can interfere with their responsiveness to a child. This interference may be dramatic or quite subtle. A parent who becomes depressively obsessed with a child's trauma to the extent of being unable to react to the child's daily needs requires additional help. A parent with more subtle difficulties might be so focused on a particular aspect of a child's trauma that he becomes unable to empathize with the actual worries and fears that are central for the child.

Children look to their parents for signals regarding the meaning of the traumatic events. They are longing for signals that, however horrible the trauma, it is something that the parents can cope with themselves and help the child with. When a child gets signals that the trauma has created overwhelming distress in the parents, the child inadvertently receives the frightening message that this experience truly is unbearable. Recovery may be significantly complicated and slowed for children who must respond daily to high levels of parental distress.[13]

Parents need to ask themselves whether they are focusing on their child's needs or whether they are too overwhelmed by their own reactions to attend sufficiently to their child. They can review their worries and compare them to the worries they know their child is having. Parents can try to identify the feelings that may be causing them to feel stuck following a child's trauma.

There is no correct parental reaction to the sudden traumatization of a child, but there are reactions that are helpful to the child and ones that are not. When parents find themselves blaming children, perceiving them as damaged or stigmatized, reacting to their behaviors with impatience, hostility, or rejection, or being simply unavailable to them, there is a need for professional help to undo these responses before they become patterned and entrenched in the parent-child relationship.[14] In addition to professional support, parents sometimes need to push themselves to seek and use their natural supports among friends, clergy, and relatives.

When You Feel That You Cannot Cope or Help a Child

There are situations of childhood trauma or trauma to multiple family members that can leave parents feeling totally depleted of inner resources.

> Anne's oldest son, Brent, died in a plane crash while traveling with his brother to visit their grandmother during school vacation. Miraculously, Anne's younger son, eight-year-old John, had survived the crash with few injuries. Anne's grief was overwhelming. Just barely making it through each day was all she could handle, and she knew it. She also knew that John was struggling to come to terms with the trauma of the accident and the loss of his older brother.
>
> Anne took John to a therapist and asked if she could turn him over to this social worker because "I have nothing to give him; I can barely help myself." John worked with the social worker for three years in therapy, and over this time his mother gradually felt her strength and resources return, to be able to give to John again.

Anne's action to protect and help her child at a time that she was emotionally overwhelmed with grief was truly courageous. Parents often do not feel that there is any permission to acknowledge a time of weakness or strain in the job of parenting. But there are times when parents need to seek the help for a child that they would like to be giving themselves but cannot.

Parental Self-Talk: Listening in on What You Are Saying to Yourself

We all engage in private conversation with ourselves. This silent internal self-talk is part of coping and problem solving. Some of it, like an inner cheerleader, promotes coping and creates energy to solve problems. Negative and pessimistic self-talk, however, can readily bog down efforts to cope. For parents faced with the difficulties of a child's trauma, it is helpful to listen in and examine this self-talk.

People have set tendencies to talk to themselves either hopefully or negatively when things go wrong in their lives.[15] Those who tend to respond to adversities by making many self-statements regarding their own stupidity and inadequacy tend to have less energy and resources for positive coping. Other people talk to themselves about difficulties more optimistically, focusing their energies on the ways they can respond and make things better.

When a child has been traumatized, parents have all sorts of things to say to themselves about themselves, about their child, and about the child's future. The shocking experience goes through the filter of a parent's typical perception of events and comes out looking more or less hopeful and manageable, depending on the nature of the filter. One parent who had to deal suddenly with his son's near-fatal fall from a cliff told himself that bad things had always happened in his life and now they would happen for his son as well. His inner conversation about his son's fall gave him little comfort or hope for helping his very injured and frightened child. For a long time, he was depressed and unavailable to a son who dearly needed him. This father could have told himself that his child was alive after a perilous fall and that the doctors were hopeful that the child's upcoming surgery would completely restore the child's capacity to walk and even run. He could have reminded himself that his lively and competent son had had many things go right in his young life precisely because of his own efforts as a father to parent him well and that he now had a new and serious opportunity to make a difference for his son.

Although everyone has tendencies to talk to themselves optimistically or negatively, it is possible for those whose thoughts tend toward the negative to interrupt and reword their own inner dialogues.[16] Some parents find it helpful to remind themselves of the unusual situation they and their family are in following a trauma to a child. In moments of frustration or despair, parents can engage in a kind of self-talk that helps to rally their sense of perspective and hope. Parents have found that reminding themselves of the following very simple thoughts can be helpful in regaining a sense of calm and distance during difficult times:

My child has been hurt and frightened; my child has every reason to act and feel the way she does.

My child does look and feel different to me, but many of these changes are temorary reactions, which will change with time. It is too soon for her to look or feel like herself again.

I need to remember that no child's healing takes a straight path; recovery involves steps forward and steps backward. Today was a difficult day, but yesterday she was doing much better. There might be some ways that I could help tomorrow go better for her.

My child has been hurt and scared. Dwelling on the ways that I could have prevented this hurt will not help her recover.

There is much that I can do to help my child, but I cannot control the timetable of her recovery.

Healing takes time, sometimes lots of time, but children can recover from traumas. My child needs my patience now.

Focusing on Images of Strength and Survival

Parents beset by fears for a child can focus on images of the child's existing strengths. One mother used the image of her son doing his exuberant karate moves during the period that he was recovering from a tragic accident. By setting her mind on the image of her son in his karate class, she got in touch with the inner strength this little boy possessed to endure and survive his accident and the subsequent year of rehabilitation. The deliberate imaging of her karate kid helped this mother speak to the resilience in her child and engage his hope and determination. At the same time, of course, she mobilized her own hope and belief in her son's future.

Children need to be reminded of their strengths and their competence. They like to hear about difficulties they have overcome in the past. Following a trauma,, parents can remind a child of problems he has solved well in the past or of difficulties he has overcome. Parents who focus on the image of their child as a strong survivor can hold this image up for the child through remembering and telling stories about the child's accomplishments. There are endless opportunities for parents to hold a mirror up for the child to see and appreciate her strengths. When a child is working hard to complete a drawing or building project, for instance, a parent can simply comment, "You know, I love the way you really stick with something until you have it just the way you want it." If a child fixes something or solves a small problem, she can be reminded what a good problem solver she is. Children welcome the images of their strengths and resilience that parents offer, particularly when they are feeling shaky and weak.

Some parents have found it similarly helpful to find images of themselves that remind them of their own strength and endurance—qualities that parents need to rely on when parenting traumatized children. One parent found it helpful to think back to a difficult time in her own childhood that she had survived, and survived well. The image was of herself as a cocky kid with pigtails swinging from her favorite tree. Another parent focused on a vivid image of himself as a young man surviving a severe storm while anchored to the side of a mountain, a thousand feet up his climb. These two parents found images of their own strength in memories of physical mastery. Some parents find it more helpful to look for images of peacefulness—a moment or time that was totally and delightfully free from stress. These peaceful images can serve as both reminders and as promises of peace in the future.

When parents have difficulty recalling comforting or strengthening images of their child or themselves, looking through family photographs can be helpful. One mother chose a much-loved photo of her son diving into a pool, his face grinning with victory, to place on the refrigerator. She kept the photo there for the whole year that it took him to get over the terror and injuries from a horse fall in which he had been trampled. Her son had been quite frightened of diving but had kept at it with great determination until he mastered it. When she looked at the photo, she remembered that determination, and it helped her believe that he would get through the months of rehabilitation and fear he had to endure.

Parents' internal images of a child and their inner dialogues can form the links to feelings of hope and endurance. Recovery from trauma has a lot to do with both hope and endurance.

Working with the Phases of Healing

Healing from trauma is often discussed in terms of predictable phases or stages. There are no absolutes when it comes to children's reactions to trauma, but there are common tasks that must be mastered in the process of recovery. Often, but not always, children approach these tasks sequentially. First, children go through an initial phase of crisis response. They tend to either overrespond or underrespond to the immediate crisis, showing extremes of distress and disruption or extremes of passivity and numbness. During this phase, children's minds and bodies are tense and hyper-alert to the possibility of danger. They need help to feel physically and psychologically safe and to regain their physiological equilibrium. Before children can tackle the emotional task of coming to terms with the trauma, they must reestablish normal patterns of eating and sleeping and loosen the grip of constant dread that pervades the first days and weeks following a traumatic event. Issues of safety may reappear at various times throughout a child's recovery, but they are most pronounced during this crisis phase.

Recovery is far from complete when the child begins to relax her guard and to trust in her immediate safety. Now she is ready to do active battle with the memories that return insistently and intrusively. The child enters a phase that adult trauma specialist Judith Herman calls "remembrance and mourning."[17] Like adults, in this phase children must find ways to acknowledge the reality of the trauma and its impact on their lives. Their work is like that of a story teller who takes an isolated horrific event and finds a place for it that yields meaning and resolution within the story.

Remembering and mourning involve great inner and external struggle for many children. The wish to forget and avoid continually clashes with the child's unwanted recall of memories and feelings. The child must confront and account for the traumatic event. There is inevitable pain, anger, and loss for children during this phase. Their inner turbulence is most often evident in the disturbed and disturbing behavior that signals their distress, in their nightmares, reenactments, and raging determination to seize control of every situation. During this phase the child struggles with all the meanings of the trauma, with the question of "why me?," "how could this possibly happen?," "how was I responsible for this?," or "how damaged am I?." She needs to find the emotional distance to convert the raw emotion of her experience into the settled form of a scary chapter in her own story. The story she thought she knew about herself has changed and must be rewritten. This work of rewriting is challenging and painful for children; it is also possible.

When the child begins the work of coming to terms with the trauma, her memories of terror exist as disjointed isolated fragments with no connection to her life. Images and impressions of her experience can jump out and frighten her at any time, recreating feelings of helplessness. Extraordinary and shocking events do not enter the memory in ordinary ways; they often remain suspended and undigested as a foreign and troubling presence in the child's awareness. If left undigested and unadmitted to the normal stream of memory, the images and feelings of trauma remain unchanged and the terror untamed. When memories of the traumatic event can find their way into the collection of ordinary memories, the terror can be transformed. This process of integrating memories of trauma occurs in the reconstruction of life stories that trauma victims of all ages engage in as part of their healing. Little by little, the child must weave her experience of trauma into her ongoing experience of herself and her life story; the trauma then takes its place as one of many events in an evolving life. Some children do this work in words, many do not. As the child proceeds with this phase, she is more able to make reference to the trauma and to tolerate reminders of the event without reacting as if she is handling an emotional hot potato. The weight of trauma lifts gradually during this phase which can last from months to years depending on the many factors that influence the severity of children's reactions.

The third and last phase of healing involves a return of energy and engagement in ordinary life. The trauma ceases to be the central reference point in the child's life. The child resumes her development with an eye more to the present and future than to the past. Herman terms this phase one of "reconnection" in adult recovery.[18] Some children begin this process of reconnecting as soon as they feel safe; they work on issues of reconnecting and resolving the trauma simultaneously. Others remain emotionally distanced and withdrawn from their prior lives during a period of resolving and only gradually resume old interests, return to previously enjoyed activities, and relax their defended posture. When the child begins to reconnect with her previous life of family, friends, and activities, the normal experiences of childhood further nurture and foster her feelings of power, competence, and pleasure. The child discovers that her story has been changed by trauma but not ended.

The progression of phases in children's recovery does not always follow a straight line. There is a unique ebb and flow to the process of recovery for each child. Progress can be uneven, occurring in fits and starts. Flashbacks, nightmares, and new encounters with fear can temporarily throw a child back to grappling with issues of safety. Some children need to cycle through the phases of recovery numerous times, revisiting issues and concerns again and again to achieve better resolution. As children develop new cognitive capacities to understand and process events, the memories of trauma may reappear to be resolved with greater insight and mastery. Ups and downs are predictable in the healing process.

Being sensitive to the tasks of each phase of recovery can help focus parents on the ways they can be helpful. When a child feels under siege during the first phase of crisis response, parents need to focus on helping a child feel safe and soothed. This is not the time to encourage a withdrawn child to return to her girl scout meetings. When the child feels safer, she will need help with the turbulent process of remembering and mourning. Now is the time to help a child understand that diffculties and distress are normal after a big scare and that the family is available to help her through this period. Children need to be able to talk about and play out their memories and feelings to whatever extent they are able during this period without fear of alarming their parents. When the child gives signals that she is ready to move on and reconnect with what is old and loved or new and exciting in her life, parents need to be ready to encourage and support her steps outward.

Points to Remember: The Healing Process

Traumatized children need and respond to lots of comforting and reassurance.

Helping a traumatized child involves adjusting expectations regarding the child's behavior and coping.

A child's spontaneous healing requires that parents be available to hear and accept the child's fears and repetitious relating of the events.

Parents need to watch their children's play and behavior at home and monitor their progress at school and out-of-home settings.

Toy props related to the trauma can help a child express feelings about the experience through play.

Listening to and accepting the very strong feelings that a child may express following a traumatic event helps a child feel safer with those feelings.

Children need to be protected against exposure to further fright. Movies, certain play activitites, and encountering actual reminders of the trauma can rearouse the feelings and memories of a trauma for children. Unnecessary separations from parents should be avoided for very anxious or young children until they are well able to tolerate a parent's absence.

Children find comfort in the continuation of regular routines and rules at home after an overwhelming event. Change of any kind at home can be unwelcome and disruptive to them.

Children who have misunderstood the cause or nature of their traumas need gentle help to correct their misunderstandings and distortions.

Children are vulnerable to the impact of their trauma on the people they love. They look to their parents to discover the meaning of what has happened to them. Parents need to be mindful of their own reactions to a child's trauma and the ways their own anxiety can increase a child's distress.

Parents can give their children messages that strengthen and support them. Holding on to the image of a child's resilience and strength during the recovery period can influence parents' and children's healing from trauma.

Complications of Trauma

When Professional Help Is Needed

Few parents request professional help for a child without some reluctance. More often than not, the idea of seeking outside help is the option of last resort. Yet it is also clear that these same parents do want to help their children. The conclusion is obvious: in many families, the idea of finding a professional helper for a child is not associated with help at all. How do we make sense of this fairly universal hesitation to seek professional assistance when a child experiences difficulties? Why is it often easier for adults to seek therapy for themselves than it is to take their child to a therapist for an equally compelling need? There are some standard answers to these questions, as well as some less obvious but bothersome obstacles for parents considering therapy for children.

Among the standard reasons for parental hesitation is the deeply rooted belief that "only crazy people see shrinks." Who would freely nominate their own child to the ranks of the "crazy" without considerable reluctance? Nevertheless, most parents can see their way beyond this popular misconception to understand that helping professionals have a meaningful role at various times of personal need in the lives of sane and well people. And yet even without subscribing to the culture's bias against mental health, parents are affected by their worries that a child will be stigmatized through involvement with the mental health profession. This fear of stigma is particularly compelling for parents whose child's trauma has involved a stigmatizing victimization. Thus, by avoiding therapy, parents often are wishing to protect a child from popular misperceptions associated with the mental health profession.

A second concern for parents is fear of being blamed by mental health professionals. When parents initially consult with a therapist, they typically wait with some dread to hear that their child's difficulties are their own fault. The fact that many parents expect to be blamed for children's problems is not too surprising. Historically the mental health profession has, in fact, placed what now seems like cruel and remarkable blame on parents of some children seeking treatment. Parents, most notably mothers, have experienced a kind of victimization by mental health theorists and clinicians in their search to help a child. Thus, parents' worries about being blamed by professionals have some grounding in the history of the mental health profession. Looking back, this "parent and mother blaming" was rooted in ignorance as well as mysogeny. Frequently, childhood disorders that could not be explained in any other reasonable manner were attributed to parental failure and maternal incompetence. With ever-increasing knowledge of the complex causes of childhood disorders coming from biological and developmental research, clinicians are now enabled to dispel rather than inflame parents' fear of blame.

But what of the blame parents so readily lay on themselves? Parents' own tendency toward self-doubt and self-blame is also a barrier to seeking treatment for children. There are few parents who are not vulnerable to the lingering fear that "if I were a better parent, my child wouldn't be needing this help." Where does this willingness to absorb blame come from in parents? Again, perhaps certain contemporary cultural attitudes toward parenting foster a tendency toward self-blame. In this culture, there is a fierce pride in the independence of parents. Despite the fact that no one is formally prepared or trained for the job of raising children, it is assumed that everyone "knows" how to do the work. New parents are carefully taught the rudiments of diapering and sent on their way. There is a lot of anxiety in "winging it" when it comes to raising a child. It would perhaps be helpful if there were very clear standards regarding what constitutes "success" in parenting, but such standards are hard to find in a society of diverse values. It is difficult for parents to find solid reassurance that their efforts in child rearing are meeting with success when "success" in parenting is so poorly defined. To one degree or other, then, parents end up looking to their children as the measures of their own adequacy as parents. When children struggle or flounder, as they inevitably do, parents tend to look within themselves for the causes. When children become the only gauge available to measure parental adequacy, the burden for children and parents can be great indeed. When a culture assumes that parents will "naturally" be prepared to parent effectively under all circumstances, parents feel vulnerable to failing this societal ideal. There is so little permission for parents to acknowledge that a particular period in a child's life is very difficult for them or that they cannot seem to find ways to help a child cope with one challenge or another.

The situation of childhood trauma poses further obstacles for parents in considering professional help for a child. Most parents experience a strong wish to get on with life, as reflected in the frequently heard statement from parents: "We just want to put this behind us." Involvement in therapy seems to be moving in exactly the wrong direction. Parents question how they or their child can "get over this" if they seem to be regularly focusing on the trauma in their treatment. Parents also often believe that children "grow out of" distressing periods. Thus, intuitively, therapeutic involvement does not make much sense to many parents of traumatized children.

The helplessness that parents feel about their child's trauma can also be a complicating factor when considering professional help for a child. Stunned by their inability to prevent the trauma, parents look for ways to undo that sense of helplessness during the child's recovery. Parents need to regain their sense of power and importance as caretakers. It is very reassuring for parents when they can see that their own acts of comforting and support make an obvious difference in the child's sense of safety and emotional healing. The suggestion that a child may need outside help can feel insulting to some parents. The idea that someone else's help is needed can be experienced as further unwelcome evidence of a parent's helplessness. Contributing to this very understandable resistance may also be long-held family beliefs that problems should stay in the family or religious beliefs that problems in the family should be dealt with through spiritual supports.

The decision to seek professional assistance is therefore a complicated and difficult one. The number of sincere hesitations that parents feel is downright overwhelming. The other side of the coin, however, is the pain that parents feel when watching a child struggle unsuccessfully with the aftermath of trauma. When a child is unable to move beyond a trauma despite the parents' best efforts to help, there is a need to know about other helping resources.

Because each situation of trauma varies dramatically in seriousness, intensity, and effect, there are few absolute guidelines regarding traumatized children's needs for professional help. It is not possible to state that all children who have experienced trauma should automatically receive professional assistance. It is possible, however, to state that in many situations of childhood trauma, professional help can provide important immediate relief and long-term benefit for a child and family recovering from an experience of trauma.

Parents need to know what behaviors constitute a child's signaling cries for help—that is, when to worry. Anxious parents want to know when they are overreacting to a child's posttraumatic behavior and when they *should* be worrying.

The following guidelines are offered to help parents sort out their worries and assist them with the difficult decisions they may be facing regarding a child's need for professional help. Our knowledge of traumatized children is good enough to flag certain signals in children's behavior that deserve professional attention. The following indicators of when to worry may be helpful in thinking through the question of whether a child needs professional help.

Guidelines for Seeking Help: When to Worry

There are a number of indicators of *immediate* concern and need for professional assistance:

A child whose posttraumatic behavior is endangering to herself or others. Children who act out in physically hurtful or emotionally frightening ways, alone or with other children, need immediate help to gain control over their behavior. Children who are driven to reenact their traumas with others compulsively need help to control their compulsions. Children who show signs of wanting to hurt themselves through incidents of extremely dangerous play, risk taking, or poor judgment may indeed be at risk of harming themselves. Similarly extreme accident proneness following a trauma may be more than coincidental and requires attention.

A child whose reaction to trauma is to talk wishfully about being dead, to dwell on issues of death and dying, or to threaten suicide. The wish to die may be expressed as a way of rejoining an important lost figure, a way of seeking punishment, or a way of finding escape. When children of any age express the wish or intent to die, they need immediate professional attention to prevent an actual attempt at self-harm.

A child whose reaction to trauma is to lose all prior grasp on the line between fantasy and reality. Children who periodically or regularly seem to lose contact with reality may repeatedly describe events that have not occurred, refer to hearing voices in their heads, engage in what seems to be extremely bizarre behavior, or speak incoherently. It can be difficult for parents to separate the magical thinking and active fantasy of young children from serious problems with reality testing. One helpful rule of thumb has to do with how strange or even "creepy" a parent feels in reaction to a child's odd behavior, thoughts, or speech. A child who is losing contact with reality under the pressure of great internal stress tends to arouse unusual feelings of confusion and anxiety in parents.

A child whose reactions to trauma are so numerous and/or severe that his daily functioning is greatly disrupted and age-appropriate activities are all but impossible to pursue. Some children have such severe initial reactions to trauma that they can find no relief from the internal barrage of feelings and memories. They appear to have no effective defenses that will permit them periods of normal activity and escape from preoccupation with the trauma. They need help learning to manage and relieve the intensity of their reactions.

Parental anxiety or depression that is so severe and disabling that regaining the family's sense of well-being feels impossible to achieve, regardless of how the traumatized child appears to be recovering. When parents feel immobilized or overwhelmed by their own reactions to a child's trauma, their needs must be addressed in order to begin restoring a sense of balance and normalcy at home.

The following indicators are predicatable during the initial stage of coping with trauma but become worrisome if they persist or intensify. While each child has a unique timetable for dealing with a trauma, the following behaviors *lasting beyond six weeks* following a traumatic event can indicate that the child has become stuck in trying to resolve the trauma and needs professional help.

A child's primary focus of conversation and play is the trauma itself. The child appears unable to invest energy in anything except trauma-related play and/or continues to retell and review the trauma with no decrease in frequency. The child's repeated play may involve exact replay of the traumatic events or play involving related themes and content that first appeared following the trauma.

A child is continuously vulnerable to reexperiencing extremes of fear, whether through nightmares, separation anxiety, extreme avoidance, or flashback-like recall of the trauma. The object of the child's fear need not be directly related to the events of the trauma if it is persistent and extreme. Children often transfer fears arising from trauma to other more ordinary objects or experiences.

A child's initial regression to the behavior of a younger child shows no sign of decreasing over time. Children at times get stuck in a regressed stance and can need help gradually regaining their former skills and abilities.

A child continues to experience more than one nightmare per week or shows no decreases in other sleep disturbances originating at the time of the trauma; for example, she continues to have marked difficulty getting to sleep, staying asleep, or rising. Ongoing sleep disturbances can be signals of continuing internal disruption, which needs to be attended to.

A child shows no decrease in social withdrawal, listlessness, or lack of pleasure in routinely enjoyable activities. After six weeks, most children are able to resume many formerly enjoyed activities that are not associated with trauma if they have not suffered physical injuries or major losses. They are able to negotiate relatively well through a routine day and show a gradual return of energy and enthusiasm. When children are unable to regain their capacity for pleasure and seem to be deflated of energy, the interference needs to be evaluated.

A child who complains frequently of physical pain or illness for which no medical explanation can be found. Such physical complaints can signal underlying emotional pain that a child is unable to put into words. Children often need help finding other ways to express and understand their distress.

A child's behaviors have a negative impact on his relationships with peers, caretakers, teachers, or parents to the point that these relationships begin to show signs of deterioration. Children whose post-traumatic behavior involves increased aggression, social inappropriateness, and/or provocative limit testing can exhaust, alienate, or infuriate the friends and adults they need most.

A child continues to experience vivid terror in response to trauma-related sensory triggers with no decrease in intensity or frequency of these reactions. The trigger may be identifiable and obvious or mysterious to the parent, but the child's sudden reaction of overwhelming fearfulness dating from the time of the trauma is startling and worrisome.

A child's distractibility interferes with attention and learning at school. Teachers may report frequent daydreaming, unsettled behavior, jumpiness, and loss of progress academically.

A child appears overly focused on self-blame and her own "badness," which may signal a continuing misinterpretation of the causes of the trauma. When children mistakenly settle on explanations for a trauma that involve self-blame, their sense of "badness" can cling with a tenacious grip.

Overall changes in the child's personality dating from the time of the trauma are dramatic and worrisome to parents and others. Those who know a child well are best able to evaluate whether a child has undergone a serious personality change; their feelings of worry are generally a good indicator of the need for help.

A child's post-traumatic reaction or behavior, even if mild, is particularly upsetting or bothersome to the child. Some symptoms can take a huge toll on a child's self-esteem and delay recovery. Children who find a period of nighttime bedwetting completely unacceptable to their sense of themselves, for instance, would benefit from consultation to gain mastery and understanding of this symptom.

One or both parents' anxiety and confusion regarding the impact of the trauma on the child continues to be so strong over time that it is interfering with the parents' ability to relax and resume a sense of normality in the family. When parents see no decrease or an actual increase in their own level of distress, there may well be a need for additional support or professional consultation. In most instances, recovery is a family matter. The help that parents get for themselves translates directly into help for their child.

The Timing of Seeking Professional Help

Crisis Intervention

Parents may seek consultation during the immediate period of crisis following a child's trauma or later when the sense of crisis has been reduced and diffused by time. Childhood trauma does create an immediate effect of crisis for the child and the family. There is a sudden need to take in a cognitively and emotionally unacceptable and overwhelming situation. Children generally have immediate reactions to trauma that may differ from their long-term reactions. These first reactions generally pull for parental concern and caretaking quite quickly, giving the parents an immediate meaningful role in helping and comforting.

In this atmosphere of crisis immediately following discovery of a child's trauma, some parents pull back within the healing comfort of the family and focus their energies on supporting the child. The tendency to retreat to the safety of the family is common enough to be discussed as the recoil phase of crisis reaction.[1] Many families initially find strength in each other and experience unusual closeness during the first phase of coping with a crisis. Thus, for some families, seeking help outside the family may not feel immediately necessary.

Other families receive or seek out immediate crisis intervention services. Emergency teams of clinicians and crisis specialists are often mobilized in response to large scale natural disasters and community tragedies. When a child's trauma involves a crime or police assistance, emergency services may be offered immediately to the child and family.

Crisis intervention, whether provided to groups, families, or individuals, offers services designed to give immediate emotional support and to facilitate coping. Victims and their parents are offered an opportunity to review and understand the event, to express their initial feelings, and to make immediate plans designed to ease recovery. Crisis clinicians help to assess the extent of traumatization and provide recommendations to parents regarding the child's immediate needs. The focus of crisis intervention is short term, and the emphasis is on coping. It is not meant to be, nor is it, a substitute for more intensive psychotherapy.

Crisis intervention can be useful for some families in gaining immediate support and in learning about the predictable reactions of children following a trauma. It can also lessen the loneliness and extreme anxiety for parents and children. A crisis interview with the child can provide information on the child's initial coping and greater understanding of what the trauma has meant to the child. An immediate interview with the child can be particularly helpful when the details of the trauma are unclear. Young children who have been molested or who have witnessed violent events are sometimes unable to explain in words exactly what has occurred. Through immediate play interviews, young children are often able to recall and clarify the actual details of the traumatic event in their play.[2] Knowing exactly what has occurred to a child is relieving to parents, who otherwise suffer with the anxiety of imagining. When a prosecutable crime is involved, early clarification of the child's trauma can have far-reaching legal implications as well. Finally, there are situations involving immediate trauma reactions of the child or other family members that are so strong and worrisome that emergency consultation is clearly needed.

"Crisis" is uniquely defined by each family. Referrals for professional help are often made by pediatricians, police, or emergency room staff during the first chaotic hours following discovery of a child's trauma. When parents feel unable to cope, when children's initial reactions are so dramatically worrisome, or when there is a need to understand further the nature of the experience, crisis intervention can be enormously helpful to children and parents.

Eventual Consultation

Many families either are not offered emergency services or do not want them. Most of the traumas addressed here have occurred primarily in the world outside the family, which may appear suddenly more dangerous and untrustworthy. When families thus seek a safe retreat within the family, their response to the assault from outside is understandable. When trauma occurs within the family, as with incest, family members may be extremely reluctant to seek outside help due to feelings of shame, conflicts over loyalty, and concerns about protecting family members. Parents who have had no contact with helpers during the initial crisis often describe taking some time to regroup and watch the child carefully in order to understand the impact of the trauma.

It is often during the period of waiting, watching, and comforting a child that the question of seeking professional consultation arises. If parents find that the immediate sense of crisis is followed by a period of consuming worry and stress, the toll on all family members can become very obvious. A family's response to extreme and sudden stress is at times similar to the response of the human body. The body can mobilize unusual power and strength as a result of a biochemical reaction in order to cope with emergencies. Families similarly can call on their own extraordinary capacities for coping initially with a child's trauma. Following this analogy, however, the body's efforts to cope with extreme stress can last only so long before reaching a point of exhaustion and eventual collapse. At some point, parenting a traumatized child also can exhaust rather than bolster the family's resources. When a child's trauma is followed by a period of relentless stress in the family, resources for coping can become depleted.

Parents who find themselves barraged by doubt and worry regarding their child's recovery may find it helpful to review the guidelines here on when to worry. When parents are uncertain about the need for professional help, it can be useful to request a consultation with a professional who is knowledgeable in childhood trauma. The consultation involves no commitment to therapy or further services and can provide a helpful opportunity to review concerns and get feedback on a child's progress and needs.

Timing Matters for the Child

The reluctance that families feel about seeking professional help is understandable but often at odds with the needs of children. The earlier that traumatized children go for professional help, the better the chances are that these children will benefit from the help.[3]

The importance of early professional intervention is related to children's internal process of healing from trauma.[4] Immediately following a trauma, the disturbing memories and feelings are fully available to a child. With time, the child needs to do something with these memories and feelings in order to resume normal functioning. Frequently children find ways to encapsulate or isolate the disturbing aspects of the trauma over time, perhaps shoving them to a dark corner of the psyche where they will not have to encounter them so frequently.[5] Children are not always aware of this process of burying the trauma, which gives them some relief from the immediacy of disruptive images and feelings. Parents, too, may notice the child's distancing from the trauma and feel relief that a child is "forgetting" about it.

Most children do not heal from serious traumas by simply "forgetting" them. Buried feelings and memories too frequently do not lose their power over the child. The memories continue to be evident in the child's behavior, disturbing the child's days and nights. As with most other human efforts to avoid strong feelings, the child's wish and attempt to avoid all memories of the trauma can backfire because the memories and feelings are being shoved aside before they have been truly coped with.[6]

Sometimes I think of the fate of traumatic memories as being similar to the laying of a brick path in mortar. In laying the bricks, one needs to think about the pattern and placement that will allow the path to hold up well against freezing and thawing. The mortar records haste and mistakes without forgiveness. Once set, there is only so much time to adjust the bricks before the mortar hardens the path into its final state. Correcting mistakes later is a troublesome job that most of us would avoid taking on. We generally would prefer to live with the uneven steps and tolerate the path's faults, which become more obvious, at least in New England after a hard winter. For children coping with the internal pressure of traumatic memories, there is also a window of time during which these memories can be worked with easily before they set. Once these memories are set by the child's attempts to distance from them, the child can be very reluctant to dig them out. A child is therefore more open and responsive to therapy in the early phases of coping with trauma than in the later phases. The work of therapy is less intrusive and more immediately relieving soon after a trauma than therapy that begins after the child has already found ways to bury the feelings and memories. It is still possible for therapy to be helpful for children long after a trauma has occurred but, like the undoing of a path set in mortar, the work is harder and can take longer.

Timing does matter when traumatized children need help sorting out what has happened. Few children are going to announce that it is time for them to see a therapist. The signs of trauma in their behavior will be their only flags that they need help. Parents need to watch for these flags and take them seriously despite the universal wish to move along with life and put the trauma behind them.

Delayed Reactions to Trauma

Children sometimes have delayed reactions to a traumatic event. Trauma can enter the memory of a child in such tricky and perplexing ways that it can lie seemingly dormant for long periods of time before erupting in unusual behavior or distress. This sleeper effect can be at work for children who have had initially strong responses with eventual good recovery or for children who have shown very mild immediate responses. Matters of memory tend to return unbidden, and when those matters have to do with trauma, they can return with jarring force. Sudden, delayed symptoms of trauma can be set off by obvious triggers such as anniversaries or by reminders so subtle that the child is not consciously aware of the connection. Delayed responses to trauma can occur within the first year following the trauma or many years later, when the connection is difficult to recognize. Generally delayed responses to trauma are seen in behavior changes. Although delayed reactions are not inevitable for traumatized children, they are common enough for parents to be mindful of them.

> A mother had reason to recall a forgotten episode that happened when her daughter, Jenny, was three years old. Jenny had become extremely distressed immediately following her grandmother's sudden disappearance from her life. The grandmother had left with no warning to get urgent treatment for a tumor at a hospital in a distant city. This grandmother had taken care of Jenny daily during the mother's work hours since birth and was clearly a most important person to this little girl. The suddenness of this major loss was im-

mediately evident in Jenny's behavior. In addition to becoming very clingy and demanding over a month's period, Jenny began making little nests out of towels and blankets all over the house. She would curl up in these nests and cuddle with her favorite bunny several times a day during the first month of her grandma's absence. Over the next four months, Jenny's mother noticed the nests being built less and less frequently as Jenny seemed to return to her sparky self. No one in the family could recall exactly when the nest building had stopped, but her mother thought that the nests had disappeared before grandmother returned from her successful treatment.

Jenny's mother had actually forgotten about the nest building until she noticed a reappearance of nests all over the house the week before Jenny was to begin kindergarten, which involved a new and challenging separation. Jenny's fears and anxieties regarding kindergarten brought up the earlier situation of loss and anxiety with her grandmother and she returned to her nesting solution to cope with it.

Jenny's situation does not clearly fit the definition of trauma because her initial nest building was a response to a sudden loss. The return of her nesting, however, is a good example of delayed reactions to anxiety-provoking events, which need further mastery. Once Jenny felt comfortable and secure in kindergarten, the nests again disappeared.

Not all children's delayed reactions to trauma are so mild or so easily mastered. Children can have severe, disabling, or endangering responses to trauma long after the original event. Living with the possibility or actuality of such delayed responses is understandably difficult for parents. It is important for parents to remind themselves that a child's delayed reaction is at times the only signal the child can give that the experience requires further resolution.

The idea that trauma gets resolved once and completely during a child's initial recovery is wishful and appealing. Some physical injuries do heal completely, but frequently even physical injuries leave some trace of vulnerability that may reappear when stressed many years later. A psychological injury such as a trauma can remain vulnerable in similar ways over time. The memories can return insistently to be mastered. When young children are traumatized, their age often prevents them from complete mastery and understanding. These memories may need to be revisited as the child gets older.[7] The return of memory is not always bad news given that children are able to resolve old worries and fears in more satisfying ways with the new abilities they acquire with age. There is, then, a new opportunity to heal involved in children's delayed responses to trauma, which parents can be grateful to notice and attend to.

Getting Beyond by Going Through Trauma

Survivors of childhood trauma who first find treatment as adults have much to teach about the enduring memories and pain that can accompany trauma victims over many years of their lives. The lessons of these survivors are sobering and disturbing. Their memories of so many years ago have a freshness and immediacy that suggests that the core of the trauma experience has been preserved with terrifying accuracy and vividness.

Mary, a thirty-year-old victim of child sexual abuse, recalls her assault with the feelings of a five-year-old victim. She has no sense of safety or distance as a competent adult looking back at a past terror as she tells her story for the first time. There appears to be no distance at all. Sitting with her pain, I wonder about the missed opportunities in Mary's life. I wish that I could have seen her when she was a skinny five-year-old carrying a secret that she thought too terrible to tell. Would it have helped? Yes. At five, she needed to tame that terror by sharing it, by understanding what really happened to her, and by correcting her assumption that it had been her own fault. Mary's own solution had been to try and go around the trauma, to forget it and move ahead with her life. She did just that, "forgetting" her abuse for years at a time, investing in her work at school and then in her successful career.

Still, at thirty, her memories tortured her; "forgetting" and sleeping became increasingly difficult. Now, in therapy for the first time, Mary does not want to hear that she must revisit the pain if it is to loosen its grip on her. She looks terribly disappointed at having to go through the pain, not around it.

Mary's parents never knew that their daughter had been raped at the age of five by Joe, their best friend and neighbor. Perhaps, though, they would recall what a difficult year Mary had in kindergarten and how they had worried about her puzzling nightmares. But Mary had been too ashamed and fearful to tell her parents or anyone else about something that happened for which she did not even have a name. The "something" of Mary's childhood remained unnamed.

Mary's adult treatment for long-ago trauma was difficult, painful, and long. It was complicated by the trauma's having been kept secret for so long.

Treatment with children of trauma can also be difficult, painful, and long but much less frequently than with adults. Children can do the work of therapy through play. Very few children under the age of eleven will tolerate or benefit from "talking" therapies. Fewer still will spend their time in therapy crying or in distress. There are indeed some frightening moments of risk and brief encounters with sorrow and terror in children's therapy, but, unlike adults, children are able to protect themselves from severely stressful episodes during therapeutic work. If they are not ready to do a particular piece of work, children are skilled at backing off and signaling their need to move away from disturbing material. Good therapists, trained in working with trauma, are constantly monitoring a child's level of anxiety and adjusting the session to prevent a child from being overwhelmed. Trauma is generally approached at the child's speed and with the child's assuming direction through choice of play and activity. The trauma must be confronted and worked with in the therapies of most children, but the process of confrontation respects a child's wishes for control. Each child directs her therapy in a unique way in combination with a co-director, the therapist, whose job it is to help the child get beyond the trauma by getting through it.

When a child needs therapy following a trauma, there is some way in which she is stuck in coping with the trauma that is hindering her moving on. Gradually, through the play and work of therapy, the child is helped to confront the obstacles that have resulted in being and feeling stuck. If confrontation could be avoided, if the child could simply be given a gentle push to go around the trauma, that would surely be the treatment of choice. What Mary and other survivors of childhood trauma have taught us is that we need to help children name and tame their traumas.

For some children, this naming and taming occur through a natural process of finding comfort and help from their families. For others, even the most comforting and loving family will not be able to contain their anxiety or tolerate their behavior in the aftermath of trauma. Children who need treatment are not children of parents who are inadequate; they are simply children who need all their parents' help *and* professional help to overcome a terrifying experience. A child may be seen in individual, family, or group therapy, but in each of these treatment approaches, the parents are critical to the success of the therapy.

Points to Remember: When Professional Help is Needed

Many families hesitate to seek help for children from mental health professionals for reasons that are entirely understandable.

Knowing whether a child needs professional help is difficult. The guidelines reviewed in this chapter are offered to clarify serious indicators of a child's need for immediate help and indicators of a child's need for help when the initial signs of trauma continue in a child's behavior beyond six weeks.

Children are best able to benefit from professional help soon after the traumatic event.

Some children can have delayed reactions to trauma, months or even years following the original event.

Many children resolve a trauma as best they can at their age but need to return to it later in their development when they are able to understand and cope with the memories and feelings in new ways.

Psychotherapy for Psychologically Traumatized Children

Once the decision to seek treatment has been made, parents face an array of choices and decisions. Many parents find it helpful to arm themselves with as much information as possible when approaching a new and challenging situation. Knowing what some of the choices involve and becoming familiar with the options and range of treatment approaches can lessen parents' feelings of vulnerability in looking for and beginning treatment. Understanding the process of psychotherapy with children and families and knowing what to expect in treatment can reduce some of the fear associated with the unknown.

Approaches to Treatment

It would be helpful if research and professional wisdom were unanimous in recommending one specific treatment approach as the best option for meeting the needs of traumatized children and their families. The reality is that different professionals practice different approaches to treatment. What exists is a rich field of different approaches and a variety of therapists with diverse talents and training. The goal is to find a good match between a therapist's expertise, the specific problems to be treated, and an individual's preferences. It is important to remember that very different approaches to the same problem can be equally effective when undertaken by a skilled and insightful therapist. In short, there are no easy or quick answers to the question of what kind of treatment to seek when dealing with childhood trauma.

There are various approaches to treatment. Children may be seen alone in a variety of individual treatments, with their families in family therapy, or in groups with peers who have similar experiences and concerns. Individual, family, and group treatment options are also often available for parents and siblings who have simultaneously experienced the trauma or are having difficulty coming to terms with one family member's traumatic experience. Understanding the different approaches is helpful in making inquiries about therapists and their services. It is important to know at the outset that some geographic areas offer lots of choices regarding therapists and some offer very few.

Individual Child Treatment Approaches

Many clinicians recommend individual treatment for children who have experienced trauma. Individual therapy can make sense for a number of reasons. When a child has been the sole victim of trauma in the family, the memories of the trauma belong to the child. Frequently, aspects of these memories or a child's feelings about them are inaccessible through ordinary conversation. The techniques of child therapy permit clinicians an unusual access to a child's thoughts, fantasies, and fears. The assumption of child therapy following childhood trauma is that the permanent meanings, memories, and feelings associated with the trauma can be altered in order to limit the long-term impact of the experience in the child's development.

Frequently used approaches in individual treatment with children are play therapy, cognitive-behavioral therapy, expressive therapy, and hypnotherapy. Children are sometimes seen as well for medication consultation and monitoring. While some clinicians work exclusively within one of these individual treatment approaches, most combine different approaches over the course of a child's treatment or within one therapy session.

PLAY THERAPY. Play therapy describes a range of treatments, all of which work through and with the child's play. Play therapies are generally useful with children between the ages of two and eleven, during the period of their development when they naturally employ play for problem solving and pleasure. For younger children, the usefulness of play therapy depends on a child's capacity to represent his experience through play and, to some extent, his capacity to communicate verbally.

An evaluation of a young child's play can be very helpful in understanding the child's experience. Treatment for children under the age of three often involves working with parents to help a child at home, but some precocious two year olds are able to benefit from play therapy. Older children, between eight and eleven, vary in their response to play therapy. For some of these older children, play therapy is relieving, and for others it is far too "babyish." Storytelling, therapeutic games, and other modified play activities are sometimes used with older children, with good results. Determining which techniques will be of most help to a particular child is part of the therapist's work during the first few sessions.

Children are seen in a therapeutic playroom where toys and materials have been selected to encourage expressive play. A child may be invited to play in an open-ended manner while the therapist looks closely at the spontaneous themes and concerns that appear in the play. As treatment progresses, a child may be encouraged to play with specific materials or to work with specific themes that address issues central to the trauma. Play therapists vary in the degree to which they direct the child's play. Some play therapists are very active directors, pushing the child to confront, rework, and examine a trauma through play and discussion. Others lean more toward letting the child assume directorship of the play, believing that children ultimately represent their central conflicts and concerns in their play. Increasingly, play therapy with children of trauma is emphasizing a more active role for therapists due to many children's tendency to avoid and become stuck with their memories of trauma.[1]

I have always sympathized with parents who have children in play therapy. It is an enormous leap of faith to pay someone a professional fee to "play" with their child. What parent has not at times wondered whether this "play" can be therapy. There is also a mystery factor that may be bothersome to parents. If something useful and therapeutic is going on behind closed doors in a child's play therapy, it is often difficult for parents to understand exactly what this beneficial experience is all about.

The work behind the child's play is, in fact, quite evident in play therapy. There can be enormous power in having a safe separate space in which to relieve the emotional burdens of trauma in the company of an accepting adult. Children can express what they may consider to be their most awful feelings and thoughts with a therapist, without the worry that they will offend or upset the most important people in their lives. It can be relieving to have this safe adult friend to borrow when the world, inside and out, is feeling dangerous and frightening.

The play permits children a needed distance from memories that may remain quite painful and unspeakable if approached directly. When I begin work with a traumatized child, I always let him know in the first session that his mom or dad have told me about what happened to him and that it is my job to help him with the worries and feelings he may be having. If he has been wetting his bed or hurting other children, I tell him that I also know about these problems and can help him with them. I do not then ask a child to tell me about the trauma in words. Instead, I invite the child to play with me. Most children whom I have seen following a trauma immediately develop a play scenario that either directly shows me the events of the trauma or indirectly shows me the most frightening features and feelings of the trauma. Some children spontaneously find the props in my office to set up the scene of the trauma itself and play it out in great detail. Other children engage in what may seem like completely unrelated play until I examine what the characters in that play are feeling.

Dana was a five year old who was molested by a babysitter. She began her first session by setting up a playground scene in which one child doll meanly pushed another on the slide. Dana proceeded to call the police and have the offending child put in jail. This seemed rather harsh to me since Dana was clearly identifying herself with the pusher and not with the victim on the slide. I grabbed the toy phone and made an emergency call to the little brute's parents to tell them that a terrible mistake had been made. "Ms. Brown, your daughter has been taken to jail for pushing another child on the slide." Speaking for the mother, Dana coolly replied, "That's just what she deserves!" and hung up the phone.

Within ten minutes of knowing each other, Dana's play allowed me to understand the overwhelming feeling of her own "badness" that clung like a heavy weight to her experience of being molested. Through play Dana could communicate this awful feeling painlessly and exactly in a way that few five year olds could find words for. Also through play, this child could then immediately have her traumatic beliefs be challenged when I proceeded to introduce a new figure to the play. This new figure, an old and very wise owl puppet who happened to be flying over the playground, landed with loud squawks of alarm and announced that children never go to jail because they are always given another chance to learn the rules.

Dana loved the drama of this owl descending and was quite taken with the fact that a gray-haired lady knew something about how to play. Dana had the girl doll who had been destined to go to jail stop to talk with the owl for a long time. She told the owl that sometimes people do go to jail for doing bad things and that she herself knew someone who was in jail. Dana's doll told the owl that this person in jail had done something "so icky" that the owl wouldn't even want to know what it was. As the owl, I was given this lovely opening to have the owl explain that many children had told me about very "icky" things that happened to them. "Oh yeah?" replied the child, her eyes widening. "What did they tell you, and how old were they?"

At no point in this conversation between the doll and the owl did Dana need to acknowledge that she was talking about herself. We were simply playing. But clearly, this was not simple play. I was encouraged that toward the end of this play, Dana came up with an alternative suggestion to deal with the pushing on the slide: "Maybe her parents could try time-out again just this one time, and maybe she'll learn to take turns." This resolution told me of Dana's remaining shreds of self-esteem and her wish to be free of the self-punitive jail in which she had all but enclosed herself since the molestation.

Not all children begin therapy with such clear announcements of their central problematic feelings. Some children hide for a long while before they can risk such disclosure, even in play. They hide under a table. They hide behind a safe game of checkers. They hide within a wall of frozen silence. Given time and safety, these children eventually come out of hiding and play. Some therapy involves accompanying the child through a period of testing and trust building after the child's trust has been devastated by a trauma involving personal violence or betrayal. Rebuilding that trust with a stranger may be the one big piece of work that child will accomplish in therapy.

Play therapy works, in part, by changing the usual rules and expectations for children. For most play therapists, the only rules that are communicated to children are rules of safety. The child quickly understands that she cannot hurt the therapist and will not be hurt by the therapist. Within this context of safety, children are encouraged to express their feelings in ways that could not, and should not, be tolerated at home or at school. Children who feel guilty and ugly inside following a trauma may need time to enact their ugly feelings through play. These children may identify with the monsters and "bad guys" in a therapist's toy collection, letting these powerful action figures destroy the "nice" little doll victims. Children who have been traumatized often do not want to identify with helpless, "nice" play figures initially. They want the power they themselves lacked when victimized by trauma. Within play therapy sessions, children can assume that power through what may look like brutal play until they are strong enough to go back and find new solutions for the helpless characters. Changing the rules allows children the freedom to express the hostile and mean feelings that often wreak havoc within them. Part of the work of therapy involves the safe expression of strong feelings. Helping a child find new solutions and a renewed sense of power following a trauma is always part of a therapist's work as well. The freedom offered within the therapy hour is most relieving to children when they can count on the rules at home and at school remaining predictable and consistent.

Play therapists use many different techniques and activities during their sessions: drawing, clay, story-making, small figures in a sand tray, puppets, or other play activities that encourage expression of feelings. Respecting the child's tolerance level, therapists also talk to children directly about their actual experience with trauma. Some therapists encourage children to engage in games and exercises that help them express troubling feelings. Many of these games and exercises have to do with naming the feelings that children sit with following a trauma.

At some point, therapy focuses on the children's anger at what has happened to them. This anger can be raw and shocking, but it is more dangerous and frightening to the child if left unacknowledged. One gifted therapist with traumatized children, Beverly James, uses many different focused exercises in her treatment sessions to help a child express painful and uncomfortable feelings. She has some children throw clay bombs at pictures of the people who have hurt them. In fact, she helps timid children feel permission by throwing them herself and by inviting the child's parents to join in the clay bomb throwing. This exercise would not be used with children who have very mixed feelings about a perpetrator.[2] Children who have been terrorized by repeated, painful medical procedures are encouraged in my office to draw the person they recall being most hurtful in the hospital. I ask these children what they might "wish" to do to this person whose image is associated with inflicted pain and fear. Little children usually take the scissors and gleefully cut these "hurters" into shreds. No one is being hurt because we are playing, but the children get to express the full measure of their outrage at having their own small bodies jabbed at, cut into, or stuck with tubes.

Psychotherapy with children does not and should not encourage children's violence, but it must begin with the child's true feelings and wishes. Particularly children who have been victimized by human violence experience anger that is potent and explosive following a traumatic event and often accompanied by violent fantasies of revenge. The anger and the fantasies can be terrifying in themselves for children, at times leading them to feel like the dangerous people who hurt them. In therapy, children learn that these wishes and feelings are natural and can be expressed safely through play without harming anyone. Children watch closely to see if their ugliest feelings and wishes produce reactions of fear and disgust in a therapist and are relieved to find themselves and their feelings accepted by a therapist who can help them find safe ways to express these feelings. Children are not practicing for violent roles in life within therapy; they are learning that strong and disturbing feelings can be tamed and expressed without actual violence or harm. Real violence tends to be perpetrated by children and adults whose feelings of anger have never been accepted or tamed.

Children of trauma need to release their feelings. For some children, release provides sufficient relief that some symptoms of distress, such as nightmares or extreme fearfulness, disappear. For most children, however, releasing feelings is only one part of their work in therapy. They generally also need to correct their misperceptions of the trauma, regain their sense of safety and power in the world, find more adaptive ways of coping at home and at school, and develop some larger perspective within which to view their experience of trauma.

Each child's life is a story being written. Trauma enters that story and threatens to foreclose the child's sense of her own story with expectations of danger and bad endings. Through therapy, we want to disrupt the child's generalized notion that because one bad thing happened to her, only more bad things will follow. We want to reengage a child's hope and optimism and her sense that her own efforts will make a difference in the story of her life. We have to go after the child's belief in her own helplessness and her melancholy view of the world as a place where she is predestined to be hurt and scared. We have to foster a new and wiser view of the world as a place where bad things can happen to good children but these children can go forward and experience the very good things that also happen in children's lives.

"My boo boos can heal now," announces Jeffie as he points to his scraped and healing knee. Jeffie has been telling me in one way or another for three years that his boo boos will never heal. Jeffie's skull was cracked by his mother's boyfriend in an episode of savage, drug-related abuse that temporarily transformed his views of himself, his life, and his caretakers. We have been working a long time on the notion that boo boos can get smaller. When he was three and just out of the hospital, I used to draw serial pictures of big blobs (his "boo boos"), which got progressively smaller with each rendering until only a speck remained. Jeffie seemed to ignore these pictures at the time. Now six, he had recently been watching the scabbing and healing of his scraped knee with total fascination. I believe Jeffie now when he tells me that his boo boos can heal, and I pretend with him, of course, that we are only talking about his knee. "Strong at the broken places" is an image (from Hemingway) used to describe this healing from devastating abuse.[3] Jeffie is feeling stronger in his broken places and for the first time is planning a future for himself. He has announced, with great excitement, that next year he will play on the town T-ball league.

Many therapists who work with traumatized children individually draw on techniques from approaches other than play therapy to address the thoughts and feelings children struggle with following a trauma. These other approaches may be integrated into play therapy or used separately.

COGNITIVE-BEHAVIORAL THERAPY. Cognitive-behavioral therapists focus directly on changing children's maladaptive behaviors and the mistaken thoughts that can fuel those behaviors. The thinking and work of these therapists are often less open-ended and more defined by specific goals than is the approach of most play therapists. There used to be no overlap between the camps of play therapists and more behaviorally oriented practitioners, but the rigidity of the boundaries between the two camps appears to be breaking down, and with good reason. Behavioral and cognitive approaches to certain problems of childhood offer impressive help.[4]

Behavioral and cognitive treatments are often combined but will be discussed separately here for simplicity. Behavioral treatments are designed to eliminate specific problem behaviors and assist a child in developing new, more appropriate behaviors. The approach is practical in emphasis and result. Specific behavioral difficulties such as bedwetting, oppositionalism, incapacitating fears, poor habits, and noncompliance with household or classroom rules are examples of childhood problems that are generally responsive to behavioral management.

Most parents find that they are already familiar with and, to some degree, practicing behavioral management. What parent has not said that a child's room must be cleaned up before he can go out and play? This statement uses the idea that rewards and privileges must be contingent on children's meeting parents' expectations, an idea emphasized in most behavioral treatments. What parent has not expressed supreme pleasure when a child does indeed clean up his room without prompting? The expression of that pleasure and pride is central to the use of rewards and praise in behavioral treatment. And what child has not been put in time-out or lost her favorite television show for breaking an important family rule? Such simple, direct, immediate consequences are also emphasized in behavioral treatment. Many parents also engage in a practice called shaping, which helps a child learn a new behavior bit by bit. The goal may be for a four year old to learn to dress himself completely in the morning, but a parent begins shaping the new behavior by first giving him the job of putting on his socks.

Behavioral interventions sound easy and familiar to parents, and they appeal to common sense. Experience suggests, however, that behavioral treatment of many childhood problems is often more complex than it appears. Almost all behavioral treatments rely heavily on the parents' serving as at-home therapists, so the treatment is very dependent on the parents' follow-through and consistency at home. Learning new ways of responding to children and being truly consistent, even when it goes against a parent's feelings at the time, can be an enormous challenge. Changing old habits does not come easily to anyone. On the other hand, when parents make new techniques and approaches work with their children, the satisfaction and sense of accomplishment can be enormous for both parents and children.

There are many applications of behavioral techniques with traumatized children. Children with extreme fears can be helped through a process called desensitization in which, with the therapist, the child is gradually exposed to less-feared objects while being taught simultaneously to relax until the child is able to confront the most-feared object successfully. Desensitization can occur in an office or in the actual situation that arouses fear, as occurred with Lindy's therapy.

Three-year-old Lindy, was terrified of going to the bathroom. She held her urine in for hours at a time and looked as uncomfortable as she felt. She was most relaxed with her potty at home but absolutely refused to use any toilet away from home; planning trips was understandably quite difficult. Lindy had suffered a severe head injury in a fall off a potty, so the source of her fear was totally comprehensible. Nevertheless, her phobic avoidance of bathrooms had to go if she was to lead a normal life.

We used several approaches to Lindy's fear of toilets. At home, Lindy's mother offered her an M+M each time she used the potty and let her know that she would get two M+Ms for using a toilet away from home. To make success easier, Lindy was at first allowed to use a portable potty to get her reward away from home.

During the same period that Lindy's mother was treating her fears at home, Lindy was bringing her fear to me. Invariably during her therapy sessions, Lindy would get a pained expression on her face and would start writhing from the pressure to urinate. Initially, we would walk up the stairs at the clinic simply to look at the bathroom. Lindy insisted at first that the potty was too high. Gradually, she was encouraged to sit on it. Despite her obvious intense need to urinate, she sat, clutching my neck in a sort of vice, but holding her urine in while I read her a happy story. We read many stories in that awkward position during our bathroom visits. Next, we began to talk to her pee—or, rather, I did. "Pee, are you there?" I would yell. Lindy would let me know the pee was there. "Well, I want to talk with you. What's this business of refusing to come out and making Lindy ache inside? It's very nice out here, and we're in a very safe bathroom. I'm holding Lindy very tightly. I won't let her get hurt, you know." The pee was resistant. "It's scared," Lindy would say of her pee as she got off the potty, the pressure unrelieved. But we persisted weekly.

Over time, Lindy began to make complimentary comments about the clinic bathroom and insisted on visiting it weekly. And then the day came when Lindy just let her urine trickle out. She let out a victory whoop and squeezed me tightly. "Dr. Cynthia, it came out!"

Behavioral treatments, such as the reduction of Lindy's fear of potties, must be tailored exactly to the child's specific needs. Some behavioral work cannot be done effectively in an office. The child and therapist must go out and face the neighborhood dog or gradually confront the feared object in the child's real environment.

Though often used in combination with behavioral treatment, cognitive approaches differ in several ways from behavioral or play therapy techniques. Cognitive techniques focus on how childrens' ways of thinking can create or maintain their behavioral problems and distress. When a discouraged child is asked to try something new in school, for instance, he often thinks to himself, "Why should I even try? I always fail anyway," a thought that keeps him trapped in a cycle of discouragement.[5] Cognitive treatment approaches help children identify self-critical and self-defeating thoughts and replace them with more positive and encouraging thoughts. In many instances, cognitive techniques teach a child to be his own inner coach in solving various problems. He might remind himself to try or, perhaps, to stop and think when he's angry and feels like punching someone.

There are various cognitive techniques and games to help children in therapy. Children who have difficulty controlling impulsive behavior are taught to take time and practice specific steps in solving the problems that set off explosive or excitable reactions. Therapists role-play challenging and provocative situations with children during therapy to help arm them with new ways of responding in difficult situations. Children are offered new ways of thinking about the problems they encounter. Old and self-deprecating beliefs are challenged, and new self-enhancing beliefs are introduced.

Because trauma generally has a strong impact on the thinking and beliefs of children, cognitive approaches are definitely relevant. When the helplessness a child has felt during a trauma generalizes to a belief that she is a helpless person, there is a need to challenge and work with this belief. When a child maintains the guilt-ridden but mistaken belief that she caused her own trauma, this belief needs to be challenged and corrected. Frequently when the meaning a child has given to a traumatic experience is changed, the feelings that accompany these meanings can also change. A child who felt tricked and duped by a molster's bribes or threats, for instance, can be helped to feel better about herself when it is explained that she in fact played the last trick on her molester by telling the secret to someone. The story the child then tells of her molestation is not just a tale of victimization but also of her own power and heroism.

EXPRESSIVE THERAPIES. Expressive therapists use art and movement to help children explore and heal from trauma. Because the impression of trauma is imprinted in the child's visual imagery and physical experience, expressive therapies can be particularly appropriate. At times, severely traumatized children can communicate an experience of trauma only in a realm that is beyond words. Trauma can be lodged in picture memory or experienced in a physical sensation. Using the power of art, music, and movement, expressive therapists help a child reach into wordless memory to explore and express inaccessible feelings.

Angie was four when her father kidnapped her from the playground near her mother's home. She was taken to Sweden, where she lived in hiding with her father for a year before her mother's efforts to have her returned were successful. Little was known about her year with the father. The local authorities were able to confirm only that Angie did not attend school in Sweden and was seldom seen to leave the father's apartment.

When Angie returned, she seemed like a different child to her mother. She spoke few words, displayed few feelings, and avoided eye contact. She was compliant but appeared numb and unchildlike. During the first weeks back at her mother's home, Angie spent her time drawing silently, unable or unwilling to talk about her pictures. The pictures themselves frightened Angie's mother. Using only a black marker, Angie created one picture after another of ghoulish monsters, knives, and guns. The tone of these pictures was dark and menacing. There were no people, but in the corner of each drawing was a box containing a small animal.

Angie worked with an art therapist for months, repetitively drawing these same pictures without comment or apparent feeling. She rejected the therapist's suggestion that words be given to the small animal. She looked puzzled when the therapist commented that the animal in the box might have some feelings. Over time, the unremitting darkness of these pictures remained, but Angie began to comment sparingly about the drawings. "Bunny's hungry. You make him some food!" she said to the therapist who drew a carrot inside the bunny's box. Discovering the bunny's hunger opened the door to further understanding of the bunny's needs. "He needs tissues," said Angie, "he's crying lots of tears in there." Around this time, Angie herself began to cry and scream in her sleep, the first signs of any distress shown in the months since being returned home. Several weeks later, Angie asked the therapist to make a sign for the bunny's box: "It needs to say 'help!'" she directed. Asked what help the bunny needed, Angie sputtered in rapid, barely intelligible speech, "the bunny's locked in there. His Daddy leaves him there so he won't get out. Get him out of there!" Using more words than the therapist had ever heard Angie speak in one session, Angie began to tell the story of her year in hiding, a frightful time that was compounded by her father's containment of her in a cage when he had to leave the apartment.

HYPNOTHERAPY. Hypnotic techniques and hypnotherapy are increasingly being used to help children with a variety of problems.

For most people, hypnosis raises images of dangling watches and magician-like practitioners doing demonstrations on a stage. The work of these stage hypnotists does not evoke much confidence, given the usual outcome that a volunteer appears to have been tricked into doing or saying something that is embarrassing or humiliating. The hypnotic techniques used with children and adults in therapy bear little similarity to this stage stereotype.

Hypnosis uses specific techniques to create a state of deep relaxation. Once relaxed at this deep level, people of all ages experience an openness to suggestion and change that may be completely contrary to their usual waking state of extreme defensiveness. With children, relaxation is induced through focusing a child's mind on specific images, usually on images that are quite pleasant and gentle. A child may be asked to picture herself floating on a lovely, fluffy white could or watching her favorite television show.

Therapists use different approaches and tailor techniques to the special interests and pleasures of each child. While the child is deeply relaxed, a therapist may introduce new images and ways of solving problems. The child is free to resist the therapist's suggestions, but often enough the child is responsive to these suggestions because he wants to feel better and wants to solve the problem bothering him. There is no hocus pocus in child hypnosis. Most children in a deeply relaxed state have their eyes open and move freely around the office.

Hypnosis can be useful with children who experience extreme fears and with those who are unable to control certain behaviors. For some extremely guarded and fearful children, hypnotic techniques may help them recall and talk about a trauma that is otherwise too painful to consider consciously. It is helpful for parents to remember that children do not lose their control when hypnotized, nor are they tricked into doing or saying anything. Therapists trained in using hypnosis with children emphasize messages of the child's safety and pleasure while introducing images of strength and power to master difficulties.[6]

MEDICATION. Some children and adolescents may need to be evaluated for medication following a trauma. Symptoms of anxiety, depression, or sleeplessness can be so intense that some regimen of medication may be enormously helpful in gaining immediate or long-term control over these symptoms. Medication is seldom, if ever, a substitute for psychotherapy with traumatized children, nor is psychopharmacological medication of children to be taken lightly. Medication, when needed, is useful in relieving immediate disabling symptoms and in helping the child to tolerate and benefit from psychotherapy. Child psychiatrists who specialize in the use of psychopharmacological drugs with children are generally the best-informed practitioners to consult regarding medication.

THE PARENT'S ROLE. Most child therapists work with parents to help them assist their children's healing. Parent guidance sessions are offered in addition to the child's individual therapy or as the sole treatment. Through parent guidance, therapists focus on helping parents understand and respond to children's behavior. Many therapists who work with children see therapy as a team effort undertaken with the parents. Given that a child may have only 1 out of 168 hours a week with the therapist, the team approach between therapist and parents makes sense.

A therapist can serve the role of coach and supporter for parents facing many challenges with a child. Many children need therapeutic parenting following a trauma, which simply means that ordinary parenting responses are insufficient to help or speed the child's recovery. What a particular child needs does not always make a lot of sense or may involve skills that a parent has never previously needed to develop. Parent guidance sessions can help identify a child's special needs.

How-to questions are frequently dealt with in parent guidance meetings. It is helpful for parents to know that they have a place to take these questions as they come up during the week. Many therapists work with parents on trying new ways of responding to a child's behavior at home. Many of the recommendations regarding new ways to respond to children are experimental; parents need to be prepared for a period of trial and error. But even a "failure" of any particular child management approach provides good information that is useful in narrowing down an approach that will be helpful.

Very young and preverbal children who have experienced a trauma are often helped solely through parent guidance. Older children who have had mild traumas may sometimes be treated indirectly solely through the parents' work with a therapist. The best therapeutic plan for each child needs to be worked out between the parents and the therapist.

Family Treatment

Family treatment approaches involve all or various family members in therapy sessions. There are many situations involving trauma for which family therapy can be extremely helpful. Families whose members have all experienced a trauma together and families whose experience of a child's trauma is affecting multiple members are likely to find family-oriented treatments helpful. When a traumatized child is very resistant to being singled out as the patient for individual therapy, the child may be more open to seeing a therapist when the family as a whole requests help. Even when a child is being seen individually, there is often a need for sessions involving all family members to identify the rippling effects of trauma and to strengthen the family's coping abilities.

Group Treatment

Group therapy can provide powerful treatment for children and parents. Groups for children who have had similarly traumatizing experiences lessen the loneliness of victimization. Many children feel singled out by trauma and interpret this as having to do with something wrong within them. Sitting with a group of peers who have all gone through a similar traumatic experience can be the most powerful experience a child can have in rethinking the meaning of her experience. Children who have been sexually abused, for instance, are generally stunned to realize that other children have also had this experience. To meet and play with some of these other children and discover that they are bright, fun, and silly can provide meaningful relief. Group treatment also offers opportunities for children to express their feelings through play, art, or mutual conversation. Shy or withdrawn children may be empowered by peer example to share or express hidden emotions. Children who have not been able to express some difficult feeling may have a chance to hear another child's account of an identical response. Groups of children, because they naturally gravitate toward fun, have a tendency to undo some of the terror and helplessness through the pleasure of their experience. Together, children can role-play empowering solutions and scenarios with each other. For adolescents who look to peers as their major source of support and identity, group therapy is particularly powerful.

In order to benefit from a group, some children first need to be involved in individual psychotherapy. In most communities, groups are frequently available for children who have experienced abuse or have been exposed with others to a natural disaster or incident of community violence. When large groups of children have been affected by earthquakes, hurricanes, or incidents of violence, group sessions are often offered on an emergency basis in schools or community centers. These brief crisis-oriented groups are offered to help children with immediate coping and do not require that children be screened to participate. For longer-term group therapy, therapists generally evaluate each child individually to determine her readiness to benefit from a group. A period of individual therapy is sometimes recommended for a child prior to involvement in a group.

It would be hard to overstate the helpfulness of groups for parents. Support groups are most commonly available for parents of children who have been sexually abused. Most parents experience relief just being with other parents who can understand their experience. Parents offer each other a special form of support and encouragement that is immediate and powerful. We know from the addictions' recovery movement that being with others who share similar challenges and suffering offers a source of hope and support that other therapies may lack.

Common Goals of Treatment

The various approaches to treatment can be confusing for parents. It may be reassuring to know that although there are various paths that can be followed, in the end all these paths are leading toward similar goals. With children of trauma, the goals of treatment include:

- The safe release of feelings
- Relief from symptoms and disturbing post-traumatic behaviors
- Recovery of a sense of mastery and control in life

- Correction of misunderstandings and self-blame
- Restoration of a sense of trust in oneself and the future
- Development of a sense of perspective and distance regarding the trauma
- Minimizing the scar of trauma

These ambitious goals serve as directional guides in treatment. We know where we would like to head with each child, but we also know that each child's recovery from trauma will be unique and, most likely, approximate. At any given time in a child's life, good therapy takes a child as far as she is able to go toward these goals. Most parents would like to know that there is some kind of guarantee of meeting the basic goals. The reality is that with the best therapist working well as a team with the parents and doing excellent work with the child, some vulnerabilities from trauma often remain and need to be returned to at a later age.

Choosing a Therapist

People have different ways of looking for therapists. Some people pick a name out of the telephone book. Others seek out recommendations and interview a number of therapists before making their final choice. For many families who have had no need to know about professional providers before, the process of finding and choosing a therapist can be confusing.

There are several issues to consider. From a practical standpoint, it is important to find a therapist who is eligible for the insurance reimbursement. Most insurance plans pay for licensed mental health providers, but licensing laws vary and so do insurance requirements. Given the high cost of professional services (ranging between $45 and $110 an hour, depending on region and provider), reviewing insurance plan information for outpatient mental health coverage is an important part of looking for a therapist.

If the plan covers the services of a number of different providers, the next question that arises has to do with the different disciplines of providers. Psychiatrists, psychologists, social workers, mental health counselors, and marriage and family counselors may all be available in a particular region. Parents want to know whether they should seek the services of one type of provider over another.

Providers vary in the number of years required for their training and in the type of knowledge in which they are trained. All three of the major choices of mental health providers—social workers, psychologists, and psychiatrists—are generally trained in doing psychotherapy. Only psychiatrists, as physicians, are trained to evaluate the medical aspects of psychological problems and to prescribe medication. Psychologists are the only providers trained in the use of psychological testing. Social workers generally receive the most training in working with the social and service network of communities. If there is a compelling need for specific services other than psychotherapy, then there may be a good argument for choosing one discipline over another. Otherwise, there is no need to be restricted by discipline of the providers. Rather than looking for which degree a therapist has, it may be most helpful to look for specialization, experience, and reputation.

Specialization

In some communities, there is a luxury of choice; in others the choices are few. When there are alternative practitioners to consider, the issue of specialization is important. In looking for a therapist to treat a child or provide parent guidance, it is preferable to look for someone who has specialized in child treatment. Within this field of child therapists, there are some providers who have further specialized in the treatment of trauma. When possible, it is important to seek out child therapists of any discipline who have developed their skills and focused their ongoing training on the treatment of trauma. Similarly, when looking for a therapist to work with other family members, those who have special interest and skill in working with issues of trauma would be recommended.

Parents should feel free to ask therapists about their specializations and their experience treating children who have suffered traumas similar to that of their own child. These questions are not insulting to providers but rather indicate the patient's seriousness in choosing the right professional.

In communities that lack specialists, the choices are narrower. Sometimes an especially well-trained person is available within a reasonable distance, and his or her expertise makes the commitment to a long drive worth the effort. In most situations, however, there is a practical need to stay close to home and find the best available therapist. In the absence of specialists, parents then need to consider the issues of experience and reputation.

Experience

Many professionals have learned their most valuable lessons about trauma and its treatment directly from children and families. In many rural communities, clinicians cannot specialize because of the pressure to respond to many different needs. Among these generalists are those who have had experience with traumatized children and their families. Parents can always ask about a particular therapist's experience. It is helpful to know how many years a clinician has been practicing and how often, if ever, a clinician has had the opportunity to work with problems similar to the ones for which help is being sought. Experience counts for a lot in psychotherapy.

Reputation

Many parents rely on the community reputation of a therapist to guide their choice. In making telephone calls, parents may find that a particular therapist is repeatedly recommended, and this rightly increases their confidence. Victim-witness advocates associated with the courts can often refer parents to specialists in childhood trauma. Having a trusted friend or other professional recommend someone on the basis of their own experience is also relieving and helpful in narrowing the search. Reputation is often a reliable indicator of someone's professional skills, but certainly there are many competent therapists who may be too new to the community to have become well known.

Initial Consultation

There are a lot of variables involved in choosing the right therapist, but the ultimate issue is the parents' personal ease and comfort with the therapist. A visit with a therapist to discuss concerns and learn about the therapist's thinking and approach gives parents a sense of the goodness of fit between them. This sense of fit is intangible and difficult to describe but readily experienced in the first several interviews. It is difficult as a consumer of professional services to pay attention to initial reservations or critical feelings, but in the long run it is very important to do so. Some parents initially consult with more than one therapist before deciding. As in any other choice of professional provider, having several initial consultations is acceptable practice.

Parental confidence in the child's therapist is key to the success of therapy. Children look to their parents for both subtle and obvious cues that this stranger who is supposed to help them is in fact trustworthy. During the first important months of child therapy, children literally borrow their parents' faith in the therapist until they have developed their own independent sense of trust in the therapist. When children pick up on parents' doubts about a therapist's reliability or skill, they will inevitably share that doubt and limit their participation in the treatment. It therefore becomes important for parents to pay attention to their own reactions to a child's therapist and to discuss concerns and hesitations openly with the therapist.

Special Considerations

LEGAL. Certain situations may require looking for a therapist with legal experience and expertise. When a child's trauma involves complex legal preparation for trial, it can be essential to find a therapist who qualifies as an expert witness under the state's legal statutes and is comfortable, experienced, and skilled in working with the legal system. The demands of managing a child's therapy and simultaneously working with attorneys on case preparation present therapists with some challenges not ordinarily confronted in clinical work. A therapist's training and experience with the legal aspects of criminal prosecution and civil litigation are a significant advantage in making this work go smoothly and successfully.

FEES. Families with limited income and those who receive public assistance have the additional burden of finding treatment that is either subsidized or reimbursed by Medicaid. Public mental health clinics that receive special state or federal funding can often offer a sliding scale for services or can accept Medicaid reimbursement. Regulations regarding which providers can be reimbursed by Medicaid vary by state. Some universities offer clinical services at a reduced fee or for free. There are also community clinicians in private practice who offer sliding scale or reduced fee services as well.

What to Expect from Therapy

Psychotherapy seems mysterious to most people, and child psychotherapy can seem even more so. Although therapists vary a good deal in their approach to child treatment, there are some similarities. Parents generally find it helpful to know what they can anticipate when a child is in treatment.

Evaluation and the Beginning of Treatment

At the beginning of treatment, therapists typically take some time to sort out the primary concerns. Some therapists want to see the child first with the parents or other family members; others prefer to see the child alone initially. Over the course of three or four initial meetings, with either various family members or with the child, a therapist is generally working toward developing a good understanding of the child, her difficulties, and her family. During this initial assessment period, some therapists find it helpful to talk with school or day care personnel and to have parents fill out developmental or behavioral questionnaires in order to round out their understanding of the child. Psychological testing is sometimes recommended initially as well. The therapist, either formally or informally, will then share an understanding of the child's needs with the parents and recommend a plan of treatment. Realistic consideration of the family's financial and time resources is an important component of the treatment planning process. Any therapy plan involves a commitment that has to be thoroughly considered if it is going to be effective. Even therapy entirely paid for by a third party involves considerable work for parents in adjusting schedules, transporting, and carving time out of a busy family's life.

There is also a commitment involved for parents in working with their child at home, which can be a major part of the child's treatment.

When the treatment plan involves psychotherapy, the child most frequently is given a regularly scheduled appointment for fifty- or sixty-minute sessions. Parents also meet with either the child's therapist or another therapist to develop supportive strategies for helping the child with daily coping and behavioral management. Parents may be invited to join in or observe a child's therapy sessions, or they may not be included in these sessions at all, depending on the therapist's style and the needs of the child. Some children need the privacy and protection of the therapy hour to take the risk of approaching their concerns. Others are quite open to or want their parents' involvement. Although it is much harder for the parents of a child in therapy to trust the process of treatment when they are unable to observe it, the deciding factor needs to be whatever condition better allows the child to work.

Rules in Child Psychotherapy

Therapists have different rules about acceptable behavior in their offices than the rules that normally apply for children at home. It is not that anything goes in therapy, but most anything does. Through experience, each therapist has carved out some basic rules regarding what is and what is not permissible behavior during the therapy hour.

The basic rules usually include no hurting of any kind. Beyond that, child therapy offices are generally designed to be sturdy and safe enough for children to express themselves in a variety of ways. There may be things to throw, furniture that can be stood on, safety guns to shoot, and dolls that can be bopped mercilessly. Child therapy offers children new opportunities to express big feelings in ways that often are unacceptable in other settings. Even very young children know that the rules of therapy apply only within the therapy office, and they do not expect that these rules, or lack of them, will now apply elsewhere. Children are smart about matters of rules and are used to adapting their behavior to different caretakers' expectations from an early age. Nevertheless, the freedom offered to children in psychotherapy can be jarring to parents, who may be finding it quite a job simply to maintain the home rules with a child. The message from the therapist to the child is that he can and should act out the gross or ugly feelings in the therapy office where he can do so safely but not at home or at school, where acting out will result in increasing his distress.

Being Prepared for the Unexpected

There are some common occurrences in child treatment that can be confusing for unprepared parents. The fact that many children look worse during the first phase of therapy comes as an unexpected shock to most parents, whose sole wish is to see improvements in the child's behavior and sense of self. It is important that parents be prepared for the regression they may see in a child's behavior at home when therapy is getting started. Particularly for children who have experienced a trauma, the first sessions of therapy may stir up the memories and feelings that had begun to settle in maladaptive ways. This stirring up is a necessary part of therapy for some children and often a signal of working with the most difficult or painful aspects of a child's experience. The temporary results of the stirring process, however, are understandably not popular with parents. It may be helpful to keep in mind that it is normal in the course of therapy for children to go backward before they go forward.

Parents may notice their children having other reactions to therapy. Many children experience strong feelings just before and after therapy sessions. Young children often express these feelings through excitement, distress, overactivity, or withdrawal and quieting. Older children may become introspective, defensive, or argumentative. The trips to and from therapy sessions can be particularly difficult or delightful depending on the child's style of coping and the stress of therapy at a particular time. Some children's reactions to the freedom of expression and the anxiety aroused within the therapy session can involve episodes of explosiveness. One three year old I was treating ended her powerful therapy sessions for several weeks in a row by running to the waiting room and picking an immediate fight with her mother. Once she bit her mother in the waiting room. Needless to say, being bitten by a child right after her therapy session is a test most parents do not have to endure. I gave this mother a lot of credit for being able to understand the power of her daughter's feelings on these occasions while reminding the child of her rule that biting and all other hurting were off- limit behaviors.

This child had other tests in store for her mother's patience during the first difficult months of therapy. Perhaps most difficult to tolerate for her mother was the child's temporary idealization of me as her therapist. It can be hard for parents when children develop strong positive and negative feelings about their therapists over the course of therapy. When children idealize their therapists, it is all but impossible for parents not to feel some disgruntlement over their child's comments about this "perfect" adult who has the easy job of playing with the child for only fifty minutes a week. But also quite difficult is the child who reaches a point of hating the therapist or putting up serious resistance to going to therapy. Excessive affection or hatred for a therapist is regularly present at any point in a child's treatment. These strong feelings may be part and parcel of treatment, but they are a handful for parents who are unprepared for them.

A child's resistance to going to therapy may come up suddenly, or it may be present from the beginning of treatment. Particularly with children who have been traumatized, the therapy itself can become associated with the trauma the child wishes to forget. Getting rid of therapy becomes the hoped-for avenue of getting rid of memories.

Most parents share with the child at least some of this wish to avoid therapy. They may be going to enormous trouble and expense to have their child in treatment and wonder about its worth. Parents wonder, too often only to themselves, if it would not be better to end the treatment, put the trauma behind them, and move on with life, particularly when the child is saying that she does not want to go anymore. The child's resistance, however, cannot be taken as a sign that he is truly ready to end therapy. What happens frequently is that a child becomes resistant during the most critical periods of the treatment. The child may be approaching a new and important piece of work during the therapy hours just at the time that the complaints about going to sessions are loudest. The caution for parents is a simple one: when a child becomes very resistant to therapy, it is a good time to talk with the therapist and find out what may be occurring that is setting off the resistance. Similarly, it is important for parents to talk freely to a therapist about their own very natural impatience and wishes to end the treatment. In the meantime, the part of the child that wants to grow, heal, and get help needs parental support and encouragement to get that help. Children's negative feelings about therapy can be accepted by parents without taking sides. Parents can encourage the child to share her negative feelings directly with the therapist.

At some time during a child's therapy, many parents wonder why they themselves cannot serve as the child's therapist if what the child needs is to be played with. Parents who feel particularly helpless and vulnerable often understandably want to take over the role of helping the child's recovery. When therapy feels like just one more insult to a parent's self-esteem, the feelings can be troubling. Actually, parents of a child in therapy are always the cotherapists. Without the parents' hard work at home, the child's involvement in therapy sessions would often be an exercise in futility. Sometimes, as with very young children, parents do serve as the primary therapists, receiving consultation as needed. Often, however, a frightened child holding horrific memories of a trauma needs a nonparent to share these memories and feelings with. Above all, children want to protect their relationships with their parents, and often they do this by holding in feelings and fears that they think would scare and upset their parents. Many children are reluctant to let their parents know about the degree of their ongoing distress.[7] These children are tuned in to their parents' worry and concern and want to protect them from further anxiety. Children in therapy have little investment in protecting a therapist; the risks for a child are much higher with parents. Following a trauma, most children want their parents to be parents, taking care of their safety, rules, nourishment, and love as they always have. As one therapist writes, "Parents must remain the gatekeepers of safety—the ones who nurture and protect while we, the therapists, open the wounds."[8]

Parents should be prepared for some of the negative and jarring surprises they might discover when a child is in treatment, but what of the positive expectations? When therapy is going well, parents can feel relieved in many ways. First, the loneliness of trying to help a child cope is lessened when there is someone else who knows the child well to consult with. Many parents welcome the support and availability of a therapist during a confusing period of parenting. Sometimes when a child begins therapy after a long period of many efforts to help the child at home, parents need hope and new ideas. It is reassuring and energizing to hear a therapist say, "Let's try this," when a parent's ideas have run dry from exhaustions and worry. It is also helpful to be able to set limits on a child's trauma-driven behavior at home or school and be able to remind the child that she has a safe place (the therapy office), where she can take and express her big feelings about what happened to her.

As a child progresses in therapy, parents have the satisfaction of watching problematic behaviors resolve as a result of the plans they themselves have carried out at home. Parents can also sense when a child is coming to terms with a trauma. A child literally lightens up when discarding the weight of trauma in therapy. The child's preoccupation lessens, and she begins to open herself to new experiences and feelings. Many parents describe this process of lightening as "being herself again."

How Long Will This Take?

One of the biggest questions that parents have about child treatment or any therapy involvement is, "How long? This is a good question but one with few certain answers. In general, the length of treatment is related to the severity of the problems a child or family is experiencing. With single incidents of trauma, the length of the treatment is also related to the severity of the trauma itself or the meaning that a child or family has given to it. The delay between the actual incident of trauma and the beginning of therapy can complicate and lengthen the therapy process.

Although an estimated length of treatment for a child can be made only after an actual evaluation of that child, the expected range of treatment time goes from several months to several years.[9] Some children are well treated in short-term psychotherapy, involving between fourteen and thirty sessions, and some are not. All therapists share every parent's wish that there were quick and effective therapy techniques for children who have experienced psychic trauma. And promising work is being done to develop time-limited treatments for specific groups of trauma victims, such as child sexual abuse victims, but there are no guarantees of quick fixes for traumatized children. The actual length of treatment to expect therefore becomes an issue to discuss thoroughly with the therapist who does the initial evaluation.

Ways to Support and Speed Your Child's Therapy

Parents sometimes worry that they will be passive, helpless observers of their child's therapy—outsiders at a time of greatest need in their child's life. But this worry can be quickly dispelled. In general, child therapy works as one part of the larger changes and healing support offered by parents and families. Child therapy, in and of itself, can have limited impact without the full involvement and support of the child's parents in the treatment.

There is often a lot of concrete work that parents do as part of the treatment plan. If a child is out of control or immobilized at home, parents are going to be making the daily changes that allow the child to regain control or begin to take risks. Parents are frequently given exercises or activities to do with children during the week between sessions. Therapists ask parents to watch their children closely in order to help understand their confusing behavior or discover the triggers for a child's unusual responses.

There is a lot of ongoing eyes-and-ears detective work to do with children that only parents can accomplish. The findings of this detective work make all the difference in the child's healing. Above and beyond any specific work parents are requested to do as part of the therapy, there is the critical job of parenting sensitively and consistently when a child is recovering from a trauma. It can be exhausting to be there for a terrified and needy child over what may be months of distress or provocative behavior. Nevertheless, this "being there" to comfort, nurture, listen to, distract, and set limits for a child is the single most important source of a child's strength to turn terror around.

Very concretely, there are also the following other ways that parents can be extremely helpful in supporting and speeding a child's treatment and recovery:

Maintain Communication with the Therapist

Therapists need to know about changes in behavior or significant events that have occurred between sessions in the child's and family's life. Some parents call in observations to therapists directly or to phone machines. Some parents come to sessions with notes they have collected over the week. The information that travels between home and the therapist is enormously helpful.

Therapists also need to know about parents' concerns and worries—whether these are about the child, themselves, or the therapy. Some parents feel embarrassed or fearful about bringing up their concerns with a therapist. Sharing worries, questions, or criticisms with a therapist is always helpful in the long run, even if uncomfortable in the short run.

The only time that it is difficult to talk about a parent's concerns is directly following a child's therapy session. It is convenient to grab a therapist for a few words at this time, but it is a very difficult time for the child. When a therapy session is over, children want their parents' full attention. Children are often stressed and tired after therapy, and they have little tolerance for standing around in the waiting room while mom or dad talk about them to the therapist. Many child therapists feel a little rude for not making themselves available to talk to parents after a child's session, but the reason for this lies in protecting the child's experience of therapy.

Respect a Child's Privacy in Therapy

Some children run out of the therapy office and relate everything they have played or worked on during the hour to their parents. Most children, however, need some time to let their sessions settle. They may be quiet on the way home, they may become very talkative about other subjects, or they may become temporarily aggressive or obnoxious. Every parent would like to know how the therapy session has been for the child, and most parents are more than a little bit curious about what the child was actually doing. It does not do much good, and it can do some harm, to ask a child questions about therapy. Just like questions about school when asked directly, most children will have vague and useless answers.

But at another time, unprompted, the child will most likely bring up some recollections or thoughts about therapy sessions and give a very vivid sense of what therapy is like.

Parents need to wait to hear about therapy rather than ask a child about therapy time. At different times in therapy, children feel the need for some privacy and boundary around their work, particularly when that work involves uncomfortable feelings or secret worries. They might be willing to check these feelings out with a stranger, but they want to protect the most important people in their lives from knowing some of their worst thoughts or wishes. Children do believe that some of the rotten things about them, if known to the people they love, will make those people love them less. Children do not "love" their therapists, so therapy can be a safe place to check out some of these feelings. It is a real challenge for any parent of a child in therapy to remember that a child's exclusion of the parent is often based on a wish to protect and ensure that parent's love.

Follow Up at Home

Therapists are full of ideas for parents to try out at home that are aimed at relieving stress or decreasing specific problem behaviors. At times the work for parents to do at home involves large commitments of time and energy. Making specific or general changes at home designed to help a child's recovery is frequently the most powerful part of treatment. There is a natural tendency for everyone to resist change, no matter how small or seemingly insignificant. Some new approaches in parenting will work well, while some ideas will prove to be useless. There is a lot to be learned about what will help a child through a process of trial and error, and a new strategy that works carries with it enormous relief.

Stick to the Basics

For therapy to be helpful, there needs to be some continuity. Parents can help by protecting a child's regular session time and making sure that a child gets to appointments on time. There is a flow between weekly sessions and within the session hour that depends on this continuity. At times during therapy, children will resume their play at exactly the point that they left off the week before. Children also develop an internal time sense for how long they have to begin, elaborate, and finish their work within the session hour. The basics of going regularly and having the full time in each session therefore have an enormous impact on the treatment.

When Treatment Is Completed

In general, any treatment can be ended whenever the client or client's parents wish to end it. Ideally, however, the end of treatment for children, families, or adults results from joint agreement and planning between the therapist and the client. How any experience is ended has a lot to do with long-term memories and feelings about that experience. Saying goodbye in therapy is an important part of the therapy. How and when to say goodbye are issues that parents, children, and therapists need to talk about and plan together.

When therapy is completed is a tricky issue. Children and families know when they are making gains. When these gains are apparent, it can be difficult to tell whether they will be sustained without therapy. There is generally an understandable tendency or wish to end psychotherapy. Children frequently abandon some of their most obvious or worrisome behaviors early in treatment. While the pain and struggle of these children may be too obvious during the therapy hour, their behavior in the outside world may be looking more and more settled. If behavior outside therapy is the only indicator considered regarding the effectiveness of therapy, then many therapies will be ended long before a child has come to terms with, or understands, the situation that led to therapy in the first place. Ideally, children are ready to end treatment when they have achieved this understanding and acceptance of a trauma and are able to resume positive coping and move forward with their development. Most children who enter treatment are coping negatively and are stuck in one or more areas of their development. For children coping with trauma, there is a need to find a perspective that releases them from extremes of fear and anxiety.

There are several things to keep in mind about the end of therapy:

1. Ending a therapy can be a big deal. Children have strong reactions to a planned termination of therapy. Some children briefly return to the original behaviors that brought them to therapy around the time that treatment is ending. Usually this return of problematic behaviors is short-lived, but it is good to be prepared for it.
2. Therapy ends best when planned and prepared for. For children whose trauma has involved a loss, the end of treatment is an opportunity to say goodbye in a new and better way. It is helpful for children to know how many more sessions they will have and to make sure that they are able to see the treatment through to the planned ending. Planned endings can often involve rituals of celebration and achievement as well as acknowledgment of loss and sadness.
3. Children and parents need to know that therapy can end for now but not forever. A therapist can always be available to provide some short-term help with specific problems that might arise down the road. There is sometimes a need to return to a trauma and make sense of it in new ways as a child grows older. For parents as well as children, the door remains open. Many therapists offer follow-up visits to check in with the child and family or welcome a child's request to visit at some point after the first period of therapy has ended.

Therapy is not magic. It involves work for the child and parents. But it can help loosen the immediate grip of trauma on a child and lighten the weight of a trauma in a child's ongoing development. When needed, therapy is one among many gifts that parents can give to a traumatized child.

Points to Remember: Psychotherapy for Psychologically Traumatized Children

Children who have been traumatized may be helped by various approaches to therapy, including individual child therapy, family therapy, and group therapy. Consultation for parents is often helpful in clarifying the therapeutic role of parents at home.

When children are struggling with the effects of trauma, there is always a need for a team approach involving the therapist and the parents as well as other important adults in the child's life.

The goals of therapy with traumatized children include:
- The safe release of feelings

- Relief from symptoms and disturbing posttraumatic behaviors

- Recovery of a sense of mastery and control in life

- Correction of misunderstandings and self-blame

- Restoration of a sense of trust in oneself and the future

- Development of a sense of perspective and distance regarding the trauma

- Minimizing the scars of trauma

In choosing a therapist, parents need to consider the professional's expertise, experience, reputation, and specialization.

Parents' open communication and comfort with a therapist contribute to the helpfulness of therapy.

Having a child in therapy is a complicated matter for parents that often involves unexpected feelings, situations, and questions.

The work of a parent and a therapist is different in many important ways. Children who have been through a trauma may need to work with someone they do not need to protect in order to come to terms with painful feelings and memories. Their temporary need for someone outside the family does not diminish their need for family support.

Parents can support and speed a child's progress in therapy in numerous ways.

Afterword

Living with Memories

Children are constantly creating and recreating their own life stories. New experiences must be woven into the stories they tell of themselves. The boy who has loved his story of being an only child must tell a new story of being the big brother when his sister is born. The little girl whose story assumes the blissful immortality of all her loved ones must change her story to make room for the death of her grandmother. As the author, the child takes events over which she has little control and finds ways to fit them meaningfully into her story. Children need these stories of themselves; through them, they know who they are and can make sense of their lives and the world they live in.

I have learned to listen closely to the stories that children like to tell about their lives. I hear about the people who love them, about the sense they have of themselves in the world, and about the important events that have already given shape and substance to their personalities. Most children tell their life stories happily. The stories in which they themselves play the leading roles are old, familiar, and comforting; their life stories make sense.

Children who have been recently traumatized do not tell their stories happily or easily. They have difficulty finding a place for senseless experiences of horror and terror. Their driven retelling of traumatic events sometimes feels like an attempt to wedge the trauma by force into the old and familiar stories of their lives. In the beginning, their stories sound chaotic and fragmented. Gradually, with time and healing, children recreate their life stories, finding a place and meaning for the trauma. As they discover that they are able to live with their memories and overcome their fears, children make room to include a traumatic event in the stories they tell of themselves. These can be stories of being loved, of surviving, and of moving on.

Parents cannot completely control what a trauma will mean in the ongoing story of a child's life but they can help a child who needs to make sense of and integrate a foreign and shocking experience. Children need their parents' help when battling memories and fears. They need help ackowledging the reality of the trauma, they need their feelings to be accepted and respected, and they need their families to provide a safe harbor for the work of healing. For some children, providing needed help is straightforward; for others, it is enormously complicated and difficult. The long-term trace of trauma in a child's life may be minimal and difficult to detect or it may be quite evident. Regardless of whether trauma changes the child's life story in small or large ways, parents can change the ways the child comes to tell and feel about that story.

Healing from trauma is not serendipitous; it does not simply occur with the passing of time or because children are inherently resilient. There is, in fact, nothing simple about childhood trauma. The workings of trauma in a child's life are devious and dogged. When ignored, the memories and distress do not go away. The fate of overlooked trauma is often a dangerous psychic burial of these memories and feelings. Rapid burial of traumatic experience and feeling tends to have a preserving effect. When buried, the child's images of terror and the distorted convictions about the traumatic event can be preserved with freshness and power, creating a lasting internal sense of danger and vulnerability. Children who are left emotionally alone to make sense of and cope with a trauma are most likely to bury their experience quickly. The task of coping for children who lack at least one person who can understand and comfort them in their pain is understandably so difficult that the defense of a quick burial makes total but tragic sense. Just one person who recognizes and responds to a child's pain, one person who can help the child look in the face of terror, can make an enormous difference.

The difference that parents and loved ones make in undoing the power of a child's trauma is often not immediately evident. The difference is in the long run, and with trauma the run can be very long indeed. For most parents, joining battle with a child against memories and ghosts of the past is one of the hardest tasks to be faced in raising children. It is also a task that carries enormous hope and power to transform the lasting meanings of trauma in a child's life.

*   *   *

There is a maple tree growing in the woods near my home that I often visit. It was many years before I realized that this tree, and the story it tells, had taken on a special meaning for me. As a young sapling, the maple grew up next to a barbed-wire fence at the edge of a tended field. Now, buried deep within the overgrown forest, the tree has incorporated the remains of the barbed wire within its sturdy trunk. The wire does not simply graze the bark; it is firmly embedded within the maple's core. And yet the tree is majestic, towering sixty feet above the undergrowth. My son loves this tree, and so do I. We love that it lived on with such determination and strength to tell its long-ago story of a sapling's encounter with a sharp and potentially quite damaging obstacle in its path.

Images of hope and transformation are necessary to anyone whose life is touched by trauma. Nevertheless, there are times when my anger at a child's violent victimization is so forceful that I find the image of a strong but scarred maple tree irrelevant or laughable. My horror at the things that happen to children never goes away. I am constantly appalled by the preventable harm to children that we, as a society, overlook and tolerate. But the image of the maple persists, as does my hope and optimism, nurtured by the children whose healing I am privileged to watch and share in.

Recently, I told Jenna the story of the maple tree. Jenna is eleven now and quite an accomplished young lady. She is one of the many reasons for my optimism about children's healing despite the scars of trauma. Vivacious and creative, Jenna is a delight to her friends and teachers. She plays the flute in the school orchestra and dances the solo parts in her recitals. Jenna's vibrant enthusiasm for life seems to be boundless.

At five, Jenna was brutally raped. At six, she seldom slept

through the night; she lay in bed waiting for her assailant to find his way to her home. "I sleep with my eyes open," explained Jenna at the time. In her mind, it was only a matter of time before she was raped again. At seven, Jenna would not testify in court; she believed that no courtroom could have the power to control this man. At eight, she was ready to start over.

It has been hard work for Jenna to become free from her fears. She has mourned deeply. She does not like the way her story went. "It's not fair that I didn't get to be a child like everyone else," Jenna says today. There is still a trace of her original worry that she was somehow to blame for her attack, but on most days she can remind herself that she was not at fault. Accompanying Jenna have been two parents whose love for her has enabled them to endure her many sieges of panic, nightmares, and rage. Jenna's parents know about hard work.

Jenna asked me recently if my book would have a picture on the cover. I asked her what picture she would draw if she were to do this cover. Without hesitating, Jenna answered that she would draw the image of a child with the top part of her head lifted up, "so that people can look inside and see all those thoughts and feelings and memories hidden in there." Jenna is not without many memories and thoughts of her own trauma. At times, the memories still sneak up on her and make her feel grumpy or tearful. She is very aware of events long ago that continue to stir her feelings. She will not forget these events but she has been able to largely disarm their power over her. As expected, it has taken Jenna longer to find some distance than children who grapple with less severe trauma. Jenna likes the way her story is turning out. More and more she feels like the creator of her success and satisfaction. The best part of her story, says Jenna, is having two parents who really love her.

I think Jenna had a purpose when she offered the image of a child whose head had to be opened up for people to see the thoughts and feelings about trauma. She knows that children are able to conceal their torment about bad things that happen to them. Jenna has also learned a lot about the troubles these thoughts and feelings can create for children. At times, Jenna has hated doing active battle with her memories in therapy. How many times has she said, "Oh let's not talk about *that* stuff!"? Now, coming out the other end, I believe she is beginning to feel that it was worth all those difficult talks we needed to have.

Jenna has very strong protective feelings toward other children. I am grateful to her for wanting to pass on this image of a child whose inner pain needs to be revealed and understood. And I am glad to pass on the strong and courageous image of Jenna herself. Her own trauma was profound. But like the maple in my fertile woods, she is growing well.

Notes

Introduction

1. Many parents whom I've been consulted with have taken great interest in the writing of this book and have been generous with their thoughts and advice. One mother, Liz, called recently to ask if I had yet found a title for the book. I was, at the time, actually searching for a title and was unhappy with the possibilities I'd thought of. "Well, I've thought of a title for you. Call it "Hard Work"! Liz sounded victorious. She had found the simplest words to describe her experience of parenting twin three-year-old sons following an oil burner explosion in their home. The boys' terror from this incident had proved to be far worse than their physical injuries. Her title struck me as totally accurate, cutting to the heart of a parent's experience. Liz had put into words the lesson which parents have repeatedly taught me: parenting a traumatized child can be incredibly "hard work". A year after the explosion, her boys can sleep again and hear a loud noise without running for cover. Now, Liz would say her work has been worth it but there were many days that Liz was simply exhausted and discouraged by the slowness of the twins' recovery. I would have been happy to follow Liz's suggestion to entitle the book "Hard Work" but my wise agent worried that inevitably it would be shelved under the "career and employment" section in the bookshops where parents would never find it!

2. L. C. Terr (1991), Childhood trauma: An outline and overview, *American Journal of Psychiatry*, 148:1, 10–19.

3. For some children, trauma does not involve a single event but a prolonged series of events, any one of which a child would find traumatic: living in a violent community, repeated abuse over a period of time, long-term emotional terrorizing. These children frequently show signs of chronic, or long-term, trauma.

   Children's reactions to single-event and long-term trauma differ in some ways. Children required to live with repeated trauma as part of their regular existence frequently "adjust" to the ever-present fear over time in ways that have far-reaching consequences for their development. These children develop a personality equipped to deal with the constant possibility of danger or terror. They find ways to block out or to "numb" feelings and thoughts. It is easier to get by if one is not aware of what has happened or might happen again at any time. Even their bodies seem to participate in their efforts to cope: they may lose much of their ability to feel physical pain, and no longer have tears when they cry, or they may become overly aggressive or overly fearful. Many blame themselves for what has happened to them, and some are actively encouraged to see themselves as the guilty party. All victimized children are likely to attribute the cause of a trauma to something within themselves rather than to the others who bear the responsibility for it. Their rage is very real but often misdirected. When the source of trauma has been long-term abuse, self-hatred can be one of the most tragic outcomes.

The path that many chronically abused or traumatized children take to protect themselves emotionally from repeated terror and danger is often a different one from the child who has encountered a single or time-limited exposure to trauma. A wall of self-protection must develop sufficient thickness to serve as an adequate barrier to emotional and physical assault. Victimized by those from whom the child expects nurturance and protection, the loss of trust can be profound. The repeatedly traumatized child's path of self-protection has different consequences for development and for the process of healing. Trauma for these children has been inextricably intertwined with their most fundamental experiences of human relationships and care.

Children who have experienced repeated trauma can be helped to heal. They can be given therapeutic parenting and be encouraged to live out new experiences. They can receive intensive and long-term psychotherapy. Healing for these victims of long-term relational abuse, requires that we acknowledge that their wounds are different from those of children who have experienced a single incident of trauma.

Chapter 1

1. L. C. Terr (1991), Childhood traumas: An outline and overview, *American Journal of Psychiatry,* 148, 10–19.
2. Ibid.
3. Ibid.; R. S. Pynoos, and S. Eth (1985), *Post-traumatic stress disorder in children* (Washington, D.C.: American Psychiatric Press).
4. C. B. Cole and E. F. Loftus (1987), The memory of children, in S. Ceci, M. Toglia, and D. Ross (eds.), *Children's eyewitness memory* (New York: Springer-Verlag), pp 178–180.
5. L. C. Terr (1988), What happens to early memories? A study of twenty children under age five at the time of documented traumatic events, *Journal of the American Academy of Child and Adolescent Psychiatry,* 27 (1), 96–104.
6. L. C. Terr (1981), Forbidden games: Post-traumatic child's play, *Journal of the American Academy of Child Psychiatry* 20, 741–760.
7. *Ibid.*

Chapter 2

1. R. S. Pynoos, and S. Eth (1985), Children traumatized by witnessing acts of personal violence: Homicide, rape, or suicide behavior, in S. Eth and R. S. Pynoos (eds.), *Post-traumatic stress Disorder in Children* (Washington, D.C.: American Psychiatric Press), pp. 17–14.

2. L. C. Terr (1991), Childhood traumas: An outline and overview, *American Journal of Psychiatry* 148 (1), 10–19

3. Y. Nir, (1985) Post-traumatic stress disorder in children with cancer, In *Post traumatic stress disorder.*

4. P. R. Adams (1984), Mt. St. Helens ashfall: Evidence for a disaster stress reaction, *American Psychologist* 39, 252–260,
   S. J. Dollinger, J. P. O'Donnell, and A. A. Staley (1984), Lightning strike disaster: Effects on children's fears and worries, *Journal of Consulting and Clinical Psychology* 52, 1028–1038,
   K. T. Erikson (1976), Loss of community at Buffalo Creek, *American Journal of Psychiatry* 133 (3), 302–305,
   C. J. Frederick (1985) Children traumatized by catastrophic situations, in *Post-traumatic stress disorder,*
   R. Galente, and D. Foa (1986), An epidemiological study of psychic trauma and treatment effectiveness for children after a natural disaster, *Journal of the American Academy of Child and Adolescent Psychiatry,* 25, 357–363,
   C. J. Newman (1976), Children of disaster: Clinical observations at Buffalo Creek, *American Journal of Psychiatry* 133 (3), 306–312,
   S. Smith (1983), Disaster: Family disruption in the wake of natural disaster, in C. R. Figley and H. I. McCubbin (eds.), *Stress and the family, Vol. 2: Coping with catastrophe* (New York: Brunner/Mazel), pp. 120–147.

5. H. A. Handford et. al. (1983), Child and parent reaction to the TMI nuclear accident, *Journal of the American Academy of Child and Adolescent Psychiatry* 25, 346–355.

6. C. R. Figley (1983), Catastrophes: An overview of family reactions, *Stress and the family*, vol. 2.

7. Erikson, Loss of community.
   R. Lifton and E. Olson (1976), The human meaning of total disaster, *Psychiatry* 39, 1–18.

8. Lifton and Olson, Human meaning.

9. Newman, Children of disaster.

10. E. Silber, S. Perry, and D. Bloch (1958), Patterns of parent-child interaction in a disaster, *Psychiatry* 21, 159–167.

11. J. D. Kinzie, W. H. Sack, R. H. Angell, and B. Rath (1986). The psychiatric effects of massive trauma on Cambodian children, *Journal of the American Academy of Child Psychiatry,* 25, 3, 370–376.

12. A. Browne, and D. Finkelhor (1986). Impact of child sexual abuse: A review of the research, *Psychological Bulletin,* 99, 1, 66–77.

J. R. Conte, and Schuerman, J. R. (1987). Factors associated with an increased impact of child sexual abuse, *Child Abuse and Neglect,* 2, 201–211.

D. Finkelhor, and A. Browne, (1988). Assessing the long-term impact of child sexual abuse: A review and conceptualization. In L.E.A. Walker (ed.), *Handbook on sexual abuse of children* (pp. 55–71). New York: Springer.

S. Kelley (1989). Stress responses of children to sexual abuse and ritual abuse in day care centers, *Nursing Research,* 39, 1, 25–29.

13. K. Zinsmeister (1990), Growing up scared, *Atlantic Monthly* 265, 49–66.

14. D. A. Wolfe, et al. (1986), Child witnesses to violence between parents: Critical issues in behavioral and social adjustment, *Journal of Abnormal Child Psychology* 14, 95–104,

K. Pruett (1979), Home treatment for two infants who witnessed their mother's murder, *Journal of the Academy of Child Psychiatry* 18, 647–657; Pynoos and Eth, Children traumatized.

15. M. Newman (1992, January 9), Victim of bias wrestles with his anger, *New York Times,* p. A1.

16. R. S. Pynoos and K. Nader (1989), Children's memory and proximity to violence, *Journal of the American Academy of Child and Adolescent Psychiatry* 28 (2), 236–241,

R. S. Pynoos, et al. (1987), Life threat and post-traumatic stress in school age children, *Archives of General Psychiatry* 44, 1057–1063;

R. S. Pynoos and K. Nader (1988), Psychological first aid and treatment approach to children exposed to community violence: Research implications, *Journal of Traumatic Stress* 1 (4), 445–473.

17. J. Garbarino, K. Kostelny, and N. Dubrow (1991), What children can tell us about living in danger, *American Psychologist* 46 (4), 376–383.

18. N. Youngstrom (1992), Inner city youth tell of life in a "war zone". *American Psychological Association Monitor* 23 (1), 36–37.

19. R. S. Pynoos, and S. Eth (1986), Witness to violence: The child interview, *Journal of the American Academy of Child Psychiatry* 25 (3), 306.

20. Ibid.

21. Ibid.

22. G. P. Koocher (1973), Childhood, death, and cognitive development, *Development Psychology* 9 (3), 369–375.

23. S. Eth, and R. S. Pynoos (1985). Interaction of trauma and grief in childhood. In S. Eth and R. S. Pynoos (Eds.), op. cit.

24. E. H. Weiss, and R. F. Berg (1982), Child victims of sexual assault: Impact of court procedures, *Journal of the American Academy of Child Psychiatry* 21 (5), 513–518.

25. L. Berliner and M. K. Barbieri (1984), The testimony of the child victim of sexual assault, *Journal of Social Issues* 40 (2), 125–137.

26. I am grateful to my friend, Larry Parnass, of the *Daily Hampshire Gazette* in Northampton, Massachusetts, for his helpful thoughts about the roles

and functions of the press following a traumatic event in a family.

27. K. MacFarlane (1985), *Please, no, not my child: Coping with sexual abuse of your preschool child* (Los Angeles: Children's Institute International).

28. M. P. Celano (1992), A developmental model of victims' internal attributions of responsibility for sexual abuse, *Journal of Interpersonal Violence* 7 (1), 57–69; S.C. Esquilin (1987), Family responses to the identification of extra-familial child sexual abuse, *Psychotherapy in Private Practice* 5 (1), 105–113.

29. Celano, A developmental model; C. M. Newberger and E. De Vos, (1988), Abuse and victimization: A life-span, developmental perspective, *American Journal of Orthopsychiatry* 58 (4), 505–511.

Chapter 3

1. R. S. Pynoos and S. Eth (1985), Children traumatized by witnessing acts of personal violence: Homicide, rape, or suicide behavior, in S. Eth and R. S. Pynoos (eds.), *Post-traumatic stress disorder in children* (Washington, D.C.: American Psychiatric Press), pp 17–44.

2. S. J. Dollinger, J. P. O'Donnell, and A. A. Staley (1984), Lightning strike disaster: Effects on children's fears and worries, *Journal of Consulting and Clinical Psychology* 52, 1028–1038.

3. Ibid., p. 1030.

4. Ibid.; R. Lifton and E. Olson (1976), The human meaning of total disaster, *Psychiatry* 39, 1–18; L. C. Terr (1990), *Too scared to cry* (New York: Harper & Row).

5. L. C. Terr (1981), Psychic trauma in children: Observations following the Chowchilla school-bus kidnapping, *American Journal of Psychiatry* 138 (1), 14–19, and Terr, *Too scared to cry.*

6. Pynoos and Eth, Children traumatized.

7. R. Ferber (1985), *Solving your child's sleep problems* (New York: Simon & Schuster).

8. L. C. Terr (1979), Children of Chowchilla: A study of psychic trauma, *Psychoanalytic Study of the Child* 34, 547–623; Terr (1981), Forbidden games: Post-traumatic child's play, *Journal of the American Academy of Child Psychiatry* 20, 741–760; Terr, Psychic trauma; Terr, *Too scared to cry.*

9. A. Browne and D. Finkelhor (1986), Impact of child sexual abuse: A review of the research, *Psychological Bulletin* 99 (1), 66–77;
J. R. Conte and J. R. Schuerman (1987), Factors associated with an increased impact of child sexual abuse, *Child Abuse and Neglect* 2, 201–211;
A. P. Mannarino and J. A. Cohen (1986), A clinical-demographic study of sexually abused children, *Child Abuse and Neglect* 10, 17–23;
M. Mian, et al. (1986), Review of 125 children six years of age and under who were sexually abused, *Child Abuse and Neglect* 10, 223–229.

10. Conte and Schuerman, Factors;
W. N. Friedrich and R. A. Reams (1987), Course of psychological symptoms in sexually abused young children, *Psychotherapy* 24, 169–170;

W. N. Friedrich, A. J. Urquiza, and R. L. Beilke (1986), Behavior problems in sexually abused young children, *Journal of Pediatric Psychology* 2 (1), 47–57;

B. Gomes-Schwartz, J. M. Horowitz, and M. Sauzier (1985), Severity of emotional distress among sexually abused preschool, school-age, and adolescent children, *Hospital and Community Psychiatry* 36, 503–508; Mian et al., Review of 125 children.

Chapter 4

1. J. Garbarino, K. Kostelny, and N. Dubrow (1991), What children can tell us about living in danger, *American Psychologist* 46 (4), 376–383;
   N. Garmezy, A. S. Masten, and A. Tellegrin (1984), The study of stress and competence in children: A building block for developmental psychopathology, *Child Development* 55, 97–111;
   S. S. Luthar and E. Zigler (1991), Vulnerability and competence: A review of research on resilience in childhood, *American Journal of Orthopsychiatry* 61 (1), 6–22;
   A. S. Masten, K. M. Best, and N. Garmezy (1991), Resilience and development: Contributions from the study of children who overcome adversity, *Development and Psychopathology* 2, 425–444;
   P. B. Mrazek, and D. A. Mrazek (1987), Resilience in child maltreatment victims: A conceptual exploration, *Child Abuse and Neglect* 11, 357–366;
   M. Rutter (1983), Stress, coping, and development: Some issues and some questions, in N. Garmezy and M. Rutter (eds.), Stress, coping, and development. (New York: McGraw-Hill.), pp. 1–142.
   Researchers looking at resilience and stress resistance in children who endure a wide range of exposure to trauma or catastrophic stress study those children who adapt well, or thrive, over time. While the research on children's resilience does not involve traumatized children exclusively, the findings regarding protective and risk factors are helpful in thinking about the forces that may influence children's response to extreme stress. These factors are best read as considerations to keep in mind rather than absolutes that have emerged from extensive research.
2. Masten, Best, and Garmezy, Resilience and development.
3. P. L. Ellis, H. L. Persma, and C. E. Grayson (1990), Interrupting the reenactment cycle, *American Journal of Psychotherapy* 4, 525–535;
   K. D. Pruett (1979), Home treatment for two infants who witnessed their mother's murder, *Journal of the Academy of Child Psychiatry* 18, 647–657;
   K. D. Pruett (1984), A chronology of defensive adaptations to severe psychological trauma, *Psychoanalytic Study of the Child* 39, 591–612;
   L. C. Terr (1988), What happens to early memories? A study of twenty children under age five at the time of documented traumatic events, *Journal of the American Academy of Child and Adolescent Psychiatry* 27 (1), 96–104.

4. Masten, Best, and Garezy, Resilience and development.
5. Luthar and Zigler, Vulnerabilty and confidence;
   Masten, Best, Garmezy, Resilience and development;
   Mrazek and Mrazek, Resilience;
   Rutter, Stress, coping, and development.
6. E. Silber, S. Perry, and D. Bloch (1958), Patterns of parent-child interaction in a disaster, *Psychiatry* 21, 159–167.
7. J. R. Conte, and L. Berliner (1988), The impact of sexual abuse on children: Empirical findings; in L. E. A. Walker, (ed.), *Handbook on the sexual abuse of children* (New York: Springer), pp. 72–93:
   Masten, Best, and Garmezy, Resilience and development;
   Rutter, Stress, coping, and development.
8. Masten, Best, and Garmezy, Resilience and coping.
9. Ibid;
   Luthar and Zigler, Vulnerability and confidence.
10. Masten, Best, and Garmezy, Resilience and coping.
11. C. J. Frederick (1985), Children traumatized by catastrophic situations, in S. Eth, and R. S. Pynoos (eds.), *Post-traumatic stress disorder in children* (Washington, D.C.: American Psychiatric Press), pp. 71–100;
    R. Lifton, and E. Olson (1976), The human meaning of disaster, *Psychiatry,* 39, 1–18.
12. R. S. Pynoos et al. (1987), Life threat and post-traumatic stress in school-age children, *Archives of General Psychiatry* 44, 1057–1063.
13. Masten, Best, and Garmezy, Resilience and coping;
    R. S. Pynoos, and S. Eth (1985), Children traumatized by witnessing acts of personal violence: Homicide, rape, or suicide behavior, in *Post-traumatic stress disorder in children,* (pp. 17–44).
14. L. C. Terr (1991), Childhood traumas: An outline and overview, *American Journal of Psychiatry* 148 (1), 10–19.
15. Masten, Best, and Garmezy, Resilience and coping.

Chapter 5

1. L. Mc Cann and L. A. Perlman (1990), *Psychological trauma and the adult survivor: Theory, therapy, and transformation* (New York: Brunner/Mazel); C. R. Figley, (1989), *Helping traumatized families* (New York: Simon & Schuster).
2. Figley, *Helping traumatized families,* p. 18.
3. R. S. Pynoos, and K. Nader (1989), Children's memory and proximity to violence, *Journal of the American Academy of Child and Adolescent Psychiatry* 28 (2), 236–241.
4. W. Shapiro, (October 26, 1987). One went right: Woes from Wall Street to the gulf—but a happy ending in Texas. Time Magazine.
5. R. Janoff-Bulman (1991, September), Coping with trauma: Rebuilding shattered assumptions (Paper presented at conference on Trauma and

Victimization: Understanding and Healing Survivors. University of Connecticut).

6. H. M. Lynd (1958), *On shame and the search for identity,* (New York: Harcourt, Brace & World).

7. S. E. Partridge (1988), The parental self-concept: A theoretical and practical application, *Journal of Orthopsychiatry* 58, 281–287.

8. D. Gelinas (1983), The persisting negative effects of incest, *Psychiatry* 46, 312–332; R. C. Summit, (1983), The child sexual abuse accommodation syndrome, *Child Abuse and Neglect* 7, 177–193.

9. E. P. Seligman (1991), *Learned optimism.* (New York: Alfred A. Knopf).

10. P. Crowley (1991), *Not My Child* (New York: Avon), p. 19.

11. I am grateful to Dr. Anne McComb for her thoughtful discussion of gender differences in processing and communicating emotion as a source of marital tension following a child's trauma.

12. S. J. Kelley (1990), Parental stress response to sexual abuse and ritualistic abuse of children in day-care centers, *Journal of Interpersonal Violence* 4(4), 502–513

13. P. R. Adams and G. R. Adams (1984), Mt. St. Helens ashfall: Evidence for a disaster reaction, *American Psychologist* 29, 252–260.
A study of families living in the communities neighboring Mount Saint Helen found a dramatic increase in residents' reports of physical as well as emotional complaints and a 46 percent increase in domestic violence during the seven months following the volcanic eruption. Incidents of vandalism and juvenile crime also increased during this same period. Clearly, the volcano's impact was far reaching in the daily experience of these families.

14. S. Smith (1983), Disaster: Family disruption in the wake of natural disaster, in C. R. Figley and H. I. McCubbin (eds.), *Stress and the family,* vol. 2 *Coping with catastrophe* (New York: Brunner/Mazel).

15. C. J. Frederick (1985), Children traumatized by catastrophic situations, in S. Eth and R. S. Pynoos (eds.), *Post-traumatic stress disorder in children,* (Washington, D.C.: American Psychiatric Press), pp. 71–100.

16. J. R. Conte and J. R. Schuerman (1987), Factors associated with an increased impact of child sexual abuse, *Child Abuse and Neglect* 2, 201–211; A. Browne and D. Finkelhor (1986), Impact of child sexual abuse: A review of the literature, Psychological Bulletin 99 (1), 66–77.

17. S. C. Esquilin (1987), Family responses to the identification of extra-familial child sexual abuse, *Psychotherapy in Private Practice* 5 (1), 105–113.

18. Kelley, Parental stress response to sexual abuse; Crowley, *Not my child.*

19. Esquilin, Family responses; W. N. Friedrich and R. A. Reams (1987), Course of psychological symptoms in sexually abused young children, *Psychotherapy* 24, 160–170; B. Gomes-Schwartz, J. M. Horowitz, and M. Sauzier (1985), Severity of emotional distress among sexually abused preschool, school-age, and adolescent children, *Hospital and Community Psychiatry* 36, 503–508; K. Macfarlane et al. (1986), *Sexual abuse of young children* (New York: Guilford).

20. D. Finkelhor (1984), *Child sexual abuse: New theory and research* (New York: Free Press), p. 197.
21. Esquilin, Family responses.
22. D. Spungen (1991, September), Secondary victimization: A personal account (paper presented at conference on Trauma and Victimization: Understanding and Healing Survivors, University of Connecticut).

Chapter 6

1. R. Ferber (1985), *Solving your child's sleep problems* (New York: Simon & Schuster).
2. B. James (1989), *Treating traumatized children: New insights and creative interventions* (Lexington, Mass.: Lexington Books).
3. J. McNamara (1990), Healing hurts: Helping adoptive children deal with flashbacks, in B. McNamara and J. McNamara (eds.), *Adoption and the sexually abused child* (Portland, Maine: University of Southern Maine), pp. 109–115.
4. Ibid.
5. Ibid., p. 112.
6. L. Terr (1981a), Forbidden games; Post-traumatic child's play, *Journal of the American Academy of Child Psychiatry* 20, 741–760.
7 I am grateful to Liz Austin, Ed. D., of the Mountain Brook Children's Center in South Deerfield, Massachusetts, for sharing this and many other stories of her creative interventions with children.
8. James, *Treating traumatized children,* p. 147.
9. Ibid.
10. B. James (1991, June), workshop on Treating Traumatized Children (Boston).
11. Ibid.
12. L. C. Terr (1981), Psychic trauma in children: Observations following the Chowchilla school-bus kidnapping, *American Journal of Psychiatry* 138 (1), 14–19.
13. E. Silber, S. Perry, and D. Bloch (1958), Patterns of parent-child interaction in a disaster, *Psychiatry* 21, 159–167.
14. S. C. Esquilin (1987), Family responses to the identification of extra-familial child sexual abuse, *Psychotherapy in Private Practice* 5 (1), 105–113.
15. E. P. Seligman (1991), *Learned Optimism* (New York: Alfred A. Knopf).
16. Ibid.
17. Herman, J. L. (1992) Trauma and recovery (New York: Basic Books).
18. Ibid.

Chapter 7

1. K. Johnson (1989), *Trauma in the lives of children: Crisis and stress management techniques for counselors and other professionals* (Claremont, Calif.: Hunter House).

2. G. S. Goodman and V. Helgeson (1985), Child sexual assault: Children's memory and the law (paper presented at the National Policy Conference on Legal Reforms in Child Sexual Abuse Cases, National Resource Center for Child Advocacy and Protection, Washington, D.C.); K. MacFarlane and S. Krebs (1986), Techniques for interviewing and evidence gathering, in K. MacFarlane et al. (eds.), *Sexual abuse of young children: Evaluation and treatment* (New York: Guilford), pp. 67–101; R. S. Pynoos and S. Eth (1986), Witness to violence: The child interview, *Journal of the American Academy of Child Psychiatry* 25 (3), 306–319.

3. L. C. Terr (1990), *Too scared to cry* (New York: Harper & Row).

4. C. R. Hartman and A. W. Burgess (1988), Information processing of trauma: Case application of a model, *Journal of interpersonal Violence* 3, 443–457.

5. Ibid.

6. Ibid.

Chapter 8

1. W. N. Friedrich (1990). *Psychotherapy of sexually abused children and their families* (New York: W. W. Norton);
B. James (1989), *Treating traumatized children: New insights and creative interventions* (Lexington, Mass.: Lexington Books).

2. James, *Treating traumatized children.*

3. L. T. Sanford (1990), *Strong at the broken places: Overcoming the trauma of childhood abuse* (New York: Random House).

4. E. Deblinger, S. McLeer, and D. Henry (1990), Cognitive behavioral treatment for sexually abused children suffering post-traumatic stress: Preliminary findings, *Journal of the American Academy of Child and Adolescent Psychiatry* 29, 747–752;
P. C. Kendall and L. Braswell (1985), *Cognitive-behavorial therapy for impulsive children* (New York: Guilford).

5. E. P. Seligman (1991), *Learned optimism* (New York: Alfred A. Knopf).

6. G. Gardner and K. Olness (1981), *Hypnosis and hypnotherapy with children* (Orlando, Fla.: Grune & Stratton).

7. H. A. Handford et al (1983), Child and parent reaction to the TMI nuclear disaster, *Journal of the American Academy of Child and Adolescent Psychiatry* 25, 346–355;
L. C. Terr (1990), *Too scared to cry,* (New York: Harper & Row);
W. Yule and R. Williams (1990), Post-traumatic stress reactions in children, *Journal of Traumatic Stress* 3 (2), 279–295.

8. C. Garrity (1992, January), personal communication.

9. There is no doubt that children whose severe trauma requires lengthy and complex treatment are poorly served by managed health care plans which mandate short-term treatments for all mental health clients. The myopic view of "cost-containment" in the health care industry shows little regard for the needs of traumatized children. Intensive, immediate treatment for traumatized children can translate into long-term savings in dollars and pain.

Bibliography

Adams, P. R., and Adams, G. R. (1984). Mt. St. Helens ashfall: Evidence for a disaster stress reaction. *American Psychologist* 39, 252–260.

Amato, P. R., and Ochiltree, G. (1986). Family resources and the development of child competence. *Journal of Marriage and Family* 48, 47–56.

Arroyo, W., and Eth, S. (1985). Children traumatized by Central American warfare. In S. Eth & R. S. Pynoos (eds.), Post-traumatic stress disorder in children (pp. 101–120). Washington, D.C.: American Psychiatric Press.

Berliner, L., and Barbieri, M. K. (1984). The testimony of the child victim of sexual assault. *Journal of Social Issues* 40 (2), 125–137.

Berliner, L., and Conte, J. R. (1990). The process of victimization: The victim's perspective. *Child Abuse and Neglect* 14, 29–40.

Brassard, M. R., Germain, R., & Hart, S. N. (1987). *Psychological maltreatment of children and youth*. New York: Pergamon.

Browne, A., & Finkelhor, D. (1986). Impact of child sexual abuse: A review of the research. *Psychological Bulletin* 99 (1), 66–77.

Burgess, A. W., Groth, A. N., Holmstrom, L. L., and Sgroi, S. M. (1978). *Sexual assault of children and adolescents*. Lexington, Mass.: Lexington Books.

Burke, J., Borus, J., Burns, B. Millstein, K., and Beaslet, M. (1982). Changes in children's behavior after a natural disaster. *American Journal of Psychiatry* 139, 1010–1014.

Ceci, S. J., Toglia, M. P., and Ross, D. F. (1987). *Children's eyewitness memory*. New York: Springer-Verlag.

Celano, M. P. (1992). A developmental model of victims' internal attributions of responsibility for sexual abuse. *Journal of Interpersonal Violence* 7 (1), 57–69.

Cole, C. B., and Loftus, E. F. (1987). The memory of children. In S. Ceci, M. Toglia, & D. Ross (eds.), *Children's eyewitness memory* (pp. 178–208). New York: Springer-Verlag.

Conte, J. R. (1984). Progress in treating the sexual abuse of children. *Social Work* 29, 258–263.

Conte, J. R., and Berliner, L. (1988). The impact of sexual abuse on children: Empirical findings. In L. E. A. Walker (ed.), *Handbook on the sexual abuse of children* (pp. 72–93). New York: Springer.

Conte, J. R., and Schuerman, J. R. (1987). Factors associated with an increased impact of child sexual abuse. *Child Abuse and Neglect* 2, 201–211.

Crowley, P. (1991). *Not my child.* New York: Avon.

Deblinger, E., McLeer, S., and Henry, D. (1990). Cognitive behavioral treatment for sexually abused children suffering post-traumatic stress: Preliminary findings. *Journal of the American Academy of Child and Adolescent Psychiatry* 29, 747–752.

Dollinger, S. J., O'Donnell, J. P., and Staley, A. A. (1984). Lightning strike disaster: Effects on children's fears and worries. *Journal of Consulting and Clinical Psychology* 52, 1028–1038.

Earls, F., Smith, E., Reich, W., and Jung, K. G. (1988). Investigating psychopathological consequences of a disaster in children: A pilot study incorporating a structured diagnosis approach. *Journal of the American Academy of Child and Adolescent Psychiatry* 27, 90–95.

Ellis, P. L., Persma, H. L., and Grayson, C. E. (1990). Interrupting the reenactment cycle. *American Journal of Psychotherapy* 44 (4), 525–535.

Erikson, K. T. (1976). Loss of community at Buffalo Creek. *American Journal of Psychiatry* 133 (3), 302–305.

Esquilin, S. C. (1987). Family responses to the identification of extra-familial child sexual abuse. *Psychotherapy in Private Practice* 5 (1), 105–113.

Eth, S., and Pynoos, R. S. (1985). Interaction of trauma and grief in childhood. In S. Eth and R. S. Pynoos (eds.), *Post-traumatic stress disorder in children* (pp. 169–186). Washington, D.C.: American Psychiatric Press.

Eth, S., and Pynoos, R. S. (1985). *Post-traumatic stress disorder in children.* Washington, D.C.: American Psychiatric Press.

Everstine, D. S., and Everstine, L. (1989). *Sexual trauma in children and adolescents.* New York: Brunner/Mazel.

Ferber, R. (1985). *Solving your child's sleep problems.* New York: Simon & Schuster.

Figley, C. R. (1983). Catastrophes: An overview of family reactions. In C. R. Figley and H. I. McCubbin (eds.), *Stress and the family.* Vol. 2: *Coping with catastrophe* (pp. 3–20). New York: Brunner/Mazel.

Figley, C. R. (1989). *Helping traumatized families.* San Francisco: Jossey-Bass.

Finkelhor, D. (1979). *Sexually victimized children.* New York: Free Press.

Finkelhor, D. (1984). *Child sexual abuse: New theory and research.* New York: Free Press.

Finkelhor, D. (1986). *A sourcebook on child sexual abuse.* Beverly Hills: Sage.

Finkelhor, D. (1988). The trauma of child sexual abuse: Two models. In G. E. Wyatt and G. J. Powell (eds.), *Lasting effects of child sexual abuse* (pp. 61–82). Beverly Hills: Sage.

Finkelhor, D., and Browne, A. (1988). Assessing the long-term impact of child sexual abuse: A review and conceptualization. In L. E. A. Walker (ed.), *Handbook on sexual abuse of children* (pp. 55–71). New York: Springer.

Frederick, C. J. (1985). Children traumatized by catastrophic situations. In S. Eth and R. S. Pynoos (eds.), *Post-traumatic stress disorder in children* (pp. 71–100). Washington, D.C.: American Psychiatric Press.

Friedrich, W. N., and Reams, R. A. (1987). Course of psychological symptoms in sexually abused young children. *Psychotherapy* 24, 160–170.

Friedrich, W. N. (1990). *Psychotherapy of sexually abused children and their families*. New York: W. W. Norton.

Friedrich, W. N., Urquiza, A. J., and Beilke, R. L. (1986). Behavior problems in sexually abused young children. *Journal of Pediatric Psychology* 2 (1), 47–57.

Furst, S. S. (ed.) (1967). *Psychic trauma*. New York: Basic Books.

Galente, R., and Foa, D. (1986). An epidemiological study of psychic trauma and treatment effectiveness for children after a natural disaster. *Journal of the American Academy of Child and Adolescent Psychiatry* 25, 357–363.

Garbarino, J. (1990). The human ecology of risk. In S. J. Meisels and J. P. Shonkoff (eds.), *Handbook of early intervention* (pp. 78–96). New York: Cambridge University Press.

Garbarino, J., Guttman, E., and Seeley, J. W. (1986). *The psychologically battered child*. San Francisco: Jossey-Bass.

Garbarino, J., Kostelny, K., and Dubrow, N. (1991). What children can tell us about living in danger. *American Psychologist* 46, (4), 376–383.

Gardner, G., and Olness, K. (1981). *Hypnosis and hypnotherapy with children*. Orlando: Grune & Stratton.

Garmezy, N. (1983). Stressors of childhood. In N. Garmezy and M. Rutter (eds.), *Stress, coping, and development in childhood* (pp. 43–84). New York: McGraw-Hill.

Garmezy, N., Masten, A. S., and Tellegen, A. (1984) The study of stress and competence in children: A building block for developmental psychopathology. *Child Development* 55, 97–111.

Garrity, C. (1992, January). Personal communication.

Gelinas, D. (1983). The persisting negative effects of incest. *Psychiatry* 46, 312–332.

Gil, E. (1987). *Foster parenting abused children*. Chicago: National Committee for Prevention of Child Abuse.

Gil, E. (1991). *The healing power of play: Working with abused children*. New York: Guilford.

Gislason, I. L., and Call, J. D. (1982). Dog bite in infancy: Trauma and personality development. *Journal of the American Academy of Child Psychiatry* 21 (2), 203–207.

Goleman, D. (1986, September 21). The roots of terrorism are found in brutality of shattered childhood. *New York Times,* C1.

Gomes-Schwartz, B., Horowitz, J. M., and Sauzier, M. (1985). Severity of emotional distress among sexually abused preschool, school-age, and adolescent children. *Hospital and Community Psychiatry* 36, 503–508.

Goodman, G. S. (1986). Age differences in eyewitness testimony. *Law and Human Behavior* 10, 317–322.

Goodman, G. S., and Helgeson, V. (1985). Child sexual assault: Children's memory and the law. Paper presented at National Policy Conference on Legal Reforms in Child Sexual Abuse Cases, National Legal Resource Center for Child Advocacy and Protection, Washington, D.C.

Green, A. H. (1978). Psychiatric treatment of abused children. *Journal of the American Academy of Child Psychiatry* 17, 356–371.

Green, B. L., Lindy, J. D., Grace, M. C., Gleser, G. C., Leonard, A. C., Korol, M., and Winget, C. (1990). Buffalo Creek survivors in the second decade: Stability of stress symptoms. *America Journal of Orthopsychiatry* 60, 43–55.

Hagans, K. B., and Case, J. (1988). *When your child has been molested.* Lexington, Mass.: Lexington Books.

Handford, H. A., Mayes, S. O., Mattison, R. E., Humphrey, F. J., Bagnato, S., Bixler, E. O., and Kales, J. D. (1983). Child and parent reaction to the TMI nuclear accident. *Journal of the American Academy of Child and Adolescent Psychiatry* 25, 346–355.

Hart, S. N., and Brassard, M. R. (1987). Psychological maltreatment: Integration and summary. In M. R. Brassard, R. Germain, and S. N. Hart (eds.), *Psychological maltreatment of children and youth* (pp. 254–266). New York: Pergamon.

Hartman, C. R., and Burgess, A. W. (1988). Information processing of trauma: Case application of a model. *Journal of Interpersonal Violence* 3, 443–457.

Haugaard, J., and N. D. (1988). *The sexual abuse of children.* San Francisco: Jossey-Bass.

Herman, J. L. (1992) Trauma and recovery. New York: Basic Books.

Hillman, D., and Solek-Tefft, J. (1988). *Spiders and flies: Help for parents and teachers of sexually abused children.* Lexington, Mass.: Lexington Books.

In, P. A., and McDermott, J. F. (1976). The treatment of child abuse: Play therapy with a 4-year-old child. *Journal of the American Academy of Child Psychiatry* 15, 430–440.

James, B. (1991, June). Workshop on Treating Traumatized Children, Boston.

James, B. (1989). *Treating traumatized children: New insights and creative interventions.* Lexington, Mass.: Lexington Books.

Janoff-Bulman, R. (1989). Assumptive worlds and the stress of traumatic events. *Social Cognition* 7, 113–136.

Janoff-Bulman, R. (1992). *Shattered assumptions: Toward a new psychology of trauma.* New York: Free Press.

Johnson, K. (1989). *Trauma in the lives of children: Crisis and stress management techniques for counselors and other professionals.* Claremont, Calif.: Hunter House.

Kagan, J. (1983). Stress and coping in early development. In N. Garmezy and M. Rutter (eds.), *Stress, coping, and development in children* (pp. 191–216). New York: McGraw-Hill.

Kaufman, J., and Zigler, E. (1987). Do abused children become abusive parents? *American Journal of Orthopsychiatry* 57 (2), 186–192.

Kelley, S. J. (1989). Stress responses of children to sexual abuse and ritual abuse in day care centers. *Journal of Interpersonal Violence* 4 (4), 502–513.

Kelley, S. J. (1990). Parental stress response to sexual abuse and ritualistic abuse of children in day-care centers. *Nursing Research* 39 (1), 25–29.

Kendall, P. C., and Braswell, L. (1985). *Cognitive-behavioral therapy for impulsive children.* New York: Guilford.

Khan, M. M. R. (1963). The concept of cumulative trauma. *Psychoanalytic Study of the Child* 18, 286–306.

Kingsolver, B. (1992, February 29). Everybody's somebody's baby. *New York Times Magazine,* 49.

Kinzie, J. D., Sack, W. H., Angell, R. H., Manson, S., and Rath, B. (1986). The psychiatric effects of massive trauma on Cambodian children. *Journal of the American Academy of Child Psychiatry* 25 (3), 370–376.

Kiser, L. J., Ackerman, B. J., Brown, E., Edwards, N. B., McColgan, E., Pugh, R., and Pruitt, D. B. (1988). Post-traumatic stress disorder in young children: A reaction to purpoted sexual abuse. *Journal of the American Academy of Child and Adolescent Psychiatry* 27 (5), 645–649.

Kluft, R. P. (1984). Multiple personality in children. *Psychiatric Clinics of North America* 7, 121–134.

Koocher, G. P. (1973). Childhood, death, and cognitive development. *Development Psychology* 9 (3), 369–375.

Krystal, H. (1978). Trauma and affects. *Psychoanalytic Study of the Child* 33, 81–116.

Levy, D. (1938). Release therapy in young children. *Psychiatry* 1, 387–390.

Lifton, R., and Olson, E. (1976). The human meaning of total disaster. *Psychiatry* 39, 1–18.

Lipsett, L. P. (1983). Stress in infancy: Toward understanding the origins of coping behavior. In N. Garmezy and M. Rutter (eds.), *Stress, coping, and development in children* (pp. 161–190). New York: McGraw-Hill.

Luthar, S. S., and Zigler, E. (1991) Vulnerability and competence: A review of research on resilience in childhood. *American Journal of Orthopsychiatry* 61 (1), 6–22.

Lynd, H. M. (1958). *On shame and the search for identity.* New York: Harcourt, Brace & World.

Lyons, J. A. Post-traumatic stress disorder in children and adolescents: A review of the literature. *Developmental and Behavioral Pediatrics* 8 (6), 349–356.

McCann, L., and Pearlman, L. A. (1990). *Psychological trauma and the adult survivor: Theory, therapy, and transformation.* New York: Brunner/Mazel.

MacFarlane, K. (1985). *Please no! Not my child.* Los Angeles: Children's Institute International.

MacFarlane, K., and Krebs, S. (1986). Techniques for interviewing and evidence gathering. In K. MacFarlane et al. (eds.), *Sexual abuse of young children: Evaluation and treatment* (pp. 67–101). New York: Guilford.

MacFarlane, K., et al. (1986). *Sexual abuse of young children: Evaluation and treatment.* New York: Guilford.

MacLean, G. (1977). Psychic trauma and traumatic neurosis: Play therapy with a four-year old boy. *Canadian Psychiatric Association Journal* 22, 71–76.

McLeer, S. V., Deblinger, E., Atkins, M. S., Foa, E. B., and Ralphe, D. L. (1988). Post-traumatic stress disorder in sexually abused children. *Journal of the American Academy of Child and Adolescent Psychiatry* 27 (5), 650–654.

McNamara, J., and McNamara, B. (eds.) (1990). *Adoption and the sexually abused child.* Portland, Maine: Human Services Development Institute, University of Southern Maine.

Mann, E., and McDermott, J. F. (1983). Play therapy for victims of child abuse and neglect. In C. Schaefer and K. O'Connor (eds.), *Handbook of play therapy* (pp. 283–307). New York: J. Wiley.

Mannarino, A. P., and Cohen, J. A. (1986). A clinical-demographic study of sexually abused children. *Child Abuse and Neglect* 10, 17–23.

Masten, A. S., Best, K. M., and Garmezy, N. (1991). Resilience and development: Contributions from the study of children who overcome adverisity. *Development and Psychopathology* 2, 425–444.

Mian, M., Wehrspann, W., Klajner-Diamon, H., Le Baron, E., and Winder, C. (1986). Review of 125 children six years of age and under who were sexually abused. *Child Abuse and Neglect* 10, 223–229.

Mrazek, P. B., and Mrazek, D. A. (1987). Resilience in child maltreatment victims: A conceptual exploration. *Child Abuse and Neglect* 11, 357–366.

Newberger, C. M., and De Vos, E. (1988). Abuse and victimization: A life-span development perspective. *American Journal of Orthopsychiatry* 58 (4), 505–511.

Newman, C. J. (1976). Children of disaster: Clinical observations at Buffalo Creek. *American Journal of Psychiatry* 133 (3), 306–312.

Newman, M. (1992, January 9). Victim of bias wrestles with his anger. *New York Times,* p. A1.

Nir, Y. (1985). Post-traumatic stress disorder in children with cancer. In S. Eth and R. S. Pynoos (eds.), *Post-traumatic stress disorder in children* (pp 121–132). Washington D.C.: American Psychiatric Press.

Parry, G. (1990). *Coping with crises.* London: British Psychological Society/Routledge Ltd.

Partridge, S. E. (1988). The parental self-concept: A theoretical and practical application. *Journal of Orthopsychiatry* 58, 281–287.

Patterson, G. R. (1983). Stress: A change agent for family process. In N. Garmezy and M. Rutter (eds.), *Stress, coping and development in children* (pp. 235–264). New York: McGraw-Hill.

Patterson, J. M., and McCubbin, H. I. (1983). Chronic illness: Family stress and coping. In C. R. Figley and H. I. McCubbin (eds.), *Stress and the family.* Vol. 2: *Coping with catastrophe* (pp. 21–36). New York: Brunner/Mazel.

Payton, J. B., and Krocker-Tuskan, M. (1988). Children's reactions to loss of parent through violence. *Journal of the American Academy of Child Psychiatry* 27 (5), 563–566.

Pruett, K. D. (1979). Home treatment for two infants who witnessed their mother's murder. *Journal of the Academy of Child Psychiatry* 18, 647–657.

Pruett, K. D. (1984). A chronology of defensive adaptations to severe psychological trauma. *Psychoanalytic Study of the Child* 39, 591–612.

Pynoos, R. S., and Eth, S. (1984). The child as witness to homicide. *Journal of Social Issues* 40 (2), 87–108.

Pynoos, R. S., and Eth, S. (1985). Children traumatized by witnessing acts of personal violence: Homicide, rape, or suicide behavior. In S. Eth andd R. S. Pynoos (eds.), *Post-traumatic stress disorder in children* (pp. 17–44). Washington, D.C.: American Psychiatric Press.

Pynoos, R. S., and Eth, S. (1986). Witness to violence: The child interview. *Journal of the American Academy of Child Psychiatry* 25 (3), 306–319.

Pynoos, R. S., Frederick, C., Nader, K., Arroyo, W., Steinberg, S., Eth, S., Nunez, F., and Fairbanks, L. (1987). Life threat and post-traumatic stress in school-age children. *Archives of General Psychiatry* 44, 1057–1063.

Pynoos, R. S., and Nader, K. (1988) Psychological first aid and treatment approach to children exposed to community violence: Research implications. *Journal of Traumatic Stress* 1 (4), 445–473.

Pynoos, R. S., and Nader, K. (1989). Children's memory and proximity to violence. *Journal of the American Academy of Child and Adolescent Psychiatry* 28 (2), 236–241.

Rieiker, P. P., and Carmen, E. (1986). The victim-to-patient process: The disconfirmation and transformation of abuse. *American Journal of Orthopsychiatry* 56 (3), 360–370.

Russell, D. E. (1983). The incidence and prevalence of intrafamilial and extrafamilial sexual abuse of female children. *Child Abuse and Neglect* 7, 133–146.

Rutter, M. (1983). Stress, coping, and development: Some issues and some questions. In N. Garmezy and M. Rutter (eds.), *Stress, coping, and development.* New York: McGraw-Hill.

Sanford, L. T. (1990). *Strong at the broken places: Overcoming the trauma of childhood abuse.* New York: Random House.

Seligman, E. P. (1991). *Learned optimism.* New York: Alfred A. Knopf.

Sesan, R., Freeark, K., and Murphy, S. (1986). The support network: Crisis intervention for extrafamilial child sexual abuse. *Professional Psychology, Research, and Practice* 17 (2), 138–146.

Sgroi, S. (1982). *Handbook of clinical intervention in child sexual abuse.* Lexington, Mass.: Lexington Books.

Silber, E., Perry, S., and Bloch, D. (1958). Patterns of parent-child interaction in a disaster. *Psychiatry* 21, 159–167.

Silver, R. L., Boon, C., and Stones, M. H. (1983). Searching for meaning in misfortune: Making sense of incest. *Journal of Social Issues* 39 (2), 81–102.

Skuse, D. (1984). Extreme deprivation in early childhood; I. Diverse outcomes for three siblings from an extraordinary family. *Journal of Child Psychology and Psychiatry* 25 (4), 523–541.

Skuse, D. (1984). Extreme deprivations in early childhood; II. Theoretical issues and a comparative review. *Journal of Child Psychology and Psychiatry* 25 (4), 543–572.

Smith, S. (1983). Disaster: Family disruption in the wake of natural disaster. In C. R. Figley and H. I. McCubbin (eds.), *Stress and the family.* Vol. 2: *Coping with catastrophe.* New York: Brunner/Mazel.

Spungen, D. (1991, September. Secondary victimization: A personal account. Paper presented at conference on Trauma and Victimization: Understanding and Healing Survivors, University of Connecticut, Vernon, Connecticut.

Stone, A. M. (1992). The role of shame in post-traumatic stress disorder. *American Journal of Orthopsychiatry* 62 (1), 131–136.

Summit, R. C. (1983). The child sexual abuse accommodation syndrome. Child Abuse and Neglect 7, 177–193.

Terr, L. C. (1979). Children of Chowchilla: A study of psychic trauma. Psychoanalytic Study of the Child 34, 547–623.

Terr, L. C. (1980). The child as a witness. In D. Schetky and E. Benedek (eds.), *Child psychiatry and the law* (pp. 207–221). New York: Brunner/Mazel.

Terr, L. C. (1981) Forbidden games: Post-traumatic child's play. *Journal of the American Academy of Child Psychiatry* 20, 741–760.

Terr, L. C. (1981). Psychic trauma in children: Observations following the Chowchilla school-bus kidnapping. *American Journal of Psychiatry* 138 (1), 14–19.

Terr, L. C. (1987) Childhood psychic trauma. In J. D. Call, R. L. Cohen, S. I. Harrison, I. N. Berlin, and L. A. Stone (eds.), *Basic handbook of child psychiatry.* vol. 5 (pp., 262–271). New York: Basic Books.

Terr, L. C. (1987). Treatment of psychic trauma in children. In J. D. Call, R. L. Cohen, S. I. Harrison, I. N. Berlin, and L. A. Stone (eds.), *Basic handbook of child psychiatry,* vol. 5 (pp. 414–420). New York: Basic Books.

Terr, L. C. (1988). What happens to early memories? A study of twenty children under age five at the time of documented traumatic events. *Journal of the American Academy of Child and Adolescent Psychiatry* 27 (1), 96–104.

Terr, L. C. (1990). *Too scared to cry.* New York: Harper & Row.

Terr, L. C. (1991). Childhood traumas: An outline and overview. *American Journal of Psychiatry* 148 (1), 10–19.

Tharinger, D. (1990). Impact of child sexual abuse on developing sexuality. Professional Psychology: Research and Practice 21 (5), 331–337.

van der Kolk, B. A. (1987). *Psychological trauma.* Washington, D.C.: American Psychiatric Press.

Walker, C. E., Bonner, B. L., and Kaufman, K. L. (1988). *The physically and sexually abused child: Evaluation and treatment.* New York: Pergamon.

Walker, L. E. A., (1988). *Handbook on sexual abuse of children.* New York: Springer.

Weiss, E. H., and Berg, R. F. (1982). Child victims of sexual assault: Impact of court procedures. *Journal of the American Academy of Child Psychiatry* 21 (5), 513–518.

Werner, E. E. (1990). Protective factors and individual resilience. In S. J. Meisels and J. P. Shonkoff (eds.), *Handbook of early intervention* (pp. 97–116). New York: Cambridge University Press.

Williams, G. J. R. (1983). Child abuse. In C. E. Walker and M. Roberts (eds.), *Handbook of clinical child psychology* (pp. 1219–1248). New York: Wiley.

Wolfe, D. A., Zak, L., Wilson, S. K., and Jaffe, P. (1986). Child witnesses to violence between parents: Critical issues in behavorial and social adjustment. *Journal of Abnormal Child Psychology* 14, 95–104.

Wyatt, G. E., and Mickey, M. R. (1988). The support by parents and others as it mediates the effects of child sexual abuse: An exploratory study. In G. E. Wyatt and G. J. Powell (eds.), *Lasting effects of child sexual abuse* (pp. 211–226). Beverly Hills: Sage.

Yates, A. (1981). Narcissistic traits in certain abused children. *American Journal of Orthopsychiatry* 51, 55–62.

Yates A. (1982). Children eroticized by incest. *American Journal of Psychiatry* 139, 482–485.

Young, M. A. (1991, September). The trauma of victimization. Paper presented at conference on Trauma and Victimization: Understanding and Healing Survivors, University of Connecticut, Vernon, Connecticut.

Youngstrom, N. (1992). Inner city youth tell of life in "a war zone." *American Psychological Association Monitor* 23 (1), 36–37.

Yule, W., and Williams, R. M. (1990). Post-traumatic stress reactions in children. *Journal of Traumatic Stress* 3 (2), 279–295.

Zinsmeister, K. (1990). Growing up scared. *Atlantic Monthly* 265, 49–66.

Further Readings for Parents and for Children

Childhood Trauma: An Overview

Terr, L. (1990). *Too Scared to Cry: Psychic Trauma in Childhoood*. New York: Harper & Row.

Childhood Injury

Lash, M. *When Your Child Is Seriously Injured: The Emotional Impact on Families*. Available from the Research and Training Center in Rehabilitation and Childhood Trauma, Department of Rehabilitation Medicine, New England Medical Center Hospitals, 750 Washington Street, Boston, Massachusetts 02111.

Child Abuse

Crowley, P. (1990). *Not My Child*. New York: Avon Books.

Gil, E. (1982). *Foster Parenting Abused Children*. Available from the National Committee for Prevention of Child Abuse, 332 South Michigan Avenue, Suite 1600, Chicago, Illinois 60604-4357.

Hagans, K. B., and Case, J. (1988). *When Your Child Has Been Molested: A Parent's Guide to Healing and Recovery*. Lexington, Mass.: Lexington Books.

Hillman, D., and Solek-Tefft, J. (1990). *Spiders and Flies: Help for Parents and Teachers of Sexually Abused Children*. New York: Free Press.

MacFarlane, K. (1985). *Please, No! Not My Child*. Available from the Marshall Resource Center, Children's Institute International, 711 South New Hampshire Avenue, Los Angeles, California 90005.

Death and Loss

Fox, S. S. (1985). *Good Grief: Helping Groups of Children When a Friend Dies*. Available from New England Association for the Education of Young Children, 35 Pilgrim Road, Boston, Massachusetts 02215.

Gaffney, D. A. (1988). *The Seasons of Grief: Helping Children Grow Through Loss*. New York: Plume.

Grollman, E. A. (1967) *Explaining Death to Children*. Boston: Beacon Press.

Jewett, C. L. (1982). *Helping Children Cope with Separation and Loss*. Harvard, Mass.: Harvard Common Press.

Schaefer, D., and Lyons, C. (1986). *How Do We Tell the Children? Helping Children Understand and Cope When Someone Dies*. New York: Newmarket Press.

Child Therapy

Doft, N. & Aria, B (1992). *When Your Child Needs Help*. New York: Harmony Books.

Parenting and Child Management

Clark, L. (1989). *The Time-Out Solution: A Practical Guide for Handling Common Everyday Behavior Problems*. Chicago: Contemporary Books.

Faber, A., and Mazlish, E. (1982). *How to Talk So Kids Will Listen*. New York: Avon.

McKay, G. D., and Dinkmeyer, D. (1989). *Systematic Training for Effective Parenting: Parents' Handbook*. Circle Pines, Mn.: American Guidance.

Marston, S. (1990). *The Magic of Encouragement: Your Child's Self-Esteem*. New York: Morrow. (also available on audiocassette.)

Kurcinka, M. S. (1991). *Raising Your Spirited Child*. New York: Harper Collins.

Schaefer, C. E., and Millman, H. L. (1989). *How to Help Children with Common Problems*. New York: Nal-Dutton.

Williamson, P. (1991). *Good Kids, Bad Behavior: Helping Children Learn Self-discipline*. New York: Simon & Schuster.

Sleep Disturbances

Ferber, R. (1985). *Solving Your Child's Sleep Problems*. New York: Simon & Schuster.

Books for Children

Abuse

Anderson, D., and Finne, M. (1986). *Margaret's Story: Sexual Abuse and Going to Court*. Minneapolis: Dillon Press. Grades 1–4.

Bass, E. (1981). *I Like You to Make Jokes with Me, But I Don't Want You to Touch Me*. Chapel Hill: Lollipop Power. Preschool-grade 3.

Drake, E., and Nelson, A. (1983). *Getting Together*. Gainesville, Fla.: Child Care Publications. For sexually abused girls.

Drake, E., and Nelson, A. (1986). *Working Together*. Gainesville, Fla.: Child Care Publications. For sexually abused boys.

Gil, E. (1983). *Outgrowing the Pain*. San Francisco: Launch Press. For older teenagers who have been sexually abused.

Gil, E. (1986). *A Book for Kids Who Were Abused*. San Francisco: Launch Press. Grade 3 and older.

Girard, L. W. (1984). *My Body Is Private*. Mortongrove, Ill.: A. Whitman. Grades K–3.

Kehoe, P. (1987). *Something Happened and I'm Scared to Tell: A Book for Young Victims of Abuse*. Seattle, Wash.: Parenting Press. Preschool–grade 2.

MacFarlane, K., and Cunningham, C. (1988). *Steps to Healthy Touching*. Mt. Dora, Fla.: KIDSRIGHTS. Grades K–7.

McGovern, K. (19xx). *Alice Doesn't Babysit Anymore*. Portland, Orc.: McGovern and Mulbacher Books. Grades K–5.

Otto, M. (1988). *Never, No Matter What*. Toronto: Women's Press. About domestic abuse and children entering a shelter for battered women with their mother.

Paris, S. (1985). *Mommy and Daddy Are Fighting*. Seattle: Seal Press. preschool–grade 4.

Polese, C. (1985). *Promise Not to Tell*. New York: Human Sciences Press. Grade 3 and older.

Russell, P., and Stone, B. (1986). *Do You Have a Secret?* Minneapolis: CompCare. Preschool–grade 3.

Sweet, P. (1985). *Something Happened to Me*. Racine, Wis.: Mother Courage. Grades 2–5.

Wachter, O. (1983). *No More Secrets for Me*. Boston: Little, Brown. Grades 1–4.

Adoption and Foster Placement

Bloomquist, G. M. (1990). *Zachary's New Home: A Story for Foster and Adopted Children*. New York: Magination Press. Preschool–grade 4.

Girard, L. (1986). *Adoption Is for Always*. Mortongrove, Ill.: A. Whitman. Grades K–6.

Children in the Courtroom

Beaudry, J., and Ketchum, L. (1987). *Carla goes to court*. New York: Human Sciences Press. Grades K–6.

Loss

de Paola, T. (1973). *Nana Upstairs and Nana Downstairs.* New York: Puffin. Grades 1–3.

Mellonie, B., and Ingpen, R. (1983). *Lifetimes: The Beautiful Way to Explain Death to Children.* New York: Bantam. Preschool–grade 3.

Varley, S. (1984). *Badger's Parting Gifts.* New York: Lothrop, Lee & Shepard. Grades K–3.

Simon, N. (1985). *The Saddest Time.* Mortongrove, Ill.: A. Whitman. Grades 1–6.

Vigna, J. (1990). *Saying Goodbye to Daddy.* Mortongrove, Ill.: A. Whitman. Grades K–2.

Play Therapy

Galvin, M. (1988). *Ignatius Finds Help: A Story About Psychotherapy for Children.* New York: Magination Press. Preschool–grade 6.

Nemiroff, M. A., and Annunziata, J. (1990). *A Child's First Book About Play Therapy.* Washington, D.C.: American Psychological Association. Preschool–Grade 2.

Self-Esteem

Moser, A. (1991). *Don't Feed the Monster on Tuesday: The Children's Self-Esteem Book.* Kansas City, Mo.: Landmark Editions. Grades K–6.

Sleep Difficulties

Dutro, J. (1991). *Night Light: A Story for Children Afraid of the Dark.* New York: Magination Press. Preschool–Grade 4.

Hill, S. (1985). *Go Away, Bad Dreams.* New York: Random House. Preschool–grade 3.

Lobby, T. (1990). *Jessica and the Wolf: A Story for Children Who Have Bad Dreams.* New York: Magination Press. Grades K–3.

Marcus, I. W., and Marcus, P. (1990). *Scary Night Visitors: A Story for Children with Bedtime Fears.* New York: Magination Press. Preschool–Grade 2.

Mayer, M. (1968). *There's a Nightmare in My Closet.* New York: Dial Press. Preschool–grade 2.

Stress

Moser, A. (1988). *Don't Pop Your Cork on Monday: The Children's Anti-Stress Book*. Kansas City, Mo.: Landmark Editions. Grades 1–6.

Sanders, C., and Turner, C. (1983). *Coping: A Guide to Stress Management*. Carthage, Ill.: Good Apple. Grades 2–8.

Toileting Problems

Mills, J. C., and Crowley, R. J. (1988). *Sammy the Elephant and Mr. Camel: A Story to Help Children Overcome Bedwetting While Discovering Self-Appreciation*. New York: Magination Press. Grade 1 and up.

Understanding Feelings

Cain, B. S. (1990). *Double Dip-Feelings: Stories to Help Children Understand Emotions*. New York: Magination Press. Grades 1–5.

Acknowledgments

The work of writing this book has held many surprises, most of them pleasant and rewarding. Surely the greatest joy has been the collaboration of colleagues and friends whose support and feedback have enriched my thinking and writing. I am sincerely grateful to my thoughtful chapter readers who generously carved time out of their busy lives to review various parts of the manuscript. This book owes much to the good thoughts and encouragement of Ed Beauvais, Marla Brassard, Nancy Dyer, Marsha Humphry, Elizabeth March, Anne McComb, Eileen Messer, Edward Plimpton, Alison Rogers, Anna Salter, Ellen Sedlis, Judith Souweine, Lisa Styles, and Ken Talan. Anne Riffle, a senior at Smith College, made my writing possible by competently assisting me with library research. I am particularly grateful to the various members of the Children's Clinic Thursday case conference group under Ken Talan's sensitive direction for the many poignant and helpful discussions we have had over the years about the traumatized children in our care.

To one reader in particular, Carla Garrity, of Denver, I owe a special debt of gratitude. Carla has accompanied me closely in the writing of this book, offering her support, her incisive thinking about the children of trauma, and her unflagging interest in the project. Just as her creative teaching at the University of Denver School of Professional Psychology has had a lasting impact on my work and thinking as a psychologist, Carla's involvement in the writing of this book has enriched the process and product. To share this project as professionals, mothers, and writers has been a pleasure that transformed many dreary hours.

There have been numerous manuscript readers whom I cannot publicly thank. The parents of children whom I have seen over the years have been instrumental in setting the direction for this book. Their thoughts and deeply felt reactions to this book in its various stages made an enormous difference in the final writing. I have tried to do justice to their faith in me and to their painful and courageous struggle with trauma in their families. As the trauma specialist Beverly James says, "There are a lot of heroic parents out there."

No grants or sabbaticals supported my work on this project, which under ordinary circumstances would have meant that the writing period would have been much longer than it has been. I am, however, blessed with extraordinary circumstances in my primary work at the Northampton Center for Children and Families. Through the unusual support of the executive director, Carl Cutchins, I was given the time and encouragement to write. The extent of my personal gratitude for this latitude is matched by my respect for the model of humanity and responsiveness in human services administration that Carl has created and maintained in this special agency.

Also at the Northampton Center for Children and Families, I am grateful to four special women for their competent support work on the manuscript and for their unrelenting humor: Lani Simmons, Chiquita Chevalier-Baker, Sandy Dunning, and Lisa Blais.

In the unfamiliar world of publishing, I have been fortunate to find the human side of the marketplace. It has been a pleasure to work with my agent, Max Gartenberg, whose expert help at every stage was offered with such graciousness. Margaret Zuskey, my editor at Lexington Books, has been the best of critics. Her thoughtful challenges and copious encouragement have made this a better book. I am particularly grateful to Margaret for her early interest in this project.

I fully intended that the writing of this book not become the source of chronic stress for my family, and to a great extent I think we have all emerged from the experience unscathed, if a bit unbalanced. Our survival I owe to my husband, Ed, whose virtues of endurance and selflessness border on the legendary. Ed has protected our son from the worst fallout of having a preoccupied mother in the house and given me much-needed support and encouragement. His commitment to making the book possible has been remarkable and unswerving at every step along the way.

My time of writing has made me more aware than ever of the

many people who grace my life with friendship and support. This book could not have been written without Jennifer Higgins, our valiant babysitter, whose resourcefulness and creativity I have depended on more than I care to acknowledge in the past year. Among the many enthusiastic cheerleaders I have been blessed with are my mother, Joan Monahon, and my good friends Judith Souweine, Lisa Styles, Sally Wilson, and Susan Partridge, and our favorite fiddler, Craig Eastman, whose music and friendship have enlivened this time of writing. No acknowledgment of support would be complete in my life without mention of one special and steadfast group of women: Ellie Axelroth, Luisa Medrano, Lena Theodorou Ehlich, and Teena Zimmerman.

Many, many children have contributed to the writing of this book. Through their pain and bravery in psychotherapy, they have taught me in such vivid ways what it is like to be young and terrified. I have tried to faithfully represent both the strength and the fragility of these children, each of whom has touched me deeply. In many ways, I have often felt like their ghostwriter, a job I have felt privileged to have.

One child in particular has taught me the most about children and about parenting. My son, Caley, a wonderful and ever-lively fellow, has patiently helped me to learn about this hard work of being a parent. I am grateful for the fortitude this six year old has shown during a busy and somewhat chaotic time in our family's life. I could not have written this book without the knowledge of what it is to love a child.

Index